GROW YOUR INVESTMENTS
with the
BEST MUTUAL
FUNDS AND ETFs

Making Long-Term Investment
Decisions with the Best Funds Today

STEPHEN L. McKEE

New York   Chicago   San Francisco   Athens   London   Madrid
Mexico City   Milan   New Delhi   Singapore   Sydney   Toronto

1 2 3 4 5 6 7 8 9 0   DOC/DOC   1 2 1 0 9 8 7 6 5

ISBN   978-0-07-181648-9
MHID   0-07-181648-8

e-ISBN   978-0-07-181649-6
e-MHID 0-07-181649-6

This publication is designed to provide accurate and authoritative information in regard to the subject matter covered. It is sold with the understanding that neither the author nor the publisher is engaged in rendering legal, accounting, securities trading, or other professional services. If legal advice or other expert assistance is required, the services of a competent professional person should be sought.

—From a Declaration of Principles Jointly Adopted by a Committee of the American Bar Association and a Committee of Publishers and Associations

McGraw-Hill Education books are available at special quantity discounts to use as premiums and sales promotions or for use in corporate training programs. To contact a representative, please visit the Contact Us pages at www.mhprofessional.com.

Disclaimer

This book is for informational purposes only. It does not consider the reader's personal information or situation. It is not to be construed in any form as providing tax, financial, investment, or legal recommendations or advice. There is no solicitation to buy or offer to sell any securities herein. The reader is solely responsible for taking all actions and determining whether any information is suitable or appropriate for you based on your own situation. All materials are gathered from sources believed reliable, but cannot be guaranteed. Information is not warranted to be accurate, complete, or timely. Neither the author nor affiliations are responsible for any damages or losses arising from any use of this information. All investments involve the potential for risk of loss. No chart, strategy, or information guarantees gains or losses. There is no guarantee that any periods used in backtesting a strategy will be identical to or similar to current or future periods. Read a fund's prospectus. The information herein is based on proprietary metrics owned by the author.

This book is dedicated to all people who work for a living,
for man is a working animal.

Contents

Preface   ix

Introduction   xiii

1 Around the Buttonwood Tree   1

2 In the Long Run, We Are All Dead   27

3 Neither a Lender nor a Borrower Be   55

4 To Diversify or Not to Diversify   79

5 Uncertainty and Choice   105

6 C-lecting Strategies   127

7 Avoiding Losses and Capturing Gains   153

8 Some Assembly Required   181

Appendix A   Secular Stock Worksheet   207

Appendix B   Secular Bond Worksheet   210

Appendix C   Mapping Your Personal Current
                       Holdings to Where They Are Ranked   212

Appendix D   Mapping Your 401(k) Choices   214

References   217

Attributions   221

Index   223

Preface

TIMELY OR TIMELESS, SHE ASKED. TIMELESS. I WANT TO PROVIDE timeless investment information to help not only the readers acquire and retain wealth but also help their children and their children's children do the same. Even a short 10 years from now, who will care about today's machinations in Washington or the actions of the Federal Reserve or the manager who has the hot hand or the mutual fund or exchange-traded fund (ETF) that sports the lowest cost? How, if at all, will the headline information and those fund facts from today help us to actually hold onto our money and make us wealthier over the years?

It is not enough to valiantly assume that the Great Depression or Great Recession with plunging stock or bond or real estate losses greater than 50% won't happen again in our lifetimes. And then when it does, to brag about how your fund's fees are less than the industry standard. Economic uncertainty will certainly happen again to us and to our children. In the meantime, we age and have less time to recover from losses. Has the standard financial industry advice to diversify, to think long term, to make decisions based primarily on age, really helped us to survive and thrive in these times? Or is there more required to achieve successful investing results?

When we factor in the human realities of age and circumstance, can we all honestly say that we're better off today by having done nothing else but buy and hold? It's been a long 14 years since the stock market made its top in 2000. Some indexes still have yet to exceed those peaks. What of bonds? Yields have dropped, and prices have rallied, but if the 30-year bond bull market is over, then when interest rates rise, does it still make sense to buy and hold bonds as a viable investment strategy? How will the standard 60% stock and 40% bond allocation perform in the future? We have in fact aged, and our lifestyles have changed over the years. Moreover, our time left in which to recover losses in the future has also shortened; it is the same with our ability to enjoy it as we once did. To say stocks have recovered to where they were 14 years ago, while ignoring the personal factors, is not to say much of anything at all.

This standard industry combination of ignoring devastating market declines and soaring market advances while disregarding our personal human realities of age and circumstance are the prompting for my writing this book. Instead, I ask and answer whether there is a way to approach investing that accounts for these variables that will help us to create and retain wealth over the generational years. Yes, selecting which funds to buy and which to avoid does matter to our wealth. And yes, avoiding bear market losses also matters.

Timeless, however, is not to say it is not timely. The reader, regardless of the amounts in his or her retirement or personal investments, should be able to use the information today. While the material transcends time in that it takes into account the various roller-coaster scenarios of the past 100 years, it is to apply the lessons learned from the past to today's market for tomorrow's market. Each generation will be able to apply the clear, proven, simple, and easy to implement conclusions.

What I want to provide the reader are answers that will both take advantage of and go beyond today's news, conflicts, machinations, and interpretations. Is the market cheap, or is it expensive? Which funds are providing the most return with the least risk? Which funds are lagging? Perhaps more important, it is not the answers today that matter the most. Instead, it is how we answer these questions. Is there a strategy behind the answers? Yes, there is.

Does human nature change? Don't we still fight over scarcity and plenty? Over the next generations, won't the same human emotions of greed and fear play out in endless cyclical repetitions in markets ranging from stocks to bonds to commodities to housing, just as they always have over the last 100 years? If we can first stand back with a sort of detached, analytical, and unemotional attitude, we will see years upon years of the same identifiable cycles of human nature that fluctuate from greed to fear and back again, generation to generation.

The crowd always thinks that this time, this market rally or collapse is different; it is going to the moon, or it is going to hell. Does it ever? Of course not, yet this irrational, reactionary cycle plays out over and over in the various markets. In the meantime, we age, and our circumstances change. How much better off would we be if we invested contrarily to our emotions and the hype? Is there a way to identify and participate in the major uptrends while avoiding the major downtrends? Can we identify those managers who have the ability to do this? Can we also consistently recognize and invest with the funds that are outperforming the markets and their peers?

We can look at ancient or recent history to see the damage done by buy-and-hold advice even when the price disassociates itself from value. We can find this from the Tulip Mania of the 1700s to the dot-com blowup in 2000 to the more recent run-up in housing that preceded the financial implosion in 2007 and 2008. While each market (commodities, bonds, stocks, housing) was different, in each instance we can find the same principles of unreasonable expectation and eventual disassociation between price and value both at the greed-infested, greater fool upside top and in the fear-instilled subsequent bottoming process.

Will there be similar cycles of greed and fear in our lifetimes and in our children's? The short answer is yes. Maybe it will be the cure for cancer or a renewable energy source, but be assured there will be something. Human nature simply does not change. Rather than be a victim and go along on the buy-and-hold roller-coaster ride with the financial industry companies, while they continuously collect their fees from you, we can learn from history and strive to profit from these secular and cyclical forces.

After over 30 years in the investing business and after talking with thousands of investors, the same question always comes up: Can you make me money and not lose it? There are no guarantees, but what matters is investing with the right funds at the right times. I measure this with a formula based on striving to maximize return and minimize risk. Get out your number 2 pencils for marking. We will be learning principles and new habits that will benefit not only you but your heirs with a rotational strategy for selecting and timing the best mutual funds and ETFs. It is time for a C change.

As you will read, C is my proprietary ranking measure of mutual funds and ETFs by their risk-adjusted relative performance. We use the C metric to rank funds with the goal of investing with the leaders and avoiding the laggards. When we select the top funds by C, it may make a substantial difference in your financial well-being over time.

Acknowledgments

I want to thank my wife Diana for her patience and support. I also want to thank my editors for their patience, feedback, and help. Writing a book—there's nothing like it to focus your thinking.

Introduction

AFTER 30 YEARS OF CHALLENGING THE FINANCIAL INDUSTRY STATUS quo by providing successful investment results based on a sound, proven strategy, I have two rules. Rule 1 is don't lose it. Rule 2 is don't forget rule 1. Sound trite? Sound familiar? It has been my statement of purpose the whole time: we strive to provide the most return with the least risk.

What's the alternative to this goal? You may be surprised to learn that there is one. Banks, brokerages, mutual funds, and insurance companies generally tell the public something different. Their first rule is this: "Buy and hold our products for the long term." Their second rule stems from their first one: "Diversify because following our rule number one may eventually hit your portfolio with potentially substantial losses of nearly 50% or worse, and it may take decades just to return to breakeven, even as your age and circumstance change."

Their standard advice does mean "Buy our products and hold them." This is not surprising, but is their typical advice the best for you? It is a problem on a number of levels. Buy and hold overlooks market valuations. It ignores the rare, but devastating disaster of a secular bear market from which it may take decades to recoup. Buy and hold disregards how funds perform relative to their peers. It takes no notice of the fact that we age. It ignores our circumstances, like how a recession may impact our financial life. It ignores the big picture of how to put the whole portfolio together in the best way for the times. Lastly, it disregards the future, specifically your future.

To be sure, those standard financial companies have flashy slick brochures, they've been in business for decades, they have organization depth, and they maintain hundreds of millions under management. But have you ever wondered why your experience hasn't lived up to their hype? Way back in the 1940s that question was phrased this way: Where are the customers' yachts?[1]

The industry publicly eschews any market timing to reduce losses, yet internally they employ timing in their funds all the time. They buy and sell daily based on whatever criteria they utilize in picking their underlying holdings in the funds. Ask them what their portfolio turnover ratio is. The turnover ratio is the percentage of buys or sells versus the fund's assets. The annual turnover ratio even for passive funds is about 25%, let alone for active funds where it might exceed 100%. The average turnover rate for all funds from 1980 to 2012 was 62%.[2] If they tell you to "buy and hold" your investments, why don't they do that with their investments? If they say to "trust me, it'll get better," "stick with us," "think long term," why are they not taking their own advice internally? As such, you'll discover that what they say is not what they do. At best, we all define it as a double standard.

How about these next issues? Have you ever wrestled with these comments, questions, and answers?

♦ They have been investing my money since the year 2000, and I still haven't made a dime. My account is still not back to breakeven. There has to be a better way to invest, but what is it? No one is doing better than the index, right?
♦ My 401(k) account looks like it has gained, but when I subtract my monthly contributions, I'm actually still losing money. How can this be?
♦ I still invest with them because the fund manager beat the market for years. After I finally bought, however, the fund did nothing but go south in value. What am I supposed to do? Won't

---

[1] *Where Are the Customers' Yachts?* This book was written in 1940 by Fred Schwed who, as a brokerage firm customer, asked this question: "If the broker has a yacht, where is *my* yacht?"

More recently, in talking with a dealer from Las Vegas, he made the observation that at blackjack, the only one who ever won always was the dealer.
[2] *Source:* Investment Company Institute, *2013 Investment Company Fact Book.*

they be great again? Was it skill or luck that drove the manager's returns? How do I know the difference?

- ◆ The fund industry tells me if I get out now, I'll miss the rally. If they know about the supposed upcoming rally, why didn't they know about the market plunge? I can't stand to even look at my statements anymore. I just don't know what happened or what to do now. All they say is, "Stay with us." They collect their fees and get their wages, but what I get are the losses.
- ◆ I feel like I'm on a roller coaster, riding the market up and down year after year, except this ignores the fact that I'm aging. I may even lose my job. I am getting closer and closer to my retirement. I just don't have the time left to recover from their buy-and-hold advice anymore.
- ◆ Now they are telling me to reallocate, to sell stocks and buy bonds simply because I am older. But it looks like I might be doing the wrong thing. I might be selling low. Why didn't they suggest selling when the market was up? Sell just because I'm five years older? What does my age have to do with an investment's value?
- ◆ Where did that magical benchmark allocation of 60% in stocks and 40% in bonds come from anyway? Why that ratio and not something else? Is it meaningful?
- ◆ They said to diversify. Is it diversification when nearly everything in my portfolio is going down in value? What kind of industry advice is this?
- ◆ The fund has billions in it. We can't all be wrong about this, can we?
- ◆ It is time to exit the roller coaster. I can't take the market's volatility anymore. I will be retiring soon, and I won't have the time to recoup the losses. I am ready to be proactive. What are my alternatives to the standard industry pitch?

Do these comments and experiences and feelings sound familiar to you? You are not alone. For the last 15 years and even much longer, thousands of investors just like you have had what amounts to the same miserable investing experience of riding the stock market zigs and zags. Make a little, lose a little, get a little hope, and then wham, the next big bear hits and half the money is gone again. Retirement now looms closer and closer, and that retirement nest egg is supposed to take over your working wage when you retire, but how?

Still, don't feel bad. Whether you are an institution or individual, they—the fund and financial industry in general—have done a fantastic marketing job of capturing and keeping your money invested in a certain way, even as they consistently underperform their peers or the indexes or lose half a fund's value in bear markets. Status quo marketing, buy and hold, is designed to keep you with their funds. They ride the market up and down with your money and get paid month after month regardless of client results. What accountability? It is, after all is said and done, how they get paid: retain the account. Regardless of whether they make you money or lose your money, they collect their fees, as long as you remain invested with them. Regardless of whether the fund uses an active or passive management approach, they get paid. Keep in mind I'm not talking about just management fees but also the fees from trading the fund's assets. Follow the money to the source of advice. Is it sound? Is it working? Is there a better way—one that accounts for your age and circumstance, as well as market valuations—to make fund choices and more?

The questions this book addresses are these: Why is "timing" a bad word for the investor, but when the fund itself uses timing to purchase and sell all the time, it's okay? Is diversifying really the answer to avoiding losses? Why shouldn't we use cash as an asset class? Is there such a thing as an overvalued or undervalued market? Is the market rational? Is the financial industry's advice about investing for the long term sound for you? Is age-based allocation a reasonable investment principle? Is there a way to measure funds against each other to take advantage of winners and avoid losers? Is there a way to take back control of your investments with a proven investment strategy? Is there a way for you to successfully manage the managers of your money?

They say, "Don't sell. Don't leave us. You'll miss the rally. Ignore the losses. It'll come back. Forget you're aging. Forget your retirement. Ignore your circumstance. Ignore the recession. Buy and hold and forget. Think long term. Diversify based on your age." I ask, "Why do they give us this advice?" Their answers will vary slightly, but two themes will dominate the answers. They say, "Market timing is impossible, and selecting in advance the next singular great fund to carry you for the subsequent 25 years is a shot in the dark." Does this sound familiar?

Except, to complicate matters, occasionally one manager does stand out, at least for a while, outperforming the S&P 500 Index for a number of years. We think the one manager must be skillful because he accomplished this for 10 years in a row. If he starts to slip in performance, we just attribute it to bad luck and stick with him. If it was skill for 10 years, then the eleventh-year failure must instead just be bad luck, we reason. So the occasional shooting star, the anomaly, does make it harder to stay the course of your taking control of managing the managers, of managing your investment account, unless you have more information. That's the information you'll find in this book.

Taking control of your investments doesn't mean buy and hold; instead, it means taking a proactive approach like selling the laggard funds and buying the leader funds. How do we know what they are? And just as important, can you sell the star fund as it starts to lag? The fund's hype nearly always lasts far longer than the performance. Recall the near hysteria of buying index funds that first peaked in 2000. It's been a long 15 years back to breakeven. We will find, until the manager's performance exceeds 15 years, there is no way to statistically separate the skillful manager or strategy from the lucky manager or strategy. By then, the investor's personal human factors like circumstance and age begin to dominate the investment equation. The reality is that you are 15 years closer to retiring. We need a strategy now.

As the star managers slip into oblivion one by one over the years, the indexers rally around the idea that since you can't beat them, join us. Buy the index funds that mimic the market. Have you ever wondered, however, how the stocks in the index are picked in the first place? Have you observed that since the year 2000, many indexes have yet to exceed those highs, especially when adjusted for inflation? And when they do, all those years of lost compounding will never be made up. Fifteen years is a long time not to make any money, even as you, the investor, continue to take the risk of market loss. Besides, we continue to age. The reality is that if you're not yet retired, retirement itself continues to edge closer and closer over the years. We'll look further into this in the bear markets of 1930, 1974, and more.

Lastly, it's a bit disingenuous to claim having the lowest-fee index fund, even as they lose 50% of investors' money and take more than a decade to get back to breakeven. Low fees didn't help the investors make money one bit. If anything, the low fees provided just another false sense of something important that really wasn't in terms of actually making money for the risk incurred. And after all, that is the point of investing—not to pay the least amount of money in fees but to make the most amount of money (net of whatever the fee is) for the risk taken.

We will explore some tools to use to help in the asset allocation process. They are akin to the same ones successful well-known managers use to pick individual stocks. The dominant theme is value. Have you ever heard a manager say, "I buy the most overvalued stocks I can find"? Of course not, yet that is what investors and managers are doing at overvalued market tops. Have you ever heard a manager say, "I am selling because of my age"? How about, "I am buying because of my age"? Of course not.

No, indexing per se is not the solution to the problem of building and retaining wealth using mutual funds and ETFs. All of the troubling issues—like losing half your investment in the next bear market—that are inherent in actively managed funds also apply to indexed funds or knowing how to assemble a portfolio designed to maximize return and minimize risk.

To be clear about this, I understand the risk of investing. There is always the potential for loss. There have been unexpected horrors like the terrorist attacks on 9/11 that shut down the markets. There have been market crashes like the one that happened in 1987. If these things happened in the past, be sure something similar can happen again. So paying attention to other factors like having an emergency fund, controlling debt, keeping your job secure, and giving diligent attention to your portfolio are required. There could be warning flags to be seen. Yet, buy and hold does not deal with these potentialities either; it will also be affected.

Today there is some $13 trillion in thousands of funds, raking in billions in fees and commissions. The managers make money, but have they done a good job at helping you make and retain money? Who has the yachts? Is there a better alternative?

The Author's Background

After joining the industry in 1982 as a stockbroker, I eventually suspected there was a better way to approach investing than the standard industry advice. This way would put the client first. Internally managed funds would not be favored for no apparent reason. There wouldn't be an attitude of do what I say, not what I do. Further it would objectively measure managers and impassionedly recognize leaders and laggards with a strategy to buy, hold, and sell no-load funds. It would quantitatively measure market valuations to determine when risk of loss is high or low. For 30 years, this way has been developed, tried, and proven. I have boiled this down to an investment approach, whereby we strive to provide the most return with the least risk.

One, identify and invest with the active or passive fund leaders over time. We know that the leaders and laggards will change. We can measure and take advantage of that rotation. It does not surprise us. It is simply a matter of fact. We do this by C, which is the risk-adjusted relative performance number.

Two, recognize and act on the knowledge that the market has intrinsic, measurable value that fluctuates from overvaluation to undervaluation. After all, the market itself is made up of thousands of actual businesses that have sales and costs and profits. Companies cycle through periods of cheap and expensive, from recession to expansion. As businesses change, so, too, will the market. The point is that the market valuations change.

Selecting and timing is my developed, tested, and perfected two-pronged strategy as we strive to provide the most return with the least risk. I recognize and try to capture the market's main moves up and avoid the main moves down based on valuation and trend metrics. I sort through all the fund choices by boiling it all down to a single selecting number, a C, for Comet. C is a fund's risk-adjusted relative performance number. The higher the C, the better; it means the fund has achieved more return per unit of risk taken. I use C instead of stars because I wanted the metaphorical comets to match the reality that funds, like comets, come into and out of prominence. Unlike comets, stars are fixed. No such thing exists in the investment world.

We want to make the most money with the least amount of risk, right? This is our guiding principle. This C strategy allows us to in effect manage the managers each month. If the fund is highly ranked based on C, we stay with it. When the C ranking drops into underperform, we sell it. It is that simple. Moreover, in a bear market, what fund is providing the most return with the least risk? It is a money market fund. This rotational strategy uses equity, bond, and cash allocations.

The independent newsletter watchdog *Hulbert Financial Digest* ranked my newsletter, the *No-Load Mutual Fund Selections & Timing Newsletter* (NLMFS&T), out of all the newsletters he tracks, number 1 for risk-adjusted performance over the 20 years ending December 31, 2013. This is through all sorts of up, down, and sideways markets, over secular and cyclical movements, following hundreds of funds, to pick the top funds, avoid the laggards, and capture the wealth-creating up moves while avoiding the wealth-destroying down markets.

Let me interject here. It really is easy enough to make money in a bull market, right? All one has to do is participate, throw a dart. It's not as easy, however, to make and keep that money over both cycles of bull and bear markets. So how do we do this? How can you do this? We want to provide you with the advice that allows you to take back your control over your investments. There are two things to keep in mind.

First, we know that the economy will change. Second, we know the markets have a thing called "value."

Unless you take control of your money, you are at the mercy of the markets and the managers, of the standard industry advice that says to buy and hold and don't compare and forget your age and circumstance. The managers must invest according to the prospectus. If it tells them to be fully invested, they will be, all the way down.

You don't have to follow that no-control outdated advice that essentially comes from the marketing department. You can manage your money. You can manage the managers and the markets. You can buy. You can sell. You can reallocate as the years go by, not based on your age but based on a proven rotational approach that combines selections and timing.

This book is about your taking back control of your own financial future from those who have educated us with information based on outdated metaphors and from those whose main goal is to collect fees off your investments.[3] This book will show you how to take back and keep control. Together we will create a plan of action that will work in all kinds of markets. It will answer important questions like, "How do we identify the leaders and laggards from the mass of funds?" "How do we know when the market has value and when irrational exuberance is reigning?" The answers are born from, nurtured by, and matured with 30 years of personal investing experience plus hundreds of hours of research on what others are doing. We care about you.

Pondering

Imagine it is 1982 when the Dow Jones Industrial Average was below 1,000. The market has been going broadly sideways since 1966, even as the economy (the GDP) has grown during that time. This period includes the devastating bear market that ended in 1974, plus other bear markets along the way. A large national brokerage firm has just hired you as one of its stockbrokers. What general advice would be the most useful for you and your clients?

Not something specific like, "Don't buy that Apple computer for $6,000, but buy the stock AAPL and hang on for the next 30 years." Not something that is known only in hindsight. But advice that is more general. Not something about basically unknown investment managers at the time like Warren Buffett or John Templeton. Or something about unknown business managers like Steve Jobs or Bill Gates. But generally speaking, what would be good advice? Something that would apply to the overall investment haystack and not just what would turn out to be about a few outlier needles you luckily stumbled upon. Guidance that will serve you well over years and years of investing, rather than advice about the big ones that got away that become so visible only years after the fact, whether they are a single manager or a single stock. After all, who knows the future? So, what general advice back in 1982 about investing would help for years and years and years in up and down and up and down markets?

---

[3] Among others, Citigroup Inc. just settled a suit for $590 million in penalties for its alleged part in the financial implosion dealing with toxic subprime debt. Quite incredible to consider that that was the only penalty. Presumably the profits were even larger; after all, they still are in business.

I remember being hired in 1982 as if it were yesterday. Here I was a twentysomething in charge of people's future well-being. In charge of whether they would live comfortably or in misery, though no one really emphasized that onerous burden on us newbies. To be sure, I was with a large, well-respected brokerage firm with lots of resources, a solid decades-old history, hundreds of millions under management, and a depth of centuries of combined managerial experience. Sound familiar? What could possibly go wrong? But in the end, some 25 years later, as it turned out, did that help them? Did it help the customers? The firm eventually went, for want of a more delicate word, bankrupt; it now exists as a bank subsidiary, which itself also required billions in government bailout and tax law[4] changes in 2009 to appear solvent as it found its footing on the ledge of depression's abyss. For all their smarts and connections and assets and experiences, in the end, the reality was that they truly didn't really have it figured out at all. They went bankrupt. And then required a bailout before their acquirer also required a bailout. So what sound advice could they really suggest to their brokers to impart to clients that would truly help? If you can't manage your own money to make money, how in the world can you manage other people's money?

Another example of where'd the smarts go question in real-time action is the Long-Term Capital Management (LTCM) firm. It was founded in 1994, and after a spectacular run with astounding gains, it went bankrupt by 1998 and dissolved finally in 2000. The company was stuffed with soon-to-be Nobel Laureates and PhDs, but in the end their algorithms lost billions for their clients.[5]

---

[4] In March 2009, the House Financial Services Committee evidently pressured the Financial Accounting Standards Board (FASB) to change its accounting rules to help banks, brokerages, and insurance companies. The committee proposed allowing companies to use "significant judgment" in valuing assets, arguing that fair value, or mark-to-the-market accounting, should be suspended during certain times. This news event marked the bottom for the stock market.

Incidentally, I believe that without this accounting rule change, we would have gone into Great Depression II, rather than as it came to be called "Great Recession."

[5] From Bennett W. Goodspeed's book *The Tao Jones Averages: A Guide to Whole-Brained Investing,* written in 1984, well in advance of LTCM's debacle, the story is told of the world's smartest man and the rabbi and the hippy all flying together when the captain rushes to the back and tells the three that the plane is going down and they have only two parachutes left between them and to save

I must say here that success oftentimes breeds blindness to the upcoming cliff. A single approach may work fantastically well for a while, but what's the exit strategy? Age? The gains were all on paper, projected and compounded forward in glorious greed. It is simply the same human nature story told in another variation of the variety of ways over and over. The haughtiness of pride typically and often follows the big success that comes before the horrible fall. Humbleness is a trait to be nurtured continuously from the mountaintop encounters with God to the next top in the stock market.[6]

After the Great Secular Bull Market started in 1982, remember the crash of 1987? Some prominent pundits were calling for the market to actually decline back to where it was in 1974. Such baloney—they had probably missed the whole advance, so wanted it to come down; their bias blinded them. What they had missed, as did nearly everyone else at the time, was that they didn't get the picture of the massive secular change taking place from bearish to bullish.

In addition to 1987's bear, recall the cyclical bear markets of 1990 and 1994? What did all three of those declines have in common that made them different from the one that ended in 1982? They were short and sweet, as far as bear markets go. They were over within months, and they were shallow on average. They were scary to be sure, but within a year or so, the markets were making higher new highs. In fact, those bear markets ended at higher lows from previous cyclical lows. Higher highs and higher lows are the very definition of a bull market.

Who can resist easy money? Finally after the market had been going up for 18 long years, the investor mantra changed. The

---

yourselves. He jumps out with his parachute, yelling "Good luck!" The world's smartest man grabs one, straps it on, and jumps, saying as he bails out that the world needs him. The rabbi looks at the hippy and says, "You take the last one my son. I've lived my life." The hippy replies, "Don't worry, padre. There are still two parachutes left. He grabbed my backpack."

[6] One wonders about Moses meeting God Almighty face-to-face on Mount Sinai and then descending to deal with his stiff-necked, blind fellows for 40 years in the wilderness. Were Moses' fellows not, after all is said and done, in reality, to benefit Moses? And yet, not learning the real lesson, he still angrily smote the rock twice, thus prohibiting his entry into the Promised Land. Just because you "get it" doesn't mean anyone else will.

standard industry advice to buy and hold was firmly in place; that's the way to fortune and fame. By the year 1998, after years of up and up, then came the final Internet boom and the magazine covers with wild-eyed day traders making thousands of apparently easy dollars in a single day. Throw a dart. Just buy something with dot-com in the name. Not to be outdone, many individuals and institutions were piling into index funds, as the active managers just didn't get it and lagged the gains. Get fully invested, and stay fully invested via an index fund, some people in the fund industry intoned. The Nifty Fifty from the 1960s had been repackaged and were reborn into S&P 500 Index funds. The clarion calls of indexing, using a buy-and-hold/forget strategy, rose in a fevered pitch.

The secular bull market had lasted from 1982 to 2000. It was getting very long-in-the-tooth by 2000. Valuation measurements were changed from earnings and dividends to click-through rates. Despite what everyone was now thinking at the time, markets don't go to the moon. The next bear market began to unfold. It, however, unexpectedly didn't act like the previous three bear markets in duration or magnitude. It wasn't over after dropping 25%; nor was it over in three short months. It still wasn't finished after a long two years. Everyone was surprised, devastated, and confused; it went down sharply and more broadly for a third year in a row. A three-year bear market was unheard of, except for the time back in the Great Depression. Surely it is not like that is it? Babies were thrown out with the bathwater at the market's bottom.

And then finally the market recovered somewhat. Time to party again the way we partied in 1999. Many got in again at higher prices after selling at the bottom just in time for the next great event, the financial implosion of 2007 and 2008. Some rode out that first bear market of 2000 to 2003, and after six long years they finally made it nearly back to breakeven. Pow. Down went the stock market by roughly 50% again. This was two devastating wealth-cutting bear markets in the same decade. What is going on? Will it happen again? How will you protect yourself from losing 50% again? Fifteen years of breakeven investing from 2000 to 2014 has been wasted. The account may be back to where it was, but not our ages. All that has been gained is personal aging: we are getting nearer to retirement with less real money to show for it. Has the standard industry advice helped? Not really. Look around and see the remains of it both in terms of financial and personal costs.

For mutual fund investors over these times, to add fund manager insult to market injury, it also turned out that some of the star managers of the nineties have been, to put it bluntly, horrible in the 2000s. The leaders are now the laggards. It hasn't helped to own the previous heroes anymore; they lost as much if not more than everyone else in the bear markets.

"Gun slingers" the managers were called back in the 1960s.[7] Young. Fearless. Nothing to lose, except other people's money. It wasn't their money, so who cares? They got their fees. In the secular bull market, as the tide lifted all boats, they were right. They were winning, the investors were winning, without thought for tomorrow. "I am invincible," cried Boris before the explosion.[8] They had skill, they thought. Luck had nothing to do with it, they thought. They were beating the (Dow) Joneses. In the 1960s, index funds hadn't been invented as alternatives. Fast forward to the 1990s, and it is not those same people anymore running the hot hands. If they survived the 1970s, which were part of the previous secular bear market, they were now the stodgy conservative types rolling bond ladders.[9] After all, their retirement had arrived. They collected their salaries, their fees, but what did the investors have to show for it? Who owns the yachts?

The new breed of hot investors born in that time, by the 1990s, became the day traders, the momentum growth investors. Young. Fearless. Nothing to lose. If you don't like it, though, you could always start using indexes. Just as it was true at the market's top in

---

[7] Adam Smith, *The Money Game, 1976.*

[8] *GoldenEye*, a James Bond novel (Ian Fleming creator) made into film presciently (in hindsight) in 1995. Popular culture, like magazine covers, may be used as a tuning fork to investor sensibilities, though sometimes they may ring early.

Prior to the National Security Agency (NSA) Edward Snowden's leak of classified information in 2013, CBS had already been airing a show for two years called *Person of Interest* whose tag line started, "You're being watched . . ."

[9] Bond ladders are a bond investment strategy that uses a scheduled series of bond maturities. For example, you might have a 10-year ladder with bonds maturing every six months (20 times over the next 10 years). As the bond matures each six months, you roll it out into a new 10-year bond. Maturities may be lengthened or shortened depending on one's view of the probable direction of interest rates. More is discussed in Chapter 3.

the 1960s, however, there seemed to be an implicit idea after 20 years of uptrends that the market wouldn't and couldn't go down. "We're on a permanent plateau. And if it goes down, it'll just be like the previous bears, short and sweet, with maybe a little of your own blood, but then it will be shortly back up and soaring again. Buy, buy, buy. Hold, hold, hold." Wrong, wrong, wrong.

As we now know, from its peak in 2007 the market lost 50%, falling back to where it had been in 1997. And frankly, if it weren't for that aforementioned accounting change, who knows where we would have ended the bear carnage.

What we need is an alternative to the outdated, self-serving star advertising message from the standard industry advice of buy and hold, of ride the market up and ride it back down, and ignore value. We need instead to take control, to actually apply the strategy of trying to make the most return with the least risk. How will we do this? I answer, follow the comets as they come into and out of prominence. As surely as it happened in the past, losses of 50% will happen again. Can you afford it again?

Through all of this history and analysis, your author has been investing and writing about investing for about 30 years. He has experienced the ups and downs of secular bull and bear markets and numerous cyclical bull and bear markets. He has watched and talked about the top managers who plunge in relative performance to become the worst managers.[10] He has tried to find a way to answer the question posed by thousands of investors: "How do I make money and not lose it?"

Let's start and find out about a proven profitable proactive rotational allocation strategy to take back control of our investments. It accounts for the reality of personal time and circumstance. It provides a way to rank and identify the top managers each month, quarter, and year. It offers how to strive to maximize return and minimize risk.

---

[10] Speaking on a radio show back in 2006, I was asked about Bill Miller's Legg Mason Value Fund (LMVTX). It had quite a record. It outperformed the S&P 500 Index for a number of years, but what did I think? How did I rank it? I answered it was now underperforming based on my C metric, on my risk-adjusted relative performance basis. From the reactions, people thought I was crazy. But I wasn't. I was just following my C approach to invest with the top risk-adjusted relative strength funds. The subsequent record speaks for how important it is to follow the C rankings. We go by the funds' current results, not their names or past performance.

Around the Buttonwood Tree

IN THE NEW WORLD, SPECULATORS AND INVESTORS GATHERED around the buttonwood tree in what would become Manhattan to make deals, to buy and sell, in what was a fairly exclusive club 200 years ago.[1] Today traders, managers, speculators, and investors gather around their computer monitors to receive instant information from around the world and make buy and sell decisions. The idea of the exchange is still the same today: like a button, it is to bring two sides together. From its humble beginnings, the financial industry has grown with the wealth of the nations to help you to create and retain your own wealth.

Imagine that today we have 20,000 professionals competing for the privilege of managing your money, whether your nest egg ranges from a tiny sum of $100 to a tidy sum of $1 billion or more. Imagine no more, however, because that is what the mutual fund and exchange-traded fund, or ETF,[2] market is doing for us today. These professionals want

---

[1] The chapter title is taken from Wall Street's first gathering place that brought together—like buttons that bring together two sides—traders, investors, and speculators in the New World.

[2] Exchange-traded funds (ETFs) operate the way mutual funds do in that they are open-end (that is, they may issue new shares at net asset value [NAV]) pooled investment vehicles. As is true of a mutual fund, one purchases shares of an ETF

our money to manage whether it comes in the form of a new 401(k) participant or a retired person's account or anywhere in between. They are scrambling over themselves to promote their firm, their investment style, and their market strategy as your best answer to the questions: What do I do now with my investment money? How do I invest it to gain the most return with the least risk of loss?

Most investors have wondered about these questions: Is my nest egg working as hard for me as I do for it? How does my broker or manager compare with other managers? Why is this fund part of my 401(k), rather than some other fund? How will I make sure I have enough money saved to retire on to not only maintain my lifestyle but perhaps even improve upon it? Should I buy and hold or try to time the market? Should I diversify? Is there a more profitable, less stressful, all-weather approach to investing? Do I have to ride the stock market roller coaster up and down just to end up where I began? What's the best way to use to choose my funds?

The funds want us, but do we want them? We have thousands of fund managers from which to choose involving hundreds of investment strategies. So, how do we decide which of them we will trust? Whom will we invest our money with? Even after we decide, new questions arise: For how long will we remain invested with them? What if our goals change over time? Will theirs? What if the markets change? Will the managers adjust? How will we measure their success or failure with our money? What will cause us to leave them, and just as important, what will cause us to stay invested with them? These questions and more are what I hope to answer in this book.

Does It Matter?

Before we look into a brief history of funds, there is one more question to ask right from the start: Does any of this really matter? Does it matter whom I pick to manage my money or which fund I use?

---

and gets professional management, diversification, and a set objective. The key difference between the two is that ETFs are tradable during the day, as stocks are. Mutual funds are priced and tradable only once a day at the close of the market.

In this book, when I say "fund," I am including both mutual funds and exchange-traded funds in the definition. Otherwise, I will specifically say "mutual fund" or "ETF" to designate each. While the two are similar investment vehicles, they are also very different in a number of ways.

Can't I just throw a dart and be done with it? Can't I just buy a low-cost index fund or choose the hot manager and not worry about it? What about buying the lifestyle- or age-based fund? Aren't they all really just about the same?"

Behind these questions are a few assumptions: Doesn't the stock market have to continue to go up over time? Won't the manager's performance eventually match an index (the technical term is *reversion to the mean*)? We will never have another Depression, right, 2008 and early 2009 notwithstanding? The market eventually recovered, and it has continued to go up, so won't it continue to go up the next 100 years? Behind the buy-and-hold advice, behind the index fund promotion, is this long-term, rising market "bailout" idea of time. These assumptions predict that the future will be like the past. It may be, but then again it may not be. Besides, as we all know, we age as we wait to get back to breakeven. For example, we have all aged since 2000, and we have less time in 2015 in which to recuperate another 50% loss like in 2000–2003 and 2007–2009. So, let's not merely agree we have questions, but let's investigate some of the assumptions. Let's be honest and forthcoming about these things.

The truth is that the market does not have to move in one direction, either up or down, especially when adjusted for inflation. The long-term trend we see in the pretty brochures ignores the personal realities of age and circumstance. I will look more closely at this in the next chapter.

The truth is that funds and managers are not at all the same. It does matter which funds and managers we choose. There is a huge performance difference between the best funds and the worst funds each and every year. I am not just talking about what might be obvious differences between, say, an international small-cap value fund and a domestic large-cap growth index fund or between a solar ETF and a health ETF. I am saying that there is a wide variance in performance between the top funds and the bottom funds each and every year, even between those funds whose objectives are identical!

It is notable that, for example, in the calendar year 2010, of the 600 equity funds we tracked, the best 5% gained 28.8%, while the bottom 5% gained a mere 1.3%. This vast performance spread between the leaders and laggards happens year after year. If you take that difference and compound it over 30 years, the difference in your retirement nest egg will be astounding.

This next table shows just one year-end comparison between all the funds in the equity asset class in the *No-Load Mutual Fund Selections & Timing Newsletter*, excluding precious metals and inverse funds:

All-Equity Fund Comparison

Year	12 months to December 31, 2010
Top 5%	28.8%
Bottom 5%	1.3%

As investors we might, however, be savvy enough to expect such a wide spread each year when comparing all the equity funds; after all, they have dissimilar goals, various strategies, and different styles. So it is even more astounding that we find this broad performance range even between the funds in the same exact style. Two examples should suffice to show this. The first one is from the small-cap funds we track. The second example is in the hybrid area:

Small-Cap Comparison

Year	12 months to May 31, 2014
Top 5% (3 at the time)	22.2%
Bottom 5% (3 at the time)	12.2%

Hybrid Comparison

Year	2010	2011	2012
Top 20%	12.1%	5.6	13.3
Bottom 20%	2.5%	−5.7	5.1

These figures are remarkable. The managers have the same objectives, and they pick from the same areas of the stock market; they actually have nearly the same "stable" of stocks from which to buy and sell. The spread nevertheless between the leaders and laggards is huge. Again, compound the difference in returns over time, and you understand why investing with the leaders is so important to your wealth.

It is the same dramatic spread of performance in the hybrid area. Hybrid funds will use some combination of stocks, bonds, and cash to achieve their goals. They all have roughly the same objectives, and they pick their holdings from the same orchard of stocks and bonds and cash, but the performance difference is eye-popping.

After just those three years, a $100,000 portfolio invested in the top funds grew to $133,800, while $100,000 in the worst 20% grew to $102,219. This is a phenomenal difference of more than 30%, or $31,581, in just three years. Imagine the difference after 20 years or more. The bottom line is that it does matter whom we use in all investment styles. As we will see in Chapter 6, we have an investment strategy designed just to take advantage of this.

Now I don't want to give the false impression that we always successfully pick the number one fund each and every year. We don't. But it is not necessary to be number one every year to achieve above average returns over time. We do recognize this performance difference, and we at least try to do something positive about it. The standard industry advice will ignore these things. After all, to recognize that another fund with the same objectives and risk is doing better than yours is akin to losing you as a client. When was the last time you heard your advisor tell you to switch advisors?

So, as we saw, it matters tremendously whom we pick to invest our money with to grow and retain our nest egg over time. Clearly, the financial and fund industry wants us to invest with them, but just as clearly, it matters whom we choose to invest with each month and each year. If we pick the top funds over time, the difference it will make to us will be life changing.

We see that, yes, it matters with whom we invest, but how do we take advantage of this information? In the first place, we have to decide to be proactive. The key here to understand up front is that the fund we choose today may or may not be the same fund we should choose six months or six years from now. The top funds change over time. That is the fact. The old days of buy and hold and forget and ignore are over. Today we have choices. We can switch easily between funds. We have a way to monitor and track this risk-adjusted, relative performance between funds. We do it because it clearly matters with whom we invest our money.

What Do We Do?

Although I will talk more about this in later chapters, right from the start I want to introduce the reader to my guiding principle. We strive to provide the most return with the least risk. That guide may sound simple and straightforward enough, but how many firms consistently practice this? To do it requires two things.

One, it requires an active approach that I call "managing the managers." We can "hire" certain funds by investing in the top funds today, and we can "fire" the same managers months or years later by moving assets away from those funds when (not if) they become laggards. A fund may have been among the best last year, but this year it may be bringing up the rear. Why do we need to remain invested with them? We don't have to in this day and age. It is simple to buy and sell. It is cheap to buy and sell. To be clear, this active approach will include index or passive funds, as well as active funds. The approach is active, even if the fund itself is passive.

Two, it requires using all asset classes as investment choices. This means including equities, bonds, and cash (money market funds). If you have invested longer than from the last bear market bottom in March 2009, you know there are times when cash is providing the most return and least risk. If our guiding principle is to make the most return with the least amount of risk, then it requires taking very defensive actions from time to time. At other times, equities may be providing the most return for the risk. Then again at other times, it might be bonds. The point is to include them all as we potentially use all funds.

Manage the Managers by C

This idea of managing the managers is probably a foreign concept to most investors. After all, we invest with particular managers in the first place because of some viable factor, like past performance or fees or familiarity. Why attempt to manage what we think we already have managed?

There is a second issue. Managing the managers in terms of moving money away from the managers we've picked implies that maybe the reason we bought in the first place was wrong. Who wants to be wrong? The truth is different: things change. There are times to move your money. The fund industry advises you not to change. It practically never advises selling; instead, it advises you only to hold on, regardless of risk and relative performance.

In Chapter 6, I will provide more details about how we manage the managers, but suffice to say here, in my monthly and weekly letters, we rank and sort and select from about 1,000 no-load mutual funds and ETFs by C; C stands for Comets. Using C, I actively asset allocate by a rotation strategy. This is managing the managers.

People ask, Why C? Most investors are familiar with stars, but comets? I wanted the metaphor to match reality. Stars are fixed. Comets, like funds, come into and out of prominence. We strive to make the most money with the least risk, not to hold onto a star falling into losses.

In a nutshell, C is the risk-adjusted relative performance number. The higher the Comet number, the better. It is a unique, simple way to answer the question that every investor has: How do I try to make money and not lose it? We identify which funds are providing the most return with the least risk across asset and style categories. For example, a fund with a C of 30 versus a fund with a C of 15 means that the first fund is better than the second because it is providing more return per unit of risk.

We know there are thousands of fund choices and hundreds of investment strategies all trying to entice us to let them manage our money. Do we have an overall approach that guides us in making this decision? For us, the answer is yes. We manage the managers by C.

Some of us participate in a 401(k) or 403(b) or other retirement plans. They are a great method to save money,[3] but unless you have a brokerage option,[4] you are limited to the investment funds in the plan. Leaving aside the question about how certain funds made it

---

[3] As an aside, but to provide additional practical advice to readers with a 401(k), you should try to at least "meet the match." For example, if your employer matches 50% of the first 3% of employee contributions, you should save at least 3% of your paycheck. If the employer matches 100% of the first 5%, then save at least the 5%. The portion you contribute is always 100% yours, and you are fully vested on that portion. The employer contribution is typically vested over time according to its schedule.

[4] The *brokerage option*, whereby 401(k) participants may open a brokerage account, is gaining some traction and becoming more common among plans. It allows participants to invest in a much wider variety of investments than what the company offers. The upside is more freedom and potentially better returns, but the downside is it may require more time and expertise on the part of the participant.

into the plan in the first place, we ask the same questions: How do you pick one fund from the others in the plan? How do you diversify? Is a rotational allocation strategy a viable alternative to a buy-and-hold strategy? If so, what formula do you use? Is it age based or value oriented or what? Even in a limited 401(k), you still have the option of actively allocating your portfolio between stocks, bonds, and cash. I will speak more to this in a later chapter, and this information is also updated at our website 401kSelections.com. In the meantime, Figure 1.1 is a composite chart showing the results from applying the proactive rotational manage-the-managers by C approach to 20 plans.

The average annual return over the 20.5-year backtest period was 13.6%; SPY (an ETF designed to mimic the S&P 500 less fees and expenses) was 8.6%; and Vanguard Wellington (VWELX) was 9.5%. The strategy forces at least a two-month holding period before rotating. Results shown assume a zero starting amount and $500 per

FIGURE 1.1 A Composite Chart Showing the Results from Applying the Proactive Rotational Manage-the-Managers by C Approach to 20 Plans

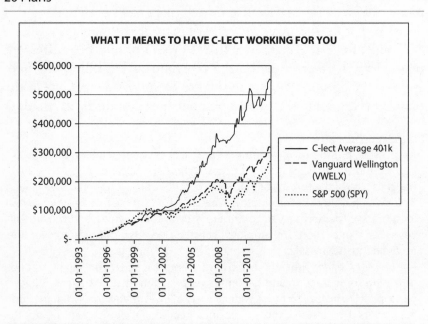

Source: Data from State Street Global Markets and Vanguard.

month contributions into each position. The top two funds as ranked by C in each 401(k) plan were used. Dividends and capital gains were reinvested. There is no assurance that future periods will be the same as or similar to past periods. This does not take into account a person's personal situation. Past performance does not guarantee future performance. See our website, http://401kSelections.com, for more information.

I advocate this proactive methodology to investing called *managing the managers*. This, in effect, is what we do. We look at the fund and ETF performance results net of fees. We look at relative performance. We consider the risk they take. We rank the managers. We make index and active fund comparisons. We make adjustments over time. We try to make the most return with the least risk. We actively manage which managers we trust with our money.

Choices

Unlike how it was even some 20 years ago, mutual fund supermarkets, like the discount brokers Fidelity, Schwab, Ameritrade, Scottrade, and E*TRADE, also all compete and make it easier than ever to use and switch between mutual funds and ETFs. They typically offer two sorts of funds. One is the *transaction-fee fund*, where it costs investors a brokerage commission to buy and sell. Two is the *no-transaction-fee fund* where it does *not* cost investors a brokerage commission to buy and to sell. The "catch" with the latter is that you must hold your position longer than the broker's short-term redemption period. Most brokerages require you to hold a fund at least 90 days, some require 60 days, while others require six months. After the holding period, we may sell without any cost. A few funds may also impose their own short-term holding period. If you sell in this period, the fund itself will charge you a fee. Once this period is over, we are free to sell without costs. Our strategy takes into account these various short-term holding periods.

ETFs are different from mutual funds in that ETFs have daily, even minute-by-minute, liquidity. Mutual funds are priced once a day at the close. That is the price at which you buy or sell. The costs to buy and sell ETFs are the brokerage commissions. There are usually no short-term holding periods for ETFs. Since 2012 some brokers have begun teaming up with ETF providers such that some ETFs are available without trading commission costs, though, as with mutual funds, they may impose a short-term holding period.

So, while the fund stores have made it easier than ever to buy and sell funds, the question of how to choose from among the thousands has not been easier to determine, until now.

With this as a very brief background to what we do and why we work our strategy of managing the managers by C, we will now begin to take a very long term historic look at markets and mutual funds spanning some 300 years. I am trying to show that things change. Buy and hold has not been a long-term viable strategy, if you are trying to maximize return and minimize risk.

History

As we begin to look at the past, one of the first things we need to recognize and readily admit to is that no one knows the future. We may make educated assumptions and hope they work out, but they are assumptions nonetheless. No one knows the future, but we often assume we do, such as when we take a passive do-nothing investment approach, regardless of the vehicle (index or active fund) chosen. This is a potential hazard to our investment health. I bring this up because of our known history of the last few thousand years. We look at the past and know that civilizations have come into and out of prominence over the centuries. Egypt, Rome, Spain, and Britain have all to a degree ruled their known worlds for a time, and all have left their imprints. Had you been a citizen of any one of those cultures, however, it would have been very easy to believe your country would dominate forever. To have said otherwise might have brought you banishment or worse. Today, for you to maintain an unwavering patriotic belief that your country's future is sure to be positive is, to put it bluntly and coldly, just an assumption. It may be an educated, well-considered, and loyal belief, to be sure, but it is a hope nonetheless.

Today, from a citizen of the world's point of view, could America's leadership role ever change? When measured by gross domestic product (GDP), China, for example, has narrowed the difference between the two output measures. According to Goldman Sachs,[5] by 2030

---

[5] Jim O'Neill, *BRICs and Beyond*, Goldman Sachs, New York, November 23, 2007.

China's GDP is expected to exceed that of the United States. By 2050 India's GDP is projected to nearly surpass that of the United States. If these trends continue, how may this change the domestic stock and bond markets? What about the international markets? And if it doesn't happen, then what do we do? Likewise, the recent energy discoveries in North America may be world changing events in the decades ahead, just as such discoveries in the Middle East were in the 1970s. To take another example, in the United States, what will be the domestic impact from entitlement program spending in the years ahead? The point here has nothing to do with patriotism; rather, it is to simply observe, based on history, that there is no guarantee that countries or markets will move solely in one direction or even that they will always recover to record all-time new highs, especially if, as it happens from time to time, your civilization is crumbling down around you. The time to have sold—that is, to recognize the value of a different investing strategy—is long gone. Aren't these the worst two words strung together for investors—too late?

And here is yet another example: we know America survived the Great Depression of the 1930s, but the majority of investor nest eggs did not. This is that personal fact that the standard industry advice may ignore as they trot out the 100-year chart and say, "See, buy and hold never fails. The market's trend in the long, long run is up." But in reality, we age, and our circumstances change. In the 1930s it would still be decades before the jobless rate came down and the stock prices rose again to where they had originally peaked in 1929. Buy and hold as a strategy may have eventually survived that debacle, but only if you, the participant, could also. And how would that be, if your savings had been wiped out in the stock market crash? Unemployment climbed to 25%. Besides, if you were 50 years old in 1929, you would have been 75 years old when the market finally recovered. How many people were able to hang in there for that long just to return to breakeven? If you were out of a job, what was the use of having a fully invested investment account that was dropping more than 50%? How much better instead to have taken a proactive approach, to have sold and let markets and economies unfold and then to have slowly rebought at what were then lower prices? A long 25-year secular bear market, where the average annual return for years was negative, would bring you that much closer to your retirement years without the hoped-and-planned-for retirement nest egg. Can you suffer through a decline like that? How about the investment that loses 50% twice in 10 years and takes a full 13 years to return to breakeven, such as we have been recently experiencing since the year 2000? If the proactive investor is to thrive, I suspect he or she needs a strategy that is different from the typical industry advice.

We know from history that the markets, like countries, will fluctuate. Some will do better than others. We know that no one knows the future. It is only with the benefit of hindsight that we can see that some things presumably worked out, but even then, those things worked out only if we ignored the personal factors of aging and circumstance.

The mistake we make is to measure only one element: price. We typically fail to consider the second and third elements: personal time as regards our age at the start and end and the time difference to recover from losses; we disassociate the personal feelings and circumstances from the numeric facts. We can see that a market eventually recovers in price to its previous level, and we think everything is then the same, but the reality is, it isn't. It ignores inflation. It ignores the human cost from a job loss or a house loss or an emergency fund loss or a myriad of other factors. We have aged. We have less time to recover losses the next time around. The market price may have returned to its former high, but the human cost most certainly will not have.

When history is actually unfolding, when we are participants therein, it is totally different from when we look back at it emotionally detached from age and circumstance. The fact is that when we are in the present living through declines and advances, there are emotions like greed and fear, lifestyle, debts, obligations, and other factors that impact our financial decisions.

Four Guides from History

Another tool we use is the simile of the four points of the compass to direct our investment results away from the rocks of passive ruin, to guide us through the do-nothing empty ocean without reference points, and to avoid the shoals of false hindsight that break apart wealth. With an active, direct manage-the-managers approach to investing, we have liquidity, transparency, measurability, and control. These things were not always available historically, but they are today. We can take advantage of this. Each of these four points will be talked about.

But first, one other thing: we recognize that most investors have a career or are retired with an active lifestyle that does not include sitting glued to the computer monitor watching blinking red and green numbers. Besides, watching the numbers blink is what we pay the fund managers for. It is for those who have our money to figure it out, to successfully invest our assets. Again, they want our money, but do we want to invest with them?

There's nothing new or earth-shattering in asking these questions. The answers we have to the questions, however, may surprise you. Since the first multinational company issuing the first stock that formed the Dutch East India Company in 1602 through 1774 when the first pooled investment account was formed,[6] investors have been trying to make some money by pooling their money together with a trusted advisor. Those pooled-money funds were the basis for mutual funds.

During this period, the first well-known bubble was recorded. It was known as Tulip Mania. At its peak, speculators willingly exchanged their land holdings for a tulip bulb. The dicey fever ran high, and it was eventually characterized by the "greater fool" strategy: it will take a greater fool than you to buy the object from you at a higher price. We know this was the strategy because prices became unhitched from their values. To be sure, bulbs do reproduce. They may be harvested and sold, just as they still are today, so it is a legitimate business with sales, costs, and profits and losses. What was happening in the 1630s, however, was that individual bulbs were selling at excessive multiples of their earnings power. Valuations were out of line. It would take hundreds of years of reproductions to ever get back your investment at the bubble's top. Today, this valuation

---

[6] The first pooled fund is attributed to Adriaan Van Ketwich who was a Dutch merchant. In 1774 he introduced *Eendragt Maakt Magt* ("unity creates strength"). The idea was to combine a number of small investments from many investors, diversify the fund, take advantage of scale, and benefit from the manager's expertise. This is still the idea behind any type of fund.

tool is known as the ubiquitous *price-to-earnings* (P/E) *ratio*. How much are you paying (price) to get net profit (earnings)? All things being equal, the lower the P/E ratio, the better.

After the Tulip Mania and the Dutch, French, and English trading companies began, the first trading agreement in the Thirteen Colonies was reached in 1792 under the metaphoric buttonwood tree in lower Manhattan. About 70 years after the Buttonwood Agreement, this first organization renamed itself the New York Stock Exchange. Its history for the next 100 years was fairly uneventful, if only because of scant records and low volume and narrow participation. One notable exception to those mundane times was the Panic of 1873. In subsequent years, there was the Panic of 1907 and the well-known crash of 1929 to be followed years later by the crash of 1987 when the Dow Industrials dropped 508 points, or 22.6%, in a single day.

It was way back in 1906 when the Dow first cleared 100. In 1956 it crossed 500—it took 50 years for it to move up 400%. Then it reached 1,000 in 1972—it took only 16 years to double. It reached 5,000 by 1996—in other words, in only 24 years, it had moved up 400%. At the end of 2012, it closed near 13,000, meaning that in just 16 years it had more than doubled.

All one had to do to participate in this rise from 100 to 13,000 was to buy and hold, right? As we saw, only if we ignore personal time and circumstances. Viewing a long-term chart is not the same thing as living through the times in which it was created. It is one thing to say I doubled my money in 10 years, but another to admit in the same breath that I did this after previously losing half of it in the years before. The question is always how would emotions and lifestyle affect the decision process? How would the fact of being older, closer to retirement, with less time to correct the losses, have affected decisions? Academic studies that show the Dow rising from 100 to 1,000 over nearly 70 years to the contrary, the reality is we don't know anyone who actually participated in this, who lived through all of the losses and recoveries.

Here's the reality of buy-and-hold and age-based allocation advice. It simply doesn't work in the real world where real people are involved. Take a look at Figure 1.2 that shows equity fund flows from the Investment Company Institute and the S&P 500 total

FIGURE 1.2 Equity Fund Flows from the Investment Company Institute and the S&P 500 Total Return During the Bear Market in 2008 That Ended in March 2009

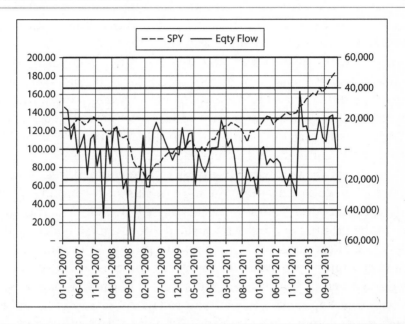

Source: Data from the Investment Company Institute and State Street Global Markets.

return during the bear market in 2008 that ended in March 2009. As you can see, from June 2008 through March 2009, investors were selling funds, except for one month in January, which may correspond to retirement contributions.

The point is that investors were selling all the way down. The reality is that investors actually do recognize age and circumstance, and they will take action to protect their nest eggs, even if funds ignore it. As such, then let's have a strategy to deal with down markets before the next one unfolds.

During those bear market times, it didn't matter if you owned a low-cost index fund or a high-cost active fund. What mattered was protecting your assets. The personal factor (age and circumstance) was substantially more important than fund cost in determining investment success. It was the asset allocation advice of buying low and selling high that mattered.

Whenever money is involved, it will always attract the shady elements. Thankfully new laws and safeguards and government agencies have arisen from the ashes of failed investment scams to help, but there is no cure for irrational exuberance, for the greater fool strategy of investing as price departs value, that continues to plague investors. Since these historic times, the four points of liquidity, transparency, measurability, and control have improved. But the all-too-human elements of greed and fear have yet to be controlled. However, with certain valuation and timing measures, we should be able to provide insight and avoid the greater fool approach.

So today, do you want to invest in a new emerging market? You don't have to determine the spice or skin or feather that is the latest hot trend and hope your advisor agrees. Nor do you have to locate a sailing captain with a sturdy boat and stable crew and convince other investors with whom to pool your money to gain some economies of scale and then wait months, if not years, to find out whether your venture was successful or not. Today we ask, What's trending now? You want out today? At what price or value? Back then there was no liquidity. You had to have other assets to sustain you, while your long-shot operation was under way. There was no transparency. How would you check whether the captain went elsewhere or lined his pockets with other assets? There was no measurability of its success. How would you have measured accountability? What was the risk? There were only three outcomes: utter failure, perhaps a return of your principal, or some success. There was no control. You were at the mercy of the forces of nature and the captain and crew. Today, it is different. Today you just open the paper or get on the Internet and find a mutual fund or ETF that invests in an emerging market. If you want to invest in a specific industry, chances are there is a mutual fund or ETF to oblige. If you want to invest in the whole market, there are also those funds to help you.

Those four points guide us. We have liquidity, transparency, measurability, and control with funds. What we still don't have yet in detail is the way to assemble and monitor and change a portfolio over time. We need a way to manage these personal advantages we have. We need somehow to take advantage of these four things by using the strategy of managing the managers over time. In turn, this requires some further background educational information.

Author's History

I graduated from college in 1978 with a degree in philosophy. I had also taken some business courses; there was some practicality there. I applied for a job at a large well-known national brokerage firm. I loved analysis, figuring out why things happened. They didn't ask me if I knew something they didn't (I didn't at that time) or whether I could make money for clients (I could sometimes, but the ability to do so was not necessarily duplicable or separable as a skill from dumb luck). Instead, they asked if I could sell. Could I gather assets for someone else to manage, preferably with one of their internally managed mutual funds?

That irrelevant question as it related to a client's financial health should have been my first warning, but I told them I could. They said, prove it and get back to us. Once convinced of something, I am tenacious and determined. So, for a few years I sold life and health insurance successfully and made a living. A few years later I returned to the brokerage firm, and they hired me.

This period was seminal in three ways not only for me but also for the financial industry as a whole. No-load funds were starting their successful ascent into the investing public's awareness. Index funds were beginning.[7] Lastly, the fee-based asset management firms, as opposed to the broker's transaction based, were also taking root.

Money Management
I won't go into this area other than to mention that it has grown with the markets. Wrap accounts and fee-based accounts have become the norm. Commission-based brokers still exist, but they are no longer the norm.

---

[7] John C. Bogle would later write a book called *Bogle on Mutual Funds*. One should at least acknowledge the pioneers upon which we stand. Good idea he had, but can it be improved upon? See the results of employing C on low-cost alternative funds in this book.

No-Load Funds

So, 1982 was near the time that no-load funds began their history. Load funds, wherein part of the investor's investment goes to the selling group, had been around since the 1920s. Everyone at the time thought that it took a salesperson to sell funds and that he or she had to be compensated. *No-load* means the fund doesn't cost the investor anything to buy or to sell the fund. There are no salespeople, but instead, the shares are directly issued from the fund company. Who would do the research and find the right fund? The easy answer initially was to just clone the market—the S&P 500. No research required; the creation of these funds was just to lower costs.

Prior to no-loads where investors buy directly from the fund companies, mutual funds were all sold by brokerage firms with front-end loads of up to 8.5%. An investor would invest, say, $10,000, and $9,150 would go to work with the other $850, the load, the commission, going to the brokerage firm. With no-loads, if you invest $10,000, then the full $10,000 goes to work. That 8.5% cut right off the bat provided a huge performance advantage to no-load funds. Yet they were slow to gain assets compared to the load funds. Why?

The issue was, How does one pick the right no-load fund? It takes education and information. The flip-side answer was that the brokers added value. They would presumably steer the clients into the right funds and in exchange for their expertise they would get the load, their paychecks. Mutual funds were sold to the customers. No-load funds, however, required some investor education. Investors had to be proactive, do the research, call the fund for a prospectus, fill out the paperwork, fund the account, and make the purchase. It wasn't easy, but over time the performance difference—the idea that the entire $10,000 investment went to work—won out over the transaction cost alternative whereby only $9,150 of the $10,000 investment went to work.

This new no-load alternative raised the question of whether the brokers truly added any value by selling that particular load fund they had picked for you. The assumption by most investors was that their brokers added value. When E.F. Hutton speaks, everyone listens, was the old commercial, right? Not anymore. No-load funds eventually turned the industry upside down in more ways than one. It turned out that in addition to financial performance comparison questions, there were lots of ethical issues raised over the years as the transition from load to no-load investing gained traction. Brokers were accused of recommending internal funds, which are those managed by their own firms, rather than external ones, even though the internal ones were often very poor performers in comparison in many cases. Internal funds also had the advantage of using the brokerage fund to trade their holdings. Furthermore, the internal funds often carried additional compensation payments to the brokers and their firm. If the brokers were motivated by money, it is easy enough to understand why their clients may have ended up owning a poorly performing load fund.

It was during the time that load funds were sold, when there were no alternatives, that what are now archaic advertising slogans arose. The product drove education, rather than vice versa. It went like this: Buy and hold for the long term. Don't switch investments. Everyone's performance is about the same. We will be back. The manager is the brains, and she is still here. This is a great concept, so buy, buy, buy. Still sound familiar? This education was tied directly to load funds. One simply can't get over the 8.5% front-end hurdle too easily. You had to buy and hold because it was far too expensive to switch funds. The product drove education.

As no-loads grew in popularity, unfortunately the same old advertising slogans became attached to the new products. After all, it does no good to educate an investor about your fund only to have her pull out her money when your no-load fund proves to be an underperformer. Buy and hold, try to ignore the competition, forget market value, don't time—these were all slogans that worked for load funds and were then tied to no-load funds.

The truth is that no-load funds solved a couple of problems. The truth had become widely known. One, the investor's cost problem of getting rid of the laggards and reinvesting with the leaders was overcome. There was no load to buy or to sell a no-load. Why not switch? Two, if the hot-handed manager left to form her own outfit, you could sell, follow the manager, and reenter a different no-load fund and have no costs to do so. An investor would invest $10,000, and $10,000 would go to work. Three months later, if the manager left, you'd sell the old no-load and buy the new no-load; your $10,000 (assuming no market change) goes back to work for you.

With those solutions, however, the same overall industry questions had still yet to be answered. Yes, a no-load fund where 100% of your money goes to work was better than one where 91.5% of your money went to work, but still, how do we know which no-load fund to buy? How do we know when to sell? How should we manage the managers?

To complicate all of this, as the years went by and it turned out investors did begin to follow the star managers, the industry learned a new thing—that is, promote fund management by committee. If it's a committee running things, whom do we blame or praise for good or bad performance? If someone left, do not worry, they said, because the committee is still here. Retain the investor money was their battle cry.

Index Funds

Also, 1982 was around the time that index funds began their history. Index funds were passive investments in the sense that the holdings did not change, until the index changed holdings, which is commonly on an annual basis. The idea behind the index funds was to match the market, both up and down. So if the market went up, your fund went up by nearly the same amount. If the market went down, your fund went down by nearly the same amount. It was simply the idea that since we can't beat the market, let's join the market, let's be the market. As we will see in the next chapter, index funds rode the tide of the new secular bull market to its frothy peak in 2000. Index funds became so popular that they were nearly called a fad. The Nifty Fifty from the 1960s had been repackaged and sold as "one-decision," large-cap S&P 500 Index funds. It was buy and hold all over again. Like all fads, it was a sign of the end, not the beginning of things. It was no surprise that they fizzled out, dropped back in price to where they were before they were popular, and then took years to recover back to their former highs. For those who know some market history, this was a similar sequence of events that took place in the 1960s and 1970s.

For our purposes, we treat index funds just like actively managed funds. We rank both of them by C (risk-adjusted relative performance) out of the same database of funds. We want the fund providing the most return with the least risk, so if it turns out to be an index fund, we may own it. If it lags, we sell it. Our loyalty belongs to achieving the goal (make the most return with the least amount of risk), not the advertising message nor the manager, broker, fund, or market.

So it was with these two emerging investment strands of no-loads and index funds as background that I returned to the brokerage firm, and they hired me. I would eventually start ignoring the self-service high-commissioned financial industry advertising message and begin wondering about the advantages to the client of no-load funds and index funds. The question became two pronged: how best to manage the managers and how best to participate in wealth-creating secular bull markets, while avoiding wealth-destroying secular bear markets.

It has been a long journey of 30-plus years from 1982 to the present. Almost none of the educational ideas about mutual fund investing changed over those years. Most investors are still told to approach investing with the same load fund investment strategy of buy and hold the fund, don't compare funds in the same style since no one knows who will be best, and ignore the fund until you retire. How's that advice working? It clearly works well for some in the industry, but for the investors? Who owns the yachts?

The latest permutation of this same idea is found with lifestyle- or age-based funds. But I will speak more on this later.

The truth is that no-load funds do not have the same restrictions on investors that load funds have. We can buy and sell no-load funds every quarter if we want without repercussion.[8] We can buy and sell ETFs daily if we want. There are no transaction costs or they are miniscule so those costs are negligible factors in deciding whether to dump a poor performer or not or in trying to avoid a bear market. It is cheap to sell and cheap to buy back in.

No-loads and ETFs are simply not the same animals as load funds, so why approach them in the same manner by employing the same old advertising messages? And there is another reason to not

---

[8] Some fund "supermarkets" like Fidelity, Schwab, E*TRADE, Ameritrade, or Scottrade may impose a holding period from 60 to 180 days to avoid short-term redemption charges. In addition, some funds may charge a redemption fee to sell within a set period, like 90 days.

FIGURE 1.3 An Example of the Buy-and-Hold/Ignore Strategy over a 60-Year Span—Age 30 to Age 90

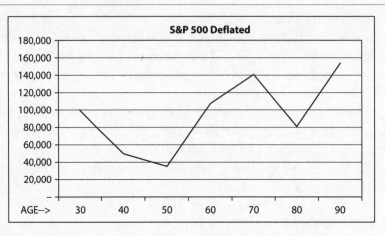

Source: Data from Standard & Poor's.

approach them in the same way. The issue with the buy-and-hold/ignore and age-based allocation investment strategy is that it looks at only one axis (price) and completely ignores the other (your age and/or circumstance, a.k.a. time). I will pull out one example, depicted in Figure 1.3, to make the point personal, as it should be.

Let's say you received $100,000 in an inheritance at the young age of 30. What would have been the common advice? Ignore valuations. Buy 100% stocks and hold. You were young with lots of time left. So you bought 100% stocks, and you held onto them, believing your advisors had your best interests at heart. The time period on the horizontal axis marks the top in September 1929. To emphasize the point, this example looks at only your inheritance and ignores any earnings from bonds or cash or job. This is the starting point of the graph.

You were young, and the market value didn't matter, the advisors said, so you bought and held. That was the standard industry advice. After all, they said, if the market declined, you were still young enough to recoup your losses. When you turned 40, your portfolio was worth about $50,000 in deflated S&P 500 "dollars." When you turned 50, your portfolio was worth less than $40,000.

At this point, if you were still following the same standard industry age-based advice, you were advised to "lighten up" on stocks and buy some bonds. After all, they said, you were older now, and you wouldn't be able to make up any losses due to your age. Too bad you followed our initial advice, but for some unknown reason you should trust us now with this advice.

By age 60, had you left it alone, your portfolio would finally have made it back to its original value of $100,000, but since you were advised to sell some at the bottom based on your age, your portfolio didn't fully recover. You were now another 10 years older at age 60. And again, the standard advice based on your age was to "lighten up" even further on stocks. As a result you missed the further substantial gains.

Finally at age 70, your portfolio was at $140,000, except that the standard industry advice kept you mostly out of those gains. At age 80, having gone through another secular bear market, your portfolio was again worth less than it was on a deflated basis (taking into account inflation) when you were age 30. And so it goes for you, your children, and their children.

Granted, this may be the worst of all examples, but it hopefully makes the point clear to all. Age-based allocation advice and buy-and-hold advice simply fail to account for market valuations, let alone the reality of age and circumstance.

Instead of blinding hindsight that obfuscates the personal age factor and smudges the reality of the rise and fall of countries and ignores the value of investments, we must have a repeatable, proven strategy to take advantage of today's power of mutual funds and ETFs. To be sure, there are remarkable managers investing successfully each and every day, but like anything else, they aren't permanent fixtures; they come into and out of prominence. There are times when a passive approach beats an active one and vice versa. There are times to be invested in stocks and bonds and times to be out in the safety of cash or money market funds. There are ways to manage the managers. Let's find out more.

These three early trends of no-loads, index funds, and fee-based money management emerged at about the same time your author had just joined a large national brokerage firm in 1982. The stock market for its part was about to embark on a wealth-changing

18-year secular[9] bull market after having been on a wealth-destroying 16-year secular bear market. What one piece of advice would have served him well not only at the start of his career but also 30 years later?[10] What guru guidance from that time 30 years ago would be just as relevant today?

Fast forward to the year 2000, and the market is about to embark on a 13-year secular bear market that includes two devastating bear market drops of nearly 50% each time, so what's that one piece of advice?

Was the advice to just hang on no matter what, to "buy and hold and forget" useful? How has the 13-year secular bear market changed that advice? We are all 13 years older, nearer to retirement, but our nest egg is where it was 13 years ago. If you remained employed and participated in a 401(k), your nest egg might be larger, but to get an accurate assessment of your annual investment returns, you have to back out those contributions. In other words, if your account started at $50,000 and it is now $75,000, it looks like a 50% gain, but if you added $5,000 per year for the last 10 years, your actual performance is a negative number. You started with $50,000 and added $50,000 for a total of $100,000, but you ended with $75,000.

Is that advice to buy and hold working or not for either active or passive fund investors? Is that advice to stay with the fund you picked or were sold 10 years ago working or not? It can't be positive, if only because we have aged and the market is where it was. We are

---

[9] *Secular* means long term. For our purposes, I define it as a period ranging anywhere from 5 to 30 years. We try to mark and monitor secular bull and bear trends in stocks, bonds, housing, and other markets. People apply the term differently to the various markets, finding different starting and ending points. From 1892 through the present, the stock market, again depending on how one defines *secular*, has gone through four secular bull markets and five secular bear markets (see Chapter 2). The bond market has experienced two secular bull markets and two secular bear markets (see Chapter 3).

[10] It is remarkable that some newsletter editors are perhaps some of the longer-living people I hear about. Joe Granville, Richard Russell, Cabot, Lutts. It could be the discipline of daily or weekly writing, of meeting deadlines, of monitoring the markets that contributes to these things.

I am regularly asked whether I plan to retire soon or not. I answer that I have no plans to ever retire. As someone once said, if you love what you do and understand your motivation, you never actually work.

nearing retirement age, but a typical buy-and-hold approach has us anchored to values from 14 years ago.

In all of this, it is essential to distinguish between the managers' motivations and yours. For them, the advice to buy and hold works great. Not because it is in fact great advice but because they continue to collect their management fees, regardless of whether you succeed or not. When was the last time you heard a fund say, "Sell us because we are lagging and buy one of our competitor's funds"?

Or again consider the Roaring Twenties to the Depression Thirties when the Dow dropped by 90%. Was the buy-and-hold advice good for you or not? Most investors were wiped out, but there were still bills to pay, children to educate, life to live. We are older now than we were. Do we have time still to recover from devastating losses of half our capital? Will the markets recover, and by when? Hindsight says it has, but hindsight is not our friend. Can't happen again, really?

Today there are thousands of fund and ETF choices. The market is sliced and diced in any number of ways from the profound to the comical. But the only thing that has changed is that the decision process for buying and selling and ranking investments is more difficult than ever.

Indexing is offered as one solution to beat the average managers, but it can't beat the averages. Furthermore, there are hundreds of index funds now. The questions are still raised, How do I pick one index over another? How do I assemble a portfolio? Indeed, another question to ask with index funds is, How do they choose which stocks to include or exclude from the index?

Conclusion

We know these things matter to our lifestyles. We know there must be a better way to choose funds. There is a huge spread in performance year after year between the leading funds and lagging funds, even within the same investment style. Once we accept this proactive, manage-the-managers approach, how do we start? What do we need to do? In the next two chapters, we will look at the secular stock and bond markets to give us an overall sense of long-term cycles and the fact that the market moves in broad, fairly easily discerned strokes and well-defined trends. We will see that what works the best in one cycle is not necessarily the best approach in the next cycle.

When these primary bull and bear trends are operating, there are always some funds doing substantially better than others. The manager does matter. There are exceptional managers, but they are exceptional only for certain time periods. There will be times when a manager outperforms his peers and the market. Someone has to lead, and someone else has to lag. But there will also be other times when the same manager underperforms his peers and the market. I will talk more about this in Chapter 7 because we will want to take advantage of both the best funds and the dominating secular trend. How do we know the secular trend? How do we take advantage of it? Let's take a look.

2

In the Long Run, We Are All Dead

THERE IS NOTHING AS CLEAR TO INVESTORS AS WHEN WE OBSERVE things in hindsight without the emotions of the present running so high.[1] The past in fact becomes crystal clear. We can see the trends, the early signals, the fake outs, the news, the failures, the successes, and the setups—they all jump out at us. Why can't we see them as they occur? Why didn't we sell before the plunge? Why didn't we buy before the run-up? What did we not see? What factors might help us in this regard to deal with current and future markets? Perhaps three things will help.

One, a sense of stock market history might help us. If there are identifiable and repeatable characteristics that show up year after year in cycle after cycle, it will help to know them.

Two, perhaps a study of the most successful investors might help,[2] but only if there are also clearly identifiable characteristics

---

[1] The chapter title is quoting Lord John Maynard Keynes who was commenting about strategies that seem to work best only in the long run; this is the buy-and-hold strategy.

[2] There have been a number of books written, such as Jack D. Schwager's *Market Wizards* and John Train's *The Money Masters*, that provide insight on

that show up in their strategies. In this regard, we have to separate two issues.

The first issue will be, Is a strategy repeatable? In other words, can you implement and follow the same strategy? Can we operate in the same way as the person who is our investment hero? For example, buying value stocks may be a viable strategy, but as we have seen, there is a huge performance difference between funds with the same value strategy. What is the difference between them?

The second issue is that we need to separate luck from skill. To do this, some studies suggest it takes at least a 15-year track record. This is part of the angst of investing and the difficulty in finding good funds and managers. It also explains how millions are still invested in consistently underperforming funds and managers. They may have had a year or two of success and may have attracted a bunch of money, but success has been elusive ever since. Who wants to admit to buying something because the manager, in all probability, was really just lucky? And what manager wants to admit that his or her track record is attributable to luck, rather than skill? Investing really is a tough business.

Three, in addition to those first two helps, "Know thyself." In my view, this is a key difference in successful investing. Why do we buy and sell at the right and wrong times? Recall Figure 1.2 from Chapter 1 that showed money flows into and out of mutual funds. What are our motivations and our goals when we buy and sell? What is our age? What is our circumstance? In these answers, we must be brutally honest with ourselves. It is no good to find one's self in the foxhole of a devastated portfolio that has lost 50% over three years with the outdated advertising message of buy and hold/ignore just when retirement or marriage or college or recession or any other of life's circumstances are now staring at us.

We won't delve further into either the second or third areas that might help us as we develop our investment strategy because there are numerous books out there for that. Rather, we will look

---

successful strategies. Warren Buffett, CEO of Berkshire Hathaway, is an example of a sort of autobiography on this; he also publishes his annual letter to shareholders, and certainly there have been a number of books written about him that try to explain his success.

to answer the first of the three helps about repeatable cycles. In this chapter we will examine the secular history of stocks. In the next chapter, we will look at the secular history of bonds.

In the previous chapter, I touched on the very long term stock history in the form of closed-end fund pools in the 1700s that morphed into open-end[3] load funds, which in turn evolved into no-loads and finally blossomed into ETFs. It helps to take a fly-by, a 30,000-mile-high view of the history, but now we begin to focus back in at ground level. I will begin to introduce my methodology for picking the best funds. I define "best" by a risk-adjusted relative performance metric called C.

I want to reiterate that this is not some academic advice divorced from emotions and reality. And it is not some Johnny-come-lately approach. Rather, it is information gained from a lifetime of actual investing. Some 30 years ago in 1982 when I entered the financial industry with a national, well-known brokerage firm, I can only wish that I had known then what I know now about the focus of this chapter and the next one in terms of secular and cyclical markets. We talk about making the most return for the least amount of risk, but who is truly doing this?

At that time of my beginning in the financial industry, the stock market had been trending sideways for years, since about 1966, in a fairly well defined sideways channel between roughly 1,000 on the upside and 600 on the downside. The assumption most people were making at that time was that those bands would never change; they were permanent fixtures. The thinking was that today is like yesterday and tomorrow will be like today.

In 1982, on the unforeseen verge of another historic secular stock market shift, I'll grant that it was, as investing always is, a very tricky time for investors for two reasons. One, the market had made another confirmed to the downside technical signal in August 1982. All of the major averages had touched new lows for the cycle. The market prospects looked bad on the surface. And so the in-house

---

[3] The difference between *open end* and *closed end* is this. *Closed end* means a fixed number of shares have been issued. *Open end* means more shares may be issued at the net asset value (net assets less net expenses divided by the number of shares outstanding).

New York chief technical analyst in charge of forecasting the market made his general recommendation that we were going lower, so sell and grow cautious. Months later as the market reached 1,000 yet again, he again advised that it was time to take profits: we're at the top of the range, as it has been since 1966.[4] Sell and wait for the assured pullback that we know is coming again just as it has for the last 15 years. The arguments sound pretty solid, right? Who can argue with 15 years of reliability?

The only way to argue was to back up and suggest we take a longer view. Learn the full extent of the market's history. The market had exploded to the upside before, as it did after World War II, and who's to say it won't happen again? This is why we started our look-back period from the 1700s; it is to give us more perspective. The rest from 1982, as they say, is history. Up and up the market rallied with nary a 25% correction.[5]

---

[4] In case you didn't catch it, it is always sort of funny, if not tragic, to read someone's advice that is separated from actual, real portfolio management—that is, advice that is separated from a real live account. Since he already told us to sell at the bottom, what were we supposed to sell now that we were back at the top?

Incidentally, this problem also surfaces in the newsletter business. Be wary of those who advocate their buys and sells without providing their advice within the confines and description of an actual portfolio, even if it is a paper portfolio. Without the actual finite portfolio, there is simply no way to ascertain whether their advice was truly profitable or not because there was no allocation of portfolio money. It is no good to list, say, 5 funds or stocks this month and the next month list another 10. The 10 are also new buys, but well, with what money are we supposed to buy the new picks? We are already fully invested in the previous month's 5 picks. And if not, then how much were we supposed to invest? To buy more, we have to sell something else; is that accounted for? The advice divorced from a finite portfolio is essentially useless in terms of knowing whether the advice worked.

[5] This is one helpful way to determine whether we are in a bull market or not. Is it easy to buy or not? If it is hard to buy, scary to enter, and a wait-for-a-pullback mentality prevails, then the odds are we are already in a bull market. It simply won't give us the chance to buy without stress and worry and fear.

Some investors will label this type of market as "climbing the wall of worry," although this typically comes later in the cycle from off the initial bottom.

The flip side to climbing the wall of worry is the bear market that descends the "slope of hope." Recall Buffett's *New York Times* editorial in 2008 that said to buy

In hindsight, however, it really wasn't his missing the cyclical bear market bottom that mattered from 1982, and it really wasn't his selling at previous tops.[6] No, what really mattered in all of this was his missing the mega picture, the huge sense of history. He failed to grasp the understanding itself of the potential for massive wealth-creating change that takes place when the market shifts from a secular bear market to a secular bull market. That was the real error, to think that today is like yesterday and tomorrow will be like today. Wrong. There are times when it is in fact different this time. This "breakout" from 1,000 was different from the previous 15 years when the market had reached 1,000. The trick of course is not to see it in hindsight but to see it as it unfolds under your very nose.

Years ago someone asked me, as we were discussing the potential merger of our two firms, were my abilities quantifiable? I was to be the analyst, the system designer, the fund picker. He was to be the marketer, the distributor. Before the deal could be done, in other words, he was asking whether my strategies for profiting using funds and allocating between markets were duplicable by someone besides me. To put it bluntly, he wanted to know whether, if something happened to me, they would be able to carry on or not without me. Was I operating from the seat of the pants or from a written, proven, quantifiable strategy? Since that time, I have been endeavoring to quantify what has been learned from 30 years of experience. This book is a sort of culmination of that; it is to put down on paper and share some of what works to create and maintain wealth.

Back to the story. So, 18 wonderful wealthy years after the secular lows in 1982, in 2000 the market finally came to its bubbly burst in dot-com click-through Nifty Nineties euphoric bliss. Since then it has moved essentially sideways now for some 14 years through 2013.

---

for a number of apparently sound reasons. We are on a solid footing. The market instead fell another 25% or so. You can be sure the market's main trend remains down when it is still operating under hope. It wasn't until the actual accounting board rule changes in March 2009 that the bottom was reached. Had the mark-to-market (MTM) valuation rules not changed, Buffett would have ended up as just another in a long line of "great" investors gone "bad."

[6] There are in fact "good trades" that fail to make money.

This period is a different animal from the previous one. It is like the market of the 1970s. For investors and analysts, it is the same failure to understand the changing dynamics of very long term trends that also applies to the wealth-destroying shift[7] that takes place from secular bull to bear.

In addition, we have seen fund after fund and strategy after strategy that fared well in the secular bull just be crushed in the secular bear. You don't bring a matador's cape into a bear's dark den and expect to walk out unscathed, yet that is what many unwittingly have done. We can recall and modify the outdated load fund advertising message as it applies to no-load funds and ETFs. Buy and hold and hope for better times. They say to pay the lowest fund management fees, and they neglect to mention you still can lose 50% or more of your wealth. This doesn't help us on a personal level as recessions shake our complacency and as we age 13 years closer to retirement. What then do we do when the certain bear prowls again and our portfolio declines 50%, but now we're 60 instead of 40?

Part of my point here is simply that, conventional wisdom aside, things in fact do change. Give it time. If you think making money in the market is easy, you simply haven't been around long enough. As we will see, inflation, deflation, deficits, surpluses, recessions, recoveries, greed, and fear—all these and other factors—affect the markets' changes over the decades. It is an investing error that blinds the stalwart to think that things won't change, either for the better or for the worst. Cycles of our fear and greed stretch back into history as far as one is inclined to look.

As Nobel Prize winner Robert J. Shiller implied,[8] short-term efficiency, where new information is priced into the market

---

[7] To reiterate from the first chapter, the shift is wealth destroying because the personal situation of age and circumstance changes. We buy at the wrong time and sell at the wrong time, not because of the market per se but because of our relationship to it based on our personal situation. Incidentally, the old saw about the rich getting richer is a nod to this exact issue. The rich have deeper pockets to sit out declines, but mostly they have the capital to take advantage of investment bargains when they appear.

[8] Robert J. Shiller, *Irrational Exuberance*, 2006.

instantaneously, does not seem as apparent over longer periods of time. In other words, other reasons, besides "efficiency" must be used to explain market rises and falls. To state the obvious, things like greed and fear influence the equation. The question is, as I was once asked, Can we quantify these things?

This is the other part of my point. It is important to at least try to recognize what type of secular market we are in. Investing strategies that work so well in secular bull markets do not work as well in bear markets and vice versa. Recall that we try to separate skill from luck. The matching admonition to this reality on Wall Street is to not confuse brains with a bull market. Again, perhaps with a bite of irony, the average secular bull lasts about that long or 15 years. Just when you think you have it figured out, wham, along comes the next secular bear market.

So, it is with this bit of personal history that I introduce this chapter on secular bull and bear markets in stocks. I will define some terms, look at some charts, comment on the two secular strategies, and forecast where the road ahead may meet our feet.

Definitions

Before moving into the details of this chapter and the next, I want to clarify a few terms I regularly use. Not everyone will agree with these definitions, but for our purposes they give us clear, concise tools by which to communicate.

Bull market means that prices move in a series of higher highs and higher lows. It generally gains at least 20% and more.

Bear market means prices move in a series of lower highs and lower lows. It generally loses at least 20% and more.

There is also, from time to time, the *sideways market* that does not have a discernible trend but remains boxed for a period between two more narrow extremes from the top to bottom of some 20%.

Secular means long term. It means years to decades, like from 5 to 30 years.

Cyclical means a period lasting from one to five years. Historically, cyclical bull stock markets average about three years, and bear markets average about one to two years. So, a full cyclical stock market of bull and bear cycles lasts about four to five years.

Within a secular bull or bear market, there will be a number of cyclical bull and bear markets.

The best picture of how these two time frames work together that I've heard about is to imagine a man with a yo-yo going up and down from his hand as he rides on a very long escalator that moves up and down. The yo-yo going up and down is the cyclical bull and bear market, within the secular escalator going either up or down. So when he is riding up, the cyclical highs and lows are higher than before; this is a secular bull market with internal cyclical bull and bear markets. When he is riding down, the cyclical lows and highs will be lower than before; this is a secular bear market with internal cyclical bull and bear markets.

With this in mind, we can see that a secular bear market will be made up of a series of cyclical markets. Even if the market ends 10 years later at the exact spot it started from 10 years earlier, there may still have been two or maybe three full cyclical bull and bear markets of better than 20% gains and losses. As one might grasp, timing and selecting strategies may vary in each kind of market, but they are still important to creating and retaining wealth.

Given that not everyone agrees with these definitions, this means that secular bull and bear markets will be measured somewhat differently by different people. Nonetheless, the point generally will remain that the market moves in secular cycles, so it gives us a framework within which to work, however imprecise it may be. Recent history is an example of this because not everyone dates the end of the current secular bear market from the same starting point. Nearly everyone does identify the Internet bubble's peak in 2000 to mark the end of the previous secular bull and start of the (current) secular bear. The difference is that some people believe the secular bear was still intact as of 2014, while others believe it basically ended in 2009. This six-year difference makes a major impact on what we might expect as we move forward. If the average secular bear market is 15 years, and if it began in 2000, we may have one more bear cycle of down 50% with which to contend. But if we date the start of the secular bull from 2009, then we may have another 10 years or so of a secular bull market, wherein peaks are higher and higher with average declines of roughly 20%. That is a big difference. Dating changes our thinking.

To help us decide, we will see that there are various characteristics that make up secular bull and bear markets. This is shown below and reiterated in Appendix A for stocks and B for bonds, which will be not only for you the reader but for your children and their children. Just as secular cycles have dominated the markets the last 100 years, they will continue to do so for the next 100 years.

Historical Charts and Data for Secular Bull and Bear Markets

To give us a better sense of all of this secular information, the following charts should help. There is a clear performance difference between the two types of secular markets. In turn, this will affect successful investing strategies. It is the rare manager who can do well in both types of markets. This is why we advocate the managing-the-managers investment approach. We rotate as the leaders change. Follow the leaders, and avoid the laggards.

Figure 2.1 shows the S&P 500 Index adjusted for inflation. It brings home more clearly the wealth creating and destroying effects of secular bull and bear markets. It is not simply that the market treads water for years and years but that, when adjusted for the depreciating value of the index because of inflation, the losses are even worse than imagined. This inflation-adjusted approach also has the benefit of more clearly identifying the historic secular market tops and bottoms.

The chart is also drawn on a logarithmic scale, so that the percentage gains and losses look the same, whether at $100 or $1,000. The period shown is from January 1871 through October 2013. The data is from various sources, including Standard & Poor's. The arrows drawn up and down with ending question marks are my own.

As the last observation with this index deflated, we can also clearly see the working definitions of bull and bear markets. Notice the series of lower highs and lower lows dating from the peak in 2000. That is the definition of a bear market. And since it has lasted more than one cyclical cycle, it is also by definition a secular bear market. In the same way, note the series of higher highs and higher lows that defined the secular bull market from 1982 through 2000.

FIGURE 2.1 Inflation-Adjusted S&P 500 Index January 1871 Through October 2013

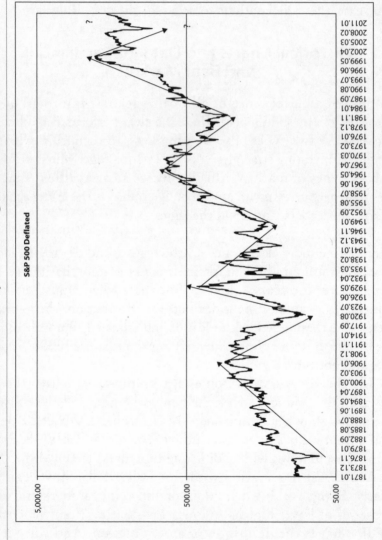

Source: Data from various sources including Standard & Poor's as cited in Robert J. Shiller, *Irrational Exuberance* (2006).

Common Characteristics of Secular Bull and Bear Markets

These clear tops and bottoms of secular bull and bear markets are drawn, unfortunately, in hindsight. The good news is that an active rotational strategy based on C allows us to move our monies to the managers who do well in the different periods. They won't be the same ones in each cycle.

Still, are there any fundamental forewarnings of potential changes we can isolate from previous cycles that might help us as we live through them in the future? There are. I'll talk about general characteristics and then specifics in the bull and bear time frames.

In the first place, toward the end of each secular period, investor attitudes totally flip-flop. Investor sentiment changes in each period. In the most recent secular change that ended in 2000, there were two seminal changes measured from the previous lows. In 1982, market timing was somewhat in vogue. By 2000, everyone believed market timing was dead, ineffective, useless, and unnecessary. As in 1929, the idea had emerged that we are in a permanently high plateau.[9] In 1982, investors preferred some sort of active management. By 2000, many investors subscribed to the theory that indexing was the key to creating and maintaining long-term wealth. In both cases, the underlying belief was that buy and hold was alive and well and asset allocation (a.k.a. a form of market timing) was dead and buried.

Sentiment has, 14 years later, somewhat changed again. Market timing has regained some respect, especially by those who lost 50% of their money twice in the last 10 years and are now 14 years older. Their time to recoup their losses is not the same as it was. Diversification using cash alternatives may be important after all.

Is there a sense yet that indexing with its buy-and-hold equivalency has lost credibility? It doesn't look that way to me. Indexing has come back stronger than ever, measured by asset flows. This may, however, be more of a rejection of active management than an

---

[9] Irving Fisher, economist, in 1929 said three days before the crash: "Stock prices have reached what looks like a permanently high plateau." He failed to recognize the impact of margin calls among other things.

endorsement of passive management. Institutions have to invest in some way.

Clearly indexing is here to stay. Not necessarily because it avoids losing money, it doesn't, but it costs us less when it happens. Does a bandage help with a concussion? One alternative remains active management. In both cases the approach of being fully invested is the same. Perhaps that is the problem, not the active-versus-passive framing of the issue. Indexing is the give-up that an active manager can beat an index over the long term. Thus investors have moved to passive index funds. We will cover this later, but obviously my solution is not to give up on active management or on passive management (indexing). My solution is to manage the managers, whether the manager is active or passive. Evolve with the leaders.

Getting back to the secular trends, while no bull or bear period is exactly like any other, there are remarkable similarities that show up consistently in all secular bull and bear periods that do not show up in the other type of market. For example, war is actually associated with secular bear markets. There is increased government spending, which some consider bullish, but the spending is for items of destruction. Bombs explode. Ships sink. It took money to build them, but then they evaporate without producing anything further. Yes, they produce peace and continued capitalism, but they don't directly produce any further goods and services. In secular bull markets, peace typically dominates the period. There is still spending, but it is for construction. We build a bridge that allows distribution to open up. We build a tractor that increases productivity. These in turn reduce cost and spur demand. The middle class typically expands and flourishes. We increase alternatives, and creativity flows freely.

In addition to war, there are other themes like regulation and innovation that show up consistently in one type of market but not the other. So, let's look at some of the generalities of each secular bull and bear stock markets from the past 130 years. This, too, will be the quick overview from 30,000 feet.

1880 to 1900 Bull Market

The golden spike was finally driven in 1869 in Utah, and the completed coast-to-coast railway was established in 1870. Growth of and eventual repercussions from the Iron Horse success spread across the country. Goods and services and people were able to move about more easily than ever. What once took months now only took weeks. Trains needed iron and coal and many other materials, which spurred industrial development across the country.

The various transportation monopolies bred power and greed, which in turn led to government regulation, which began to cap the power of industry.

1900 to 1920 Bear Market

The rise of regulation helped end the bull market of the time. Railroad rates became too onerous and burdensome for some, and government was employed to cap the rates. This eventually hurt the value of railroad stocks in 1906. Collateral values declined. Margin (the use of borrowed money to buy stocks) calls went up. Selling was forced. The decline was also helped by a Black Swan event: the earthquake of 1906 in San Francisco.[10] These events in turn led to the Panic of 1907. Liquidity further dried up. Bank runs were common. Recession lingered. J. P. Morgan would offer to pledge his money to ease the panic, foreshadowing later whales (big investors) who step into the panics of others to profit therefrom. Morgan wasn't the first; he was taking his cue from an earlier Rothschild.

A world war would escalate during this time in 1914. It was the ending of World War I at the eleventh hour on the eleventh day of the eleventh month in 1918 that helped usher in the next secular bull market.

1920 to 1929 Bull Market

The Roaring Twenties remains in everyone's lexicons even by those who have no direct connection to it. *The Great Gatsby* and Prohibition and jazz combined with the growth in automobile production and rising wages to produce the next great secular bull market. Forget "a turkey in every oven"; the mantra was "a car in every driveway." Productivity increased along with leisure time. Toward the end of the rise, shoeshine boys were giving stock advice. The article "Everyone Ought to Be Rich" by John J. Raskob came out

---

[10] I talk about Black Swan events in Chapter 7. Basically, they are unforeseen calamities.

in the *Ladies' Home Journal* about two months before the crash of 1929.[11] The public was electrified by the rising tide, just as much as it was hundreds of years earlier with Tulip Mania. And some 80 years later by dot-coms.

All you had to do to make money was participate in it and buy something—get on board, the train was leaving.[12] Like any investment approach that departs from value and ends up relying on what eventually becomes nothing more than the greater fool strategy,[13] it all ended badly.

1929 to 1949 Bear Market

The devastating bear market would destroy generations of wealth as age and circumstance compounded with falling prices to end in disaster and ruin. America caught cold and coughed, and the Great Depression spread around the globe. Breadlines formed. Unemployment in America spiked above 20%. Construction came to a halt. Food prices dropped some 60%. Government-sponsored plans and programs expanded to help the country, but malaise lingered. Nothing worked. Investors would swear off ever again investing in equities. World War II started and helped destroy confidence and increase fears of loss.

1949 to 1968 Bull Market

The ending of World War II in 1945 eventually led to prosperity at home and abroad. The Marshall Plan passed and helped fund construction projects here and abroad, just as much as the war had led to destruction. The returning GIs all needed places to work and live. Trade picked up again. As Wall Street rallied, it attracted some of the

---

[11] In our own time, we recall books about how to grow rich in real estate with no money down. Like all bubbles, this one ended horribly too.

[12] It is all too easy to forget certain lessons of history in the pounding of the hooves. The *Titanic* had sunk only a mere 15 years earlier, but new ships continued to ply the seas.

[13] The greater fool strategy is relying on a fool greater than you to enter the market and buy whatever is being sold that is divorced from its real value. It is all too easy to believe that rising prices actually mean something. They do not, not in and of themselves. It is always the underlying value that matters.

best and brightest. As well, like the transcontinental railroad before it, it was the interstate road system military-industrial complex born in 1956 that helped the country grow and prosper. Men went to the moon. The future was the brightest it had been in a long time. Of course, this eventually led to overconfidence and overvaluations as many thought the market would join Neil Armstrong on the moon.

1968 to 1982 Bear Market

Rising prices led to out-of-control inflation, and rising interest rates provided too much competition for an overpriced stock market. Why risk your money in stocks when Treasuries yielded north of 12%? Government operated under the mistaken assumption that we could maintain our lifestyle by printing more money; the erroneous policy was nicknamed Guns and Butter. The Vietnam War escalated and spilled into other countries near Vietnam. The Cold War continued. Recessions became more commonplace. Malaise again took hold throughout the country. Turn off your lights, and lower your thermostats. We spun our wheels and got nowhere.

1982 to 2000 Bull Market

The emerging market countries like China and Brazil and regions like the Far East began to rise up as forces to be recognized. Democracy, capitalism, and the rise of the middle class around the globe strengthened and blossomed in this period. At home, new leadership took place fiscally and financially. Inflation was unwound by raising short-term interest rates to near 18%, even as America's place in the world rebounded. The Cold War eventually ended. You don't bomb your customers. An old 1920s term was reminted: *conspicuous consumption*. We wanted stuff. The crash of 1987 ended without a depression, which helped breed investors' confidence in getting into and staying with stocks.

The naysayers were wrong. Enthusiasm picked up again. The advances in technology, especially in electronics, computers, and the Internet, were gaining steam, which led to an inevitable market bubble where, again, valuations eventually didn't matter. This time would be different. Just get on board at whatever the cost. Buy something. But then pop went the weasel, just like every other time.

2000 to ???? Bear Market

The same two things have helped define this period, like other secular bear markets: war and the unwinding of the greater fool strategy. The War on Terror became commonplace, costing billions. The aftermath of bubbles is not kind, said Alan Greenspan. We entered a very rare 3-year bear market with losses wiping out nearly 10 years' worth of gains. Toss compounding gains out the window. The stock market eventually recovered, only to be slammed again as collateral damage from another pocket of irrational exuberance in housing spread through the financial system. Stock prices dropped as the Great Recession began. Questions about the solvency of the banking system arose. Housing values were dropping by much more than the 3% or 0% down payment requirement. The loan was still there, but the equity had disappeared. It was the accounting change (the Financial Accounting Standards Board [FASB] Statement 157) in March 2009 that saved us from the second Great Depression. The change allowed banks, brokerages, and insurance companies to essentially price assets without regard necessarily to the current market value of their assets that are not actively traded or that are distressed (housing). That was the "bell that rung" at the bottom; the markets have recovered again.

Some are now thinking that the secular bear market ended in 2009, while others believe it still has further to run. Based on previous secular bull and bear markets, how might we answer the question whether it is over or not?

The massive War on Terror fought primarily in the Middle East has wound down. This is clearly a positive, just as it was at the end of previous major wars in the secular change. Wars cost money that simply ends up being destroyed. This end suggests a bullish fundamental global change.

At the same time, is there taking place currently a major industrial innovation change, such as occurred with the automobile in the 1920s or the space exploration and interstate build-out of the 1950s or the computer revolution or emerging markets advances of the 1990s? The closest comparison to those things today is the exploration and build-out of the domestic energy industry from fracking to solar to electric. Some project that the United States will be the number one energy exporter in the world by 2020. To be in the top

1% of income for a resident in North Dakota, you need to make more than $500,000; this is more than what's required in California and about identical to those in New York.[14]

So, a case based on three indicators can be made that the market may have made a secular turn beginning in March 2009. The primary argument against this is valuation. The market did not get as undervalued as it did before at previous secular bottoms. We will see this chart shortly.

20?? to 20?? Bull Market

If we look ahead past the secular bear market, what do we see? Barring a national collapse of some sort due to runaway debt, like entitlements, we know the stock market will cycle back up. The world will generally be at peace during this time. Construction will rule, not destruction. New roads, dams, bridges, and other infrastructure building will take place here and abroad. New technologies from robotics and alternative energy and industries from biotech to Internet-based businesses will boom. Inflation may start off muted, but it should eventually begin to rise.

At some point, as with every other bull market, valuations will again eventually reach extremes. The greater fool will step in again, drawn in by greed and apparently easy money. And the whole process will continue into the next wealth-destroying secular bear market for those who are unprepared or who think it is different this time or who follow the standard industry advice to buy and hold.

20?? to 20?? Bear Market

The market will again become severely overvalued as measured by various value ratios like price versus earnings or dividends or book value or sales or replacement cost. Perhaps another costly major war will start. Maybe an industry will have squeezed out the obvious paths of growth and prosperity, becoming a monopoly in need of regulation. Maybe there will be too much wealth concentration.

Whatever the cause, whatever the time frame, a secular bull and secular bear market will take place again. If you can stand apart from the pounding herd of greedy bulls and sell when everyone else

---

[14] *Source:* 2012 Economic Policy Institute report.

is thinking the next stop is beyond the moon, if you can stand apart from the clawing, decimating pawed apart portfolio of a bear market, then this will save and help you and your heirs build and keep your fortune.

Tools to Help

After these broad secular comments, let's now move back into some specifics.

Rate of Change

Figure 2.2 shows the S&P 500 deflated for inflation and its 10-year rolling rate of change (ROC).

As you can see, whenever the ROC-10 nears −50%, which means the deflated S&P 500 is down 50% from 10 years ago, it was a good time to start accumulating stocks. Whenever the ROC-10 nears

FIGURE 2.2   The S&P 500 Deflated for Inflation and Its 10-Year Rolling Rate of Change

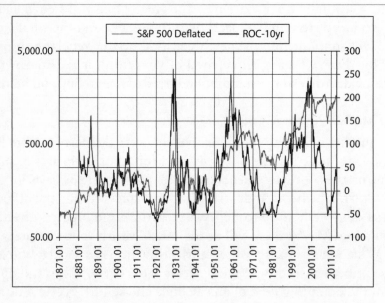

Source: Data from Standard & Poor's.

+100%, it is time to grow cautious. When it spikes above 200%, the top is all but assured. For updates to this and other materials, please visit http://SelectionsAndTiming.com.

Interest Rates and Stocks

Another tool to consider is the relationship between interest rates and secular bull and bear markets in stocks. As in other things, sometimes our assumptions are not borne out by the facts. As we will see in the next chapter on bonds, there is practically no long-term relationship between the two series. This is because the directions of interest rates and the underlying economics are more important than the absolute level of rates. The economy functioned in the 1980s with interest rates at 5%, just as it did in the 2000s with interest rates nearer to 3%.

Strategies for Secular Markets

As you might have already ascertained, it is abundantly clear that what works well in a bear market is not necessarily what works well in a bull market. For long-term investing success, it really is important to know what type of secular market we're in. The strategies that make one successful in each will change.

Some investors will still not be convinced about these things. That really is okay and actually works to our advantage. If everyone were a value investor, for example, would the great value investors have success in finding any value stocks?

To bring this point home about changes in risks and returns over the decades, consider Figure 2.3 from Rydex/SGI (now Guggenheim Partners). It shows the efficient frontier from Modern Portfolio Theory (MPT) over different decades. The point is very clear that what works best to make the most return with the least risk truly does shift, change, and flip-flop. Assuming we all define our investment goals the same way—that is, we want the most return and least risk—there are times, as in secular bear markets, where any stock allocation from 100% down to 10% is the worst investment. There are other times when a stock allocation even up to 100% makes the most sense in terms of risk and reward. There are still other times when bonds are the best place to invest. Consider Figure 2.3.

FIGURE 2.3 The Efficient Frontier from Modern Portfolio Theory over Different Decades

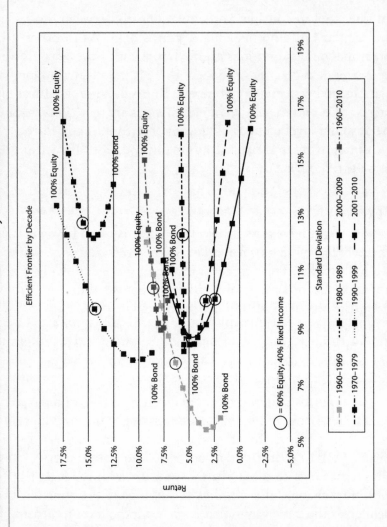

Source: Data from Rydex/SGI (now Guggenheim Partners). Copyright © Guggenheim Investments 2014 (guggenheiminvestments.com).

The *efficient frontier* is the mathematical points at which the most return with the least risk is earned using some combination of stocks and bonds. As mentioned already, my guiding principle is striving to provide the most return with the least risk. If you agree that is the goal, it forces us to make active allocation decisions.

The frontier shifts. It is not fixed. What worked well in the 1990s is not the same as what worked well in the first decade of this century. Look at the flip-flop of the equity point from positive to negative. We know this intuitively, experientially, and mathematically. To do something about it, what is most helpful to know is that fund managers may or may not be able to adjust their portfolios for this; they may be restricted from making changes because of their prospectus. We will have to do this by selling those funds and buying other funds. Later in the book I will speak much more about this proactive rotational allocation strategy.

To sum this up for now, based on the facts, the old outdated standard industry 60% stock and 40% bond allocation strategy is a useless tool to help us achieve our goal of the most return and least risk. From where did the standard 60/40 allocation arise? It most likely arose from measuring a single snapshot of market capitalizations in the 1950s! The world has changed substantially since then. We agree that asset allocation to achieve the most return and least risk matters. What this truly means is the allocation itself between stocks and bonds will and must vary over time. This brings me to my next point about the secular bull and bear markets and how they influence funds and managers.

Luck or Skill

Various studies have concluded that we need at least a 15-year horizon to separate the managers with luck from those with skill. This is interesting because that time frame encompasses just about the average length of bull and bear secular markets. An example may serve to illustrate the point. Generally speaking, in the secular bull market of the 1990s, you wanted to be fully invested, pedal to the metal, and you could make some money just by throwing darts. Basically, you just had to buy something. This "investment strategy," however, simply encompassed the secular bull market of the time. The success that arose from using the approach of being 100% always invested turned out to be due more to luck than to skill. How do we know this? This same strategy has not worked as well the past 13 years, unless you consider returning to breakeven successful.

Another example showing the importance of this 15-year time frame is the well-known example of the Legg Mason Value Fund. For 15 years it outperformed the S&P 500. Investors thought it invincible. As the fund climbed upward, it attracted more and more money. But then the fund famously collapsed in 2007 and 2008, and it gave back the gains from years earlier. It appeared to have the right value strategy that worked for a time, but when the times changed, the strategy failed the investors. For our part, the C metric we had for the fund was "avoid" before and during 2007 and 2008 because the fund's returns did not justify the risk.

Let's get back to the bigger picture, the secular trends. See how that works? We love to think the market is efficient or rational. We can mathematically measure it, and there is always some efficient market when measured over one set of indicators from a very long period of time. Something has to define success, after all. If we drill down into the decades, however, we find the markets are actually much more fluid than our fixed approach. If we add in personal age and circumstance, then the whole buy-and-hold/ignore approach practically and completely falls apart.

As to secular bear markets, the same question may be raised. At the end of the 1970s secular bear, timing was in vogue. Not losing was a winning strategy. It worked as the channel between tops and bottoms worked, but again, was it skill or luck? Was it your timing ability, or was it simply that your investments were coinciding with the market times? Sell about 1,000 on the Dow Industrials, and buy back around 600. It had worked for years. And so when I entered the business, as I noted earlier, that was the mantra from the gurus in the company and elsewhere.

Fast forward some 20 years, and timing is practically dead by the year 2000. Since then, after two devastating bear markets with 50% losses from peaks to troughs in each, you'll find that timing has a bit more respect.

The point in all of this is the markets change, and we can change with them. If we can recognize these things, the reality is that an active allocation process that incorporates stocks, bonds, and cash is useful when used correctly in both secular bull and bear markets.

The proactive rotational allocation selection process to invest with the leaders and avoid the laggards helps because there are always some managers in tune with the market (secular, cyclical, up, down, and so on). And again, as mentioned, it won't necessarily be—and in fact, it probably won't be—those previous leaders who make the successful transition from one secular market to the next secular market. The managers have their prospectuses that they must follow. Our selecting strategy simply tries to find the current managers that are leading the groups based on the risk-adjusted relative performance number that we call C.

To put it bluntly, let's just assume that nearly all managers operate at some level between luck and skill. Does this free us to look at them without emotion? Call their success "skill" and call their failure "bad luck"? Call their success "good luck" and their failure "lack of skill"? Call it however we want, my job is simply to rank the funds, active or passive, to find the leaders and avoid the laggards.

With all of that said, I am, of course, well aware of my 20-year ranking through December 31, 2013, at number one on a risk-adjusted performance basis per the *Hulbert Financial Digest*. I would point out that this period encompassed both secular and cyclical bull and bear markets. I hope there is at least a modicum of skill behind that record. As well, if I have successfully accomplished my goal, striving to provide the most return with the least risk, it is the skill of those underlying managers whose funds I've moved into and out of over the decades as they provided the most return with the least risk.

Forecasting from Where We Are Now

What is ahead? We saw that the negative impact from war is winding down. We also know that the rise of America as a net energy producer and exporter may be a game changer. Those are the positives. The negative is still value. The market was undervalued in 2009, but only on a price basis from where it had been. Since then the rapid price rise has made the market overvalued as it has been at other secular peaks. I suspect the real issue is not that stocks are attractive, because they're not on a valuation basis, but instead that the alternative to stocks in the form of interest-bearing accounts is not attractive with short-term rates near zero.

One value measure is the fairly well known *cyclically adjusted price-to-earnings* (CAPE) *ratio*. This is also known as the *Shiller P/E ratio*, which computes the well-known P/E ratio (price divided by earnings) to the average 10-year inflation-adjusted P/E ratio. Remarkably it has worked well over the years to identify when the market is expensive and when it is cheap. Most recently, however, it has been nearly continuously signaling that the market is overvalued since 1999, if CAPE of 10 is the top line measure of undervalued. I'd simply toss out, as happened at the bottom in March 2009, that accounting rule changes may change investment tools that worked previously.

As you can see from Figure 2.4, the end of previous secular bear market corresponded to relatively cheap prices in relation to earnings (below 10X) (right scale). The tops of secular bull markets

FIGURE 2.4 The S&P 500 Index in Relation to CAPE Readings for the Period of 1871 Through 2013

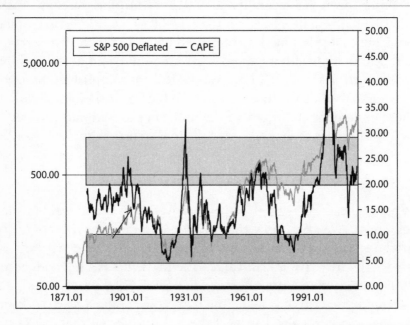

Source: Data from Standard & Poor's and Robert Shiller's website at http://irrationalexuberance.com.

correspond to CAPE readings above 20X. While it may have worked well in the past, either accounting rule changes or CAPE's popularity have contributed to making it less useful the last 15 years.

Another way to measure the comparison between value and price in the stock market is with *Tobin's Q ratio*. This ratio was made famous by Smithers & Co. It is the quotient that compares the market value of stocks over the corporate net worth. When the replacement cost is high, it implies that the stock market valuation is high also. When the cost to replace assets is low or below 1, then it implies the market valuation is also low. Like other valuation metrics, it will move between overvalued and undervalued within the confines of secular bull and bear markets. Figure 2.5 shows the S&P 500 in relation to the Q ratio from 1945 through 2013.

The Q ratio is similar to Warren Buffett's supposedly favorite valuation indicator, which is the comparison between market capitalization and gross domestic product (GDP). This valuation may be used for countries as well as companies.

FIGURE 2.5 The S&P 500 Index in Relation to the Q Ratio for the Period of 1945 Through 2013

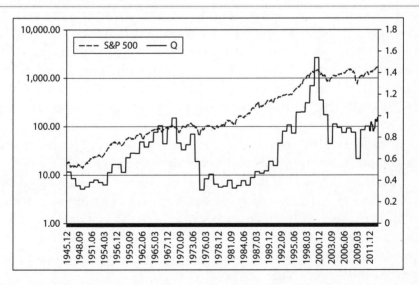

Source: Data from Standard & Poor's and the Board of Governors of the Federal Reserve System (U.S.), Federal Reserve Economic Data (FRED), Federal Reserve Bank of St. Louis.

There are additional measures to show where we are in the secular market, such as the earnings yield and the dividend yield. The *earnings yield* is simply the inverse of the P/E ratio. The *dividend yield* is the dividend paid divided by the price of the stock or mutual fund. Both measures may provide additional information. And there is one more indicator to talk about.

The Fed Model

I briefly talked about this above when describing how P/E ratios fluctuate between cheap and expensive and the alternative investments to stocks. The bottoms of secular bear markets are typically accompanied by single-digit P/E ratios. If the secular bear that began in 2000 ended in 2009 but it was not accompanied by single-digit P/E ratios as in the past, then we need some explanation for this possible anomaly. Popularity and accounting rule changes may apply, but also the Fed model may help us in this regard.

This model compares the relative yields between 10-year Treasury bonds and the inverted P/E ratio on the S&P 500, which gives us the *earnings yield*. For example, if the P/E ratio is 10, then the earnings yield on stocks is 10% (1/10). If the P/E ratio is 20, then the earnings yield is 5%. The lower the P/E ratio, the "cheaper" the market is—that is, the faster you will get back your investment, all other things being equal. The P/E ratio tells us how many years it will take for the company to earn the price you paid. For example, if the price of the stock is $10 per share and it earns $1, then its P/E ratio is 10. It will take 10 years, assuming no growth and equivalency, for the company to earn the price you paid for the stock. The faster you earn back your investment, the greater the return, and the faster you compound your investment, all other things being equal.

Back to the point: in both cases, this number, the earnings yield, alone doesn't yield too much information. We don't invest in a vacuum but rather within a construct of alternative choices. We could buy real estate or bonds or commodities as well as stocks. For our purposes, however, this stock earnings yield is typically compared against the 10-year Treasury bond yield.

The idea is that if the stock earnings yield is greater than the bond yield, then stocks are relatively cheap and should be bought.

You would be compensated for taking the additional risk of stocks over the "guaranteed" government yield. If stock yields are less than government Treasury bond yields, stocks are considered expensive and should be sold.

That's the theory. What's the reality? The model has worked fairly well recently, but its long-term track record is shaky. It is beyond the scope of this book to go into more detail about this. My point is simply to offer one possible explanation for why stocks have rallied strongly without coming out of the trough of undervaluation.

Conclusion

It's been a long, grinding 13 years in which many investors, especially indexers, have not made any money. If, however, you have been employing some market timing and fund selecting strategies, then the 13 years could have been very profitable. Selling high and buying low, staying with the leaders, while avoiding the laggards has helped in this environment, just as it does in a secular bull market. But if instead you have been an indexer or a buy-and-hold investor using outdated advice, you've broke even at best after 13 years. When priced in current dollars (deflated), that strategy has been a horrible investing approach. A simple T-bill portfolio beat the stock index. This is not the way to achieve *the most return with the least risk*. We've shown that. The efficient frontier shifts over time.

To make this even more poignant, we are older now than we were in 2000. Our circumstances have changed. This has to be acknowledged if we want to do something about industry standard results. In Chapters 6 and 7, we will look at how we do things differently in both these areas of selecting and timing so that we take into account, first and foremost, personal age and circumstance.

3

Neither a Lender nor a Borrower Be

THE CHAPTER TITLE IS FROM SHAKESPEARE, BUT LET IT BE KNOWN that borrowing to buy something productive is not inherently wrong or dumb.[1] Borrowing to buy something consumable or disposable, however, is. Those are the things that have no collateral value or are quickly consumed, like borrowing to buy a meal. The difference is between buying clothes on credit and a car on credit. Both depreciate, but in the former case the rate of depreciation is so quick and complete that there is never a way to sell the clothes if you have to at anywhere near what you paid and thus fully pay off the loan. Cars, planes, and RVs (things with wheels)—they, too, depreciate, but at least they are assets that will presumably pay off the loan if worse comes to worst and they have to be sold. The next step up is borrowing to buy an asset like real estate that might appreciate. It *might* appreciate because, as we all know by now, there is no guarantee that the value of a house or any other asset—including stocks—must go up.

---

[1] Shakespeare was speaking about borrowing from and loaning to friends and family. Good advice then as it is now.

The last step in the debt continuum is to borrow to buy a productive, profitable business that continues in that manner.

In the last chapter we explored the history of the stock market and saw how it fluctuates over time in relation to its underlying valuation: its price compared to earnings, replacement costs, dividends, book values, and cash flows. In this chapter we look at the history of the bond market. What drives interest rates up and down? We will also look at whether there is some correlation between interest rates and stocks, which is important as we discuss asset allocation or market timing.

The first myth I've already put to bed is the idea that there is some sort of magical static allocation between stocks and bonds, like 60% and 40%, that is the panacea for all the ailing swings in the stock and bond markets. In fact, the success or failure of any allocation strategy depends on your time frame and your personal age and circumstance. As we saw in the last chapter from the Guggenheim Partners' (formerly Rydex/SGI) chart in Figure 2.3 on the efficient market, there are decades when bonds are the place to invest, even up to 100% of the portfolio, rather than equities, in order to manifest the most return with the least risk. Following this goal means that we will have to adjust what we do from maintaining a static approach to pursuing a dynamic one. Basically, there are times when equities provide all of the risk and none of the reward, and a 100% allocation to bonds (or cash) is the better course of action. To be sure there are other times when equities provide a tremendous upside with little of the "normal" risk; this happens at the ends of secular bear markets when the stock market is cheap. It is the same with the bond market. Both stock and bond markets move in broad discernible trends that last anywhere from 5 to 30 years.

Incidentally, we think of cash[2] or money markets or CDs as the nearly riskless end of the bond spectrum. After all, a CD or a money market fund is simply our loaning our cash to a bank or the Treasury, and in return we receive interest from them until maturity (assuming no bankruptcy). Cash serves the same purpose as a bond,

---

[2] When I use the term *cash*, I mean it to include *CDs* or *money market funds* as synonyms. I'm not talking about the cash we might have in our billfolds.

except that it is employed for a very limited duration. In the case of money market funds, the duration can be as short as a day.

Cash is practically riskless with its daily duration. At the other end of the risk spectrum are junk bonds that may provide a higher yield than other investments but with substantially more risk of default.

With this in mind, that cash is a very short term duration bond, it becomes much easier to consider the idea that there are times to utilize cash. This is the next myth to explode. The first myth was that a static 60% stock and 40% bond allocation is ideal to achieve the most return and least risk. The second myth is that cash should never be used. This is untrue, if one wants to achieve the most return with the least risk. Hopefully we will learn this long before the next bear market pummels us. We no longer want to be in the emotional position that sets us up to sell at the bottom.[3] The standard industry advice that timing doesn't work has credence if only because most people sell low and buy high. They act in tandem with their emotions. The point is that if one uses bonds anyway to mitigate stock risk, and cash is a bond, then clearly cash is an alternative to stocks as well as to bonds. Most of the investment world pooh-poohs this idea as market timing, but facts are facts. The real issue to address is why some advisors will not use cash in their portfolio allocation recommendations. Clearly there are times when cash is providing the most return and least risk. If that is the goal, then why not use cash? In a later chapter, I'll speak more to these objections.

Getting on with bonds, we will now look at some basics. Bonds are debt instruments. To be issued, they require a party on each side of the transaction: one who is the lender and the other who is the borrower. Bonds may also be known as *fixed-income securities*. They run the gamut in terms of quality and duration from bank-issued, government-backed up to $250,000 insured CDs to 30-year junk bonds, but they function in the same way. Each is an IOU (I owe you) between the borrower and lender.

Bonds are used in a variety of ways to fund different operations, ranging from meeting day-to-day expenses to making long-term investments by individuals, companies, and governments. Bonds may

---

[3] No one of course will admit to selling at the bottom.

be backed by underlying assets (secured) or by a promise to repay (unsecured). The holder of the bond is the creditor, the lender, who has loaned money to the issuer. The issuer is the borrower, the debtor. Bonds are usually issued at par value, which is 100% of the face value. This is the amount that is borrowed and must be repaid. Like stocks, bonds also trade in the secondary market at different prices from their par values between their issue date and maturity. The bond's face value is normally measured in increments of $1,000.

There are all sorts of bonds issued by numerous borrowers, ranging from the very safest to the very riskiest and from the shortest to the longest duration. The interest the issuer pays to the lender relative to the market at the time of issuance usually reflects the issuer's risk of default and the bond's duration. The higher the risk of default by the issuer, the greater the interest rate paid by the issuer. The lower the risk of default, the lower the interest rate. Normally the longer the term to maturity, the higher the interest rate. Typically the issuer pays interest to the lender every six months until the bond matures. At maturity, assuming no bankruptcy of the borrower, the bonds mature at par value, and the loan is paid back. Basically the debtor borrows the money from the lender, pays the lender interest, and then pays back the full amount borrowed at maturity.

When talking about bonds, we also need to be clear about the relationship between prices and yields (interest rates). The two move inversely. When yields fall, bond prices go up. When yields rise, bond prices go down. The reason for this is that the value of cash flows (the interest paid) will change relative to the interest that newly issued bonds pay compared with the old bonds. The interest rate of the bond is normally fixed over its term, but the bond market itself, interest rate levels, will change. For example, if an old bond yields 10% of par maturing in 25 years and it has been outstanding for two years and if new 25-year bonds are issued to yield 11%, then the price for the old bond must go down in order to be competitive with the higher yields of the new bond. In this example, the price will fall roughly 10%. New buyers of the old already issued bond would then also receive roughly 11% current yield. In this case, if the bondholders had to sell the bond prior to maturity, the bondholders would incur a loss. If they held to maturity, however, they would receive back their original principal. Conversely, if investors bought a bond with a 10% coupon at par and interest rates subsequently fell, then the bond price would go up; its cash flow, its yield, would be worth more to the current market. At maturity, though, it, too, would return to par value.

Bond buyers face a number of risks between the dates of issuance and payback. Aside from fluctuating interest rates and having to cash out early, the primary risk is default. If the issuer goes bankrupt, the bondholder may or may not get back the full original principal amount invested. He may receive back only a portion, and it may take longer to receive than the stated maturity date. In the pecking order of payback in the event of a default, bonds as debt rank higher than stocks as ownership equity.[4] Another risk is that interest rates will change. As mentioned, if rates rise, then bond prices fall. Again, though, if investors hold their bonds to maturity, then they will get back their principal.

Both of these risks function as trade-offs when buying a bond fund, as opposed to buying a bond directly. With one investment in the bond fund, you could be lowering your risk of default because the fund had diversified among hundreds of issuers. But the trade-off is that because the bond fund itself has no par value, you are never assured of receiving back your principal. That is the trade-off between the two: immediate diversification today but no assurance of a future par value. To be clear, the fund has a net asset value, which is the price of all of its assets less its liabilities, but the net asset value is not the fund's underlying bonds' future par value. This is an important point.

In addition to the risk of default, this fluctuation in a bond's value is also associated with its quality and time to maturity. Usually, the shorter the time to maturity, the lower the interest rate. And usually, the greater the quality of the issuer, the lower the interest rate.

In periods of easy money and normal economic expansion, interest rates are in what is called a *positive yield curve* where short-term bonds pay less than intermediate-term bonds, which also pay less than long-term bonds. In periods of tight money, when economic expansion is too hot or inflation is heating up, short-term bonds typically will pay

---

[4] This is why the anticipated return from stocks must be higher than from bonds, to compensate for the additional risk incurred.

more than long-term bonds. This is known as an *inverted yield curve.* Usually, an inverted yield curve is a precursor to and forecaster of a recession. In turn, this may forecast a stock market top.

Lastly, as you will see below, the bond market is no different from the stock market in that prices move in both secular (5- to 30-year) cycles and cyclical (1- to 4-year) cycles. With this information, just as we evaluate stocks, we won't make the easy mistake of thinking things will never change. For investors who buy bond funds, as opposed to individual bonds, this is critical information.

Strategy

Typically, investors use bonds to make money on their money. They make the loan and receive the interest. At maturity, assuming no bankruptcy, they receive back their principal. The second way to use bonds is as a hedge for some of the stock market's volatility. For example, in a typical bear stock market, equities may easily lose more than 25% of their value. A portfolio invested only in stocks would thus lose one-fourth of its value. And as mentioned in the last chapter, there is no assurance that the market will eventually recover to its former peaks within one's lifetime.

This is unacceptable to numerous investors. So many individuals and institutions use some combination of stocks and bonds, like the well-known historic 60% stock and 40% bond allocation. In a recession-induced bear stock market where earnings are declining, there are times when interest rates will then begin to also decline. Bond prices will move inversely, which in this case of falling interest rates, will mean that prices will move up. This bond price increase may offset some of the loss in the stock portion. Further details of this common strategy are beyond the scope of this chapter, but I would ask the question whether this strategy will work as well in the future as it has historically, when rates are already so near to zero? How much of an offset to a stock loss of 25% could a decline from interest rates at their current levels (in 2015) help, given that they are already so low? The answer may suggest to some investors that they should actually move out of longer-term bonds and use the full bond spectrum, including near cash, like CDs or money market funds, as an asset class to hedge.

Take a look at the following table for an example of the impact on bond prices when interest rates rise. This assumes the bond is issued with a 4% coupon:

Years to Maturity	Rates Rise 1%	Rates Fall 1%	Rates Rise 2%	Rates Fall 2%
1	−1.0%	1.0%	−1.9%	2.0%
5	−4.4	4.6	−8.5	9.5
10	−7.8	8.6	−14.9	18.0
20	−12.6	15.0	−23.1	32.8
30	−15.5	19.7	−27.7	45.0

Source: Calculations from the American Association of Individual Investors (AAII.com).

As you can see, the mathematics of yield and price moves bears out this consideration. With long-term rates already roughly at 3%, a drop of 1% to 2% will increase 10-year bond prices by 8.6%. So, if stocks drop 30% in a normal bear market and you have 60% of your portfolio in stocks, then you lose 18% (60% of −30%). What of the bond portion? In this example, 40% of your portfolio is invested in bonds. Based on the table above, with a 1% drop in rates, it would yield a bond price gain of about 9%, which would translate into a gain of about 4% (40% of 9%) for the bond portion. The total portfolio, therefore, declines by "only" 14% (−18 + 4).

So, while the idea that a balanced portfolio is a way to offset stock declines may have worked well in the past, in today's environment, it may not be the case. Interest rates may already be at the bottom of their 30-year secular bull market.

I want to focus a bit more now on what to watch out for if you are a bond fund investor, rather than a buyer of individual bonds. We know that if interest rates go up, bond prices will fall (as can be seen in the table above). At maturity, however, an *individual bond* will return to its par value, which is usually 100. This assumes no default by the issuer. You will receive back your investment. For a *bond fund* investor, however, the key point is that there is no par value per se in a bond fund. So investors are never assured of receiving their principal back. While the bond fund holds individual bonds that mature at par, the fund itself does not have a par value. Its value is simply the values of all the bonds it holds on that particular day less accrued expenses.

This fact about a fund's nonrealizable par value usually does not affect the investor in a secular bond bull market because rates are falling and bond prices are rising. The risk of loss is there, but it is not apparent to everyone. In a period of expected interest rate increases, however, the bond fund's bonds will decrease in value. Because of bond fund cash flows from new fund buyers and fund sellers, the fund may be forced to sell those depreciated bonds, rather than having the ability to wait until their maturity at full par value. Thus the fund may be forced to sell a holding at a steep loss, which is passed on to the fund holder at the marked-down net asset value (NAV). Then, should interest rates return to where they were, the fund's NAV may not. The bonds had been sold for a loss. The point in this is that in a bond bear market, rather than buy bond funds, one should instead strongly consider purchasing individual bonds.

This bond bear market guidance assumes a couple of things. One, it assumes an investor has a large enough portfolio to properly diversify among different issuers in order to offset potential default risk. Investors can use rating companies like Moody's or Standard & Poor's to help them assess risk, enabling them to buy bonds from only the most highly rated issuers with ratings of AA or AAA. However, investors should keep the caveat in mind that we have all learned, which is that the rating companies' evaluations are not always accurate or timely. Two, it assumes that the costs of trading bonds are not prohibitive—costs that include the spreads between bid and ask and the commissions. Plus, there are the investors' personal costs to research, monitor, and trade bonds. Three, it assumes one can accurately forecast expected interest rate changes.

One strategy to use when buying individual bonds is bond laddering. This strategy buys individual bonds or CDs that mature as rungs of a ladder over a period of time. For example, if an investor has $100,000, he might buy 10 issues of $10,000 each ranging in maturity from 1 to 10 years, or he might buy 20 issues of $5,000 each ranging in maturity from 1 to 5 years, or any combination. Those years are the rungs. When the nearest bond matures, the investor rolls it out to extend the ladder back to the ladder's original configuration; in the first example, the investor would buy a new 10-year bond. Or the investor can buy 10 CDs that would mature each month and roll them out as they mature. If interest rates rise and the investor needs liquidity, the shorter-term bonds, which are less sensitive to rate changes, can be sold.

In sum, in a secular bond bull market where yields are falling and prices are rising, the easiest investment approach is to buy a bond fund. There is built-in diversification. There is also daily professional management. Costs of ownership may be less. In a bond bear market where yields are rising and prices are falling, the best approach, depending on your personal situation, may be to buy individual bonds.

Bond Market History

The history of the bond market is not dissimilar to the history of the stock market. It moves in very broad wide-ranging trends that may last for years and years. Since 1900, in fact, there have been two secular bull markets in bonds and two secular bear markets in bonds. These very long term trends that have ranged from 5 to 35 years are shown in Figure 3.1.

The first secular bond bear market (rising rates and falling prices) lasted from January 1900 through June 1920 (reference the graph line labeled AAA Yield Bear in the chart). Interest rates then dropped, entering a secular bond bull market (reference the graph line labeled AAA Yield Bull). Rates dropped from 6.4% to 2.5% over the next 26 years from July 1920 to August 1946. Rates then began another secular bear market, when rates rose from less than 3% to more than 15% over some 35 years from September 1946 to September 1981 (again, reference the graph line labeled AAA Yield Bear). Since that peak, rates have dropped again in the current secular bond bull market from October 1981 through the present (again, reference the graph line labeled AAA Yield Bull). In total, over the last 100 years, there have been two secular bull markets and two secular bear markets in bonds. Over the next 100 years no doubt there will be a few more secular bull and bear markets in bonds.

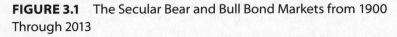

FIGURE 3.1   The Secular Bear and Bull Bond Markets from 1900 Through 2013

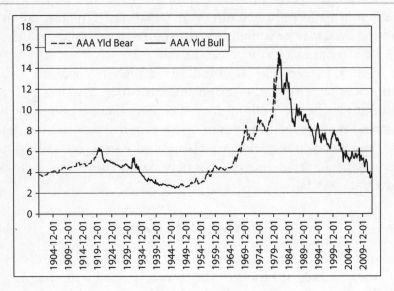

Source: Board of Governors of the Federal Reserve System (U.S.), Federal Reserve Economic Data (FRED), Federal Reserve Bank of St. Louis.

Timing Factors

The relationship between interest rates and other factors is much more interesting than it might appear to be on the surface. The obvious connection, for example, between recessions and interest rates is anything but clear except on a shorter-term cyclical basis of one to five years. One might intuitively believe that in a recession, interest rates will decline. Or in an expansion, interest rates will increase. But that is not the case, as can be seen in Figure 3.2, which shows the relationship between interest rates and recession periods. While it is true that interest rates generally decline during recessions, what is less obvious is how interest rates might behave subsequent to recessions. Interestingly, that movement depends more on their secular trend than it does on the economy generally. In other words, other factors influence the ultimate direction of interest rates more than recessions and recoveries.

FIGURE 3.2 Moody's Seasoned Aaa Corporate Bond Yield (AAA) from 1910 Through 2020

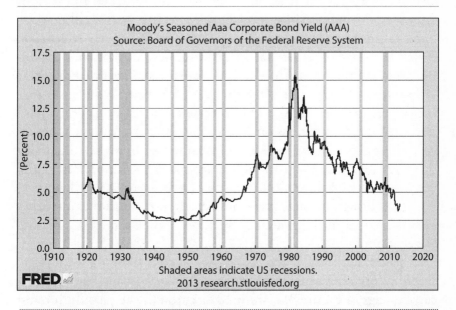

Source: Board of Governors of the Federal Reserve System (U.S.), Federal Reserve Economic Data (FRED), Federal Reserve Bank of St. Louis.

The grayed portions show recessionary periods, but in the secular bear market for yields (where rates rise and prices fall), while yields fell during recessions, they subsequently rose above recession levels. In secular bull markets (yields fall and prices rise), yields also fell during recessions, but then they fell below prerecession levels. So, other long-term factors, besides recessions, were at work on the ultimate level of interest rates. I will look at these other factors shortly.

Basically, this relationship between pre- and postrecession levels of interest rates is one of the best ways to determine whether bond yields are in a secular bull or bear market. As of the recession of 2008, yields have continued to fall below their prerecession levels. (The period prior to 1919 is not shown for Moody's Aaa corporate bond yields in Figure 3.2, but the secular trend on interest rates is clear enough; they had been rising during those marked recession periods.)

So, as Figure 3.2 shows, in secular bond bear markets (rates rising), yields in the economic expansion went above prerecession levels. In subsequent recessions, levels never returned to previous rates seen during previous recessions. In secular bond bull markets (rates falling), yields went below prerecession levels. My conclusion is that there are other key factors at work besides economic expansions and contractions. The two key secular turns that marked these long-term changes were after the recession near 1949 (rates rose above prerecession levels) and in reverse after the recession in 1982 (rates fell below prerecession levels). For the current time as this is written in 2014, unless we enter another recession to give us a lower starting yield, the level to watch is around 5.5% set back in 2008. (As of the date of this report, the risk of a recession is very low.)

The following charts are a further attempt to find those other factors at work in the secular correlation between interest rates and the economy.

The first indicator I investigated was to compare inflation as measured by the consumer price index (CPI) against interest rates. As can be seen in Figure 3.3, from 1871 through the peak in interest

FIGURE 3.3 Inflation in Comparison to Interest Rates from 1871 Through 2013

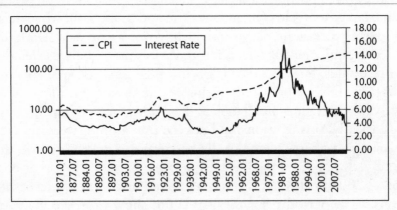

Source: Robert Shiller, *Irrational Exuberance*, 2006. Used with permission.

rates in September 1981, there was some correlation between the two series. Since then, however, the CPI has continued to climb, while interest rates have fallen. This happened before, during the late 1930s and 1940s. As a timing tool, it is not very precise, but this indicator does show how relationships change.

The next thing I looked at was the value of the U.S. dollar compared to other currencies (Figure 3.4). As you can see, this is much more helpful in forecasting rate trends. The peak value of the dollar corresponds to the peak interest rate yield back near 1984. There was, however, a dollar rally from 1995 through 2003, even though interest rates continued to decline, but this may be more of a "safe haven" factor than it is a more permanent fundamental factor. The same uncoupling happened in the financial crisis of 2007 and 2008

FIGURE 3.4   Real Trade Weighted U.S. Dollar Index: Broad

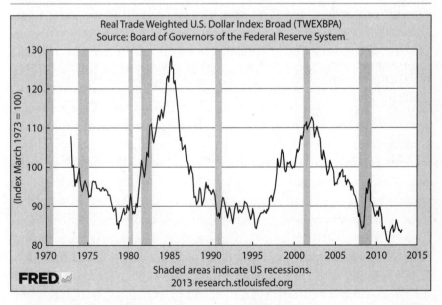

Source: Board of Governors of the Federal Reserve System (U.S.), Federal Reserve Economic Data (FRED), Federal Reserve Bank of St. Louis.

when rates fell but the dollar value went up. Since then, the relentless loss of a dollar's purchasing power has been dropping along with the falling interest rate yield.

They generally move closely with each other. So an analysis of the direction of interest rates should include a review of the value of the U.S. dollar relative to other currencies. As Figure 3.4 indicates, currently the United States is "on sale" or is "cheap" relative to other currencies, and it has been dating back to 1977.

This brings me to what I find is the most interesting relationship, which is between the level of federal debt as a percentage of gross domestic product (GDP) and interest rates. Although the Federal Reserve is independent of political influence, it may not be that independent. In fact, it is subject to congressional oversight. That said, lowering the federal government's cost of borrowing is, perhaps, in the Fed's best interest. Is it on purpose or just an anomaly? You may be the judge.

Please note in this example that it is not the absolute level of debt that is important but rather the ratio of debt to GDP. Some pundits will play to fear and forecast the end of the world by using the singular idea of the large amount of debt. As a way to counter this unfounded fear, think instead of levels of debt in personal terms. When you were younger, like the country, in your twenties, you could support maybe $10,000 of debt. When you were in your fifties, you could support maybe $100,000 of debt. What's the difference? The absolute level of debt is clearly greater, but the difference that matters is in your earnings power. At the country level, this is known as gross domestic product. Should we look for falling skies, like Chicken Little, just because the level of debt is so much greater today than it has been? We should not. While the absolute level of debt is 10 times greater than it was, so, too, is the level of income as measured by GDP. In addition to income, asset levels have grown. It is those things that are important in determining how much debt is too much debt. The ratios of income to debt or of assets to debt are the main factors. This is true on the personal and national levels. Clearly the federal government has more debt on an absolute basis than ever before, but also just as clearly, the nation's GDP is greater than ever before. The important factor is the ratio of debt to GDP, not the absolute level.

FIGURE 3.5   The Federal Debt: Total Public Debt from 1965 Through 2013

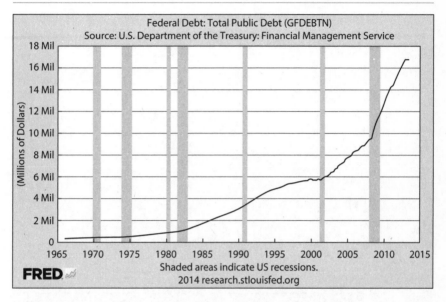

Source: Data from the U.S. Department of the Treasury, Financial Management Service. Board of Governors of the Federal Reserve System (U.S.), Federal Reserve Economic Data (FRED), Federal Reserve Bank of St. Louis.

Figure 3.5 shows the large increase in absolute levels of debt, and Figure 3.6 shows the more important relationship of the federal debt as a percentage of GDP.

As you can see, the ratio has risen and fallen in broad swings over the decades. It has ranged from lows of 32% to highs of 122%. The big question is not about the level of debt but about the ratio of that debt to income or assets.

Figure 3.7 is very interesting. It provides a better visual picture of the inverse relationship between interest rates and the gross federal debt as a percentage of GDP. The takeaway from this chart is the obvious long-term relationship between the federal debt as a percentage of GDP and interest rates. Federal debt as a percentage of GDP is inverted; reference the graph line labeled federal debt.

FIGURE 3.6   The Gross Federal Debt as a Percentage of Gross
Domestic Product from 1930 Through 2013

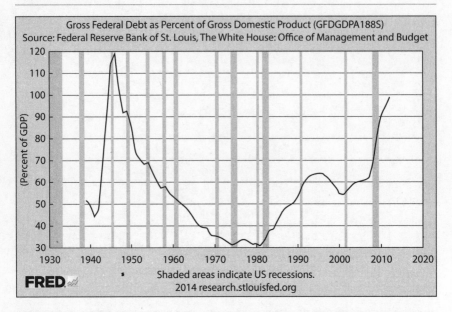

Source: Data from the Federal Reserve Bank of St. Louis and the White
House Office of Management and Budget. Board of Governors of
the Federal Reserve System (U.S.), Federal Reserve Economic Data
(FRED), Federal Reserve Bank of St. Louis.

When federal debt as a percentage of GDP declines, interest rates
(reference the AAA Yield graph line) rise. When debt as a percentage
of GDP increases, then interest rates generally fall.

The last secular bull market in bonds ended about the time
World War II was ending. Debt as a percentage of GDP was around
100%. As the war wound down and spending was redirected from
destruction to construction, the GDP expanded. Debt decreased.
Interest rates fell.

The secular bull market in bonds eventually ended, and the
secular bear market in bonds began, running from the late 1940s to
the late 1970s. This is similar to the same situation as today.

As mentioned, the Fed operates independently of Congress,
but it also functions within the government's approval process.

FIGURE 3.7   The Inverse Relationship Between Interest Rates and the Gross Federal Debt as a Percentage of GDP from 1939 Through 2013

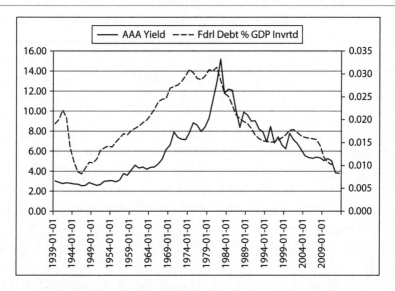

Source: Board of Governors of the Federal Reserve System (U.S.), Federal Reserve Economic Data (FRED), Federal Reserve Bank of St. Louis.

The chairperson is an appointed position. As such, if this relationship continues to hold in the future, we really shouldn't expect the secular trend of interest rates to change from down to up until the federal government begins to reduce its debt as a percentage of GDP. When might this happen? As we look at this, keep in mind that GDP is reported with a lag of more than three months to current interest rates.

It is also perhaps more than a coincidence that today's situation is very similar to the period in the 1940s when the ratio also exceeded 100%. Back then, World War II was ending. Wars cost a lot of money to conduct, but this one was finally winding down, which meant that resources would be devoted to construction instead of destruction. As mentioned in the previous chapter in relation to the secular bull and bear markets in stocks, it wasn't war that helped the market. It was the Marshall Plan and the GI Bill that helped stocks boom.

In 2013, the United States was winding down the wars in the Middle East that began September 11, 2001, from Iraq to Afghanistan. Today the rebuilding process is in place.

On a citizenship level, things are in place now to suggest a secular change in the bond market. More than that, however, are the recent tax increases and sequestration (wherein Congress was cutting their spending) in 2012, 2013, and 2014. They did these things, and the economy is still expanding. This changing ratio between falling spending and increasing GDP is part of the forecasting tool that also suggests the secular bond bull market is ending. To be sure, this forecast, like any forecast, requires constant vigilance. Updates may be found at our website SelectionsAndTiming.com. But we now have a few additional tools with which to watch this potential secular change that will impact your financial health and wealth.

For one thing, the government has been spending less than it did the year before for two years in a row. This hasn't happened since the Korean War. For a second thing, the Congressional Budget Office (CBO) in a report dated August 22, 2012, was projecting a possible reduction in federal debt as a percentage of GDP beginning in 2014 to 2015 and declining steadily, though slowly, thereafter.

Both of these factors contribute to the sense that the 30-year secular bull market in bonds is coming to an end.

One- to Five-Year Cycles

As I did in the previous chapter on stock market cycles, I want to also expand on the idea that within secular bull and bear markets, there are cyclical (one to five years) bull and bear bond markets. These shorter-term trends may also impact the investment decision-making process.

We should look at any correlation between stocks and bonds. As you can see in Figure 3.8, there is no direct correlation between the direction or level of interest rates and stock prices. For example, interest rates have been falling ever since 1982, and they are continuing to do so through the present. Stocks have both rallied and fallen numerous times.

FIGURE 3.8 The Lack of Correlation Between Interest Rates and Stock Prices from 1871 Through 2013

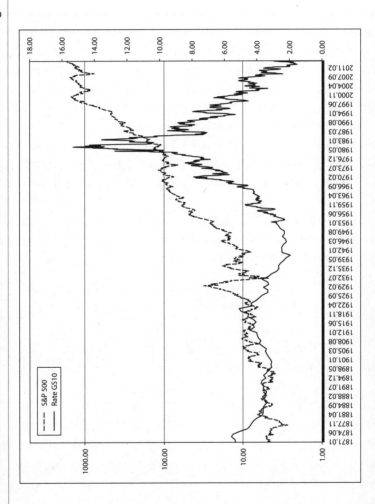

Source: Data from Standard & Poor's.

Sentiment

Lastly, I want to mention bond investor sentiment. Just as it is with the stock or gold markets, this is also a useful measure. Sentiment is a contrary indicator; that is, the more bullish investors are, the more cautious one should become, and the more bearish investors are, the more aggressive one might become. So consider Figure 3.9 that shows the yields of Treasury Inflation-Protected Securities (TIPS). TIPS provide some safety against inflation. They pay a nominal yield, and the principal is adjusted for the inflation or deflation rate. At maturity, they pay either the original principal or the adjusted principal, whichever is greater.

As you can see from this chart, investor sentiment was so strongly bullish on bonds at the lows that the yield on TIPS was near a negative 1%. Investors were paying the government for the privilege of

FIGURE 3.9 Ten-Year Treasury Inflation-Indexed Security, Constant Maturity, from 2002 Through 2013

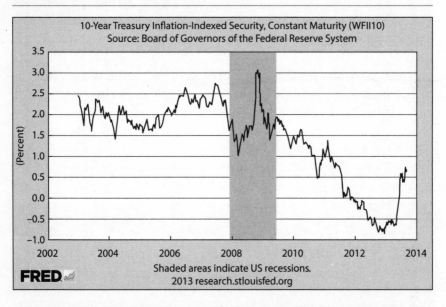

Source: Board of Governors of the Federal Reserve System (U.S.), retrieved from Federal Reserve Economic Data (FRED), Federal Reserve Bank of St. Louis, https://research.stlouisfed.org/fred2/series/WFII10/.

owning its bonds.[5] This sentiment measure, like the turn in federal debt to GDP, may also suggest that the 30-year secular bond bull market is coming to an end.

Just as there are advantages to knowing the stock market's trend, there are numerous advantages to knowing the direction of interest rates. This is true whether one is a borrower or a lender, a consumer or a business. For example, if you know rates are trending higher and prices lower, then it behooves you to lock in low rates for as long a time as possible. If rates are trending lower, then you should invest in longer-dated bonds.

Conclusion

As we have seen in this chapter, interest rates and bond prices move in secular trends that may last for decades. When interest rates fall, bond prices climb. When rates rise, prices fall. I would emphasize these two main takeaways about a bond fund's net asset value and a resulting strategy.

A bond fund's net asset value is not equal to the sum of its bonds' par values, but rather, it is equal to their current prices at today's interest rates, not at the rates when the bonds were issued. What this means is that the bond fund investor is never assured of getting back his principal in a bond fund. Certainly this is true when rates rise and remain higher, but it is also true even if rates rise and then fall back to where they had been. There is no par value in a bond fund.

The strategy therefore to use when buying bonds should be different in secular bull and bear markets. In a secular bond bull market, when interest rates are falling and bond prices are rising, for most investors, the use of bond funds should be emphasized. For one investment, you receive immediate diversification, professional management, and easy price tracking. In a secular bond bear market, however, individual bonds should be considered. They have a maturity date at which, all things being equal, they will price back to their par value.

---

[5] I should mention, hopefully as an anomaly, that trial balloons are floated to see whether the public would be willing to pay banks "interest" for the privilege of letting the banks hold our cash.

One strategy, therefore, to use in a secular bond bear market is a bond ladder. As we saw, using a bond ladder is investing the same amount over a variety of maturities and when the nearest one matures, rolling it out to the longest maturity. In this way, your portfolio's par value of all the bonds is like a sidewalk escalator: it is flat and constantly rotating.

To determine when interest rates are in a secular bond or bull market, certainly a visual inspection of a long-term chart will help. In Chapter 7 we will look at moving averages in this regard. On a more fundamental basis, these secular movements that last decades appear to be unrelated to the economy, to GDP, or to inflation. The two main factors identified to use when forecasting the long-term trend of interest rates are the trends of federal government debt as a percentage of GDP and the value of the U.S. dollar.

On a cyclical basis, ranging from one to five years, other technical tools, such as moving averages, correlations, and fundamental indicators, such as the yield curve and the strength or weakness of the underlying economies, both domestic and foreign, may be employed to help determine the interest rate direction.

Like any ratio, this one (federal government debt to GDP) also has two components. Half of the assumption is that GDP will continue to expand, which is to say that there will not be a recession for the foreseeable future. The information in Figure 3.10 would help to monitor this part of the equation. It shows the probability of a U.S. recession.

An increase above 10% is a very good indication that the United States either is or soon will be in a recession. (Note that there were two false signals out of nine total signals; one was in 1978, and the other was in 2006.) When this indicator increases, it suggests that the GDP will turn negative. This in turn suggests interest rates will eventually fall.

Finally, as long as we're talking about government Treasuries, I should mention there is a useful website: http://TreasuryDirect.gov. If nothing else, you can use it to search to see if you have any lost savings bonds (after the issuance date of 1974).

In addition, there is another service that would help provide further information for this part of the equation. The Conference Board

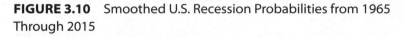

FIGURE 3.10   Smoothed U.S. Recession Probabilities from 1965 Through 2015

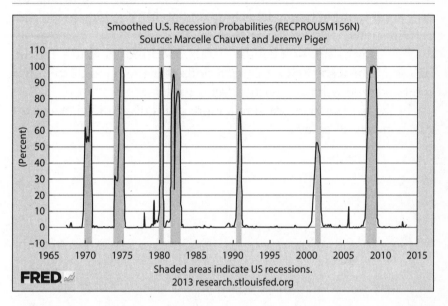

Source: Board of Governors of the Federal Reserve System (U.S.), Federal Reserve Economic Data (FRED), Federal Reserve Bank of St. Louis.

publishes a leading economic indicator each month. It, too, should be monitored for economic clues about the economy's future.

The second half of the ratio is the federal debt. This, too, must be monitored. The nonpartisan Congressional Budget Office will help us in this regard. We know that government spending is projected to decline for two years in a row beginning in September 2013. Taxes are going up. As a result, we also know that federal debt as a percentage of GDP is forecast to continue to decline slowly over the next few years. This forecast, of course, should be monitored carefully and updated regularly. If the federal debt as a percentage of GDP does indeed begin to decline, this means on a secular basis that interest rates should reverse course from down to up. A confirmation of this would be when rates rise above their prerecession levels.

It would thus mean that the 30-year secular bull market in bonds has come to an end.

As regards an investment policy, if we are fairly certain that the long-term trend in bond yields is up and bond prices are down, then certain strategic changes should be made.

Buy shorter-duration bonds. Avoid bond funds, and use individual bonds instead. Reduce expectations that the bond portion of a total portfolio will necessarily offset stock losses.

In the next chapter, I will talk more about diversification and the role bonds might play.

4

To Diversify or Not to Diversify

I WILL RECAP WHAT WE'VE LEARNED SO FAR. FROM CHAPTER 1, WE saw that the standard financial industry advice on how to make a return with the least risk falls short on a number of levels. Rather, we must include the personal factors, like age and circumstance, in the investment strategy. Diversification as a way to reduce risk is addressed by using cash, in addition to stocks and bonds. There are times when cash provides the most return with the least risk. There is simply no assurance that market trends up or down will remain in place. From Chapters 2 and 3, we saw in fact that stocks and bonds move in secular trends wherein gains and losses ranged from −90% to +100%. With the typical buy-and-hold approach, one's investment success is largely influenced only by where the market is in its secular cycle. If you buy when the market is "cheap" versus buying when it is "expensive," your results will differ substantially. The better alternative is to employ asset allocation or market timing based on measurable indicators.

With these things in mind, how do we respond to this information to help us form a new, updated, reliable, and cohesive investment strategy? If our selecting and timing are important each year or even each month to our financial well-being, and they are, what should we do about it? Can we do anything about it?

Just like anyone else in the financial industry, I can look at the 100-year chart of the S&P 500 or the Dow Jones Industrials and say that, had we bought and held the index for 100 years, we would have made money. This is that standard analysis behind the financial industry's usual recommendation to buy and hold. With a nod to the reality of devastating bear markets and recessions, and so to smooth the peaks and valleys and reduce that market risk, some advisors recommend that a portion of the total portfolio be invested in bonds. That one-time snapshot of stocks and bonds has been the basis for the industry standard advice to allocate a fixed 60% of your portfolio to stocks and a fixed 40% of your portfolio to bonds. The advice was based on the market cap of equities and fixed income that were prescribed when Modern Portfolio Theory had its beginnings in the 1950s. As we are learning, however, this standard advice completely ignores the personal time and circumstance factors, not to mention the numerous gains and losses of more than 50% from stocks over those years. It also ignores that some managers perform better than the indexes and their peers, though they aren't necessarily the same managers who do so year in and year out. It ignores the fact that global market caps have changed. Lastly, it ignores the most fundamental of investor goals: to make the most return with the least risk. How much better off would we be if we could somehow account for these facts?

The industry recognizes these possible 50% or worse losses not by dealing with them directly, but indirectly by recommending that you diversify. Reduce your overall portfolio loss by reducing your portfolio's exposure to that area. It is akin to saying that if you build a mansion here, chances are good that a tornado will hit it, so build a shack instead and hope for the best. They say to buy bonds instead of stocks. Buy real estate in addition to bonds or stocks. Buy gold as a hedge. Yet the fact is that the part of your portfolio in stocks will still decline by whatever amount the stock market declines. If the market drops 50%, your stock portfolio drops 50%. The standard diversification advice recognizes that there are substantial losses, but it doesn't really solve the problem. If the water is poisonous, it won't help to swallow only half a glass, rather than drink the full glass.

We've also seen that the efficient market hypothesis wherein the mathematical horizon of the stock and bond allocation that defines the most return for the least amount of risk, to which everyone presumably aims, actually changes and shifts and migrates over the decades and from bull to bear markets. It is a myth that a 60/40 strategy has consistently worked the best. Additionally, it is a myth that the same 60/40 allocation will continue to necessarily work in the future. Is there any reason whatsoever to think the next 100 years will contain the same factors and events as the past 100 years? The wheel has been invented, so let's not invest as if it will be reinvented over and over. Whatever combination of stocks and bonds that worked the best over any period in the past tells us nothing about what will work the best in the future.

As we know from high school history, the reality is that things change over time, whether measured in eras, centuries, decades, or years. Kingdoms and nations rise and fall. Cultures ascend and descend. Many of us can tick off the once dominant ancient empires from Egypt, to Assyria/Babylonia, to Greece and Rome. We also know of countries that commanded great respect over large parts of the globe for a time, like Spain and Portugal, Russia and Great Britain. Given these past documented nationhood changes, what makes us think that the world we live in today will always remain the same for our children and for theirs? Already in our present lifetimes we've seen the ascendency and prosperity and reward that came from the rising once-emerging markets like Japan, Brazil, Russia, and China. Most analysts predict these trends will continue. Will China's GDP surpass that of the United States—presently number one—in the next 50 years? What will it mean if it does or if it does not?

Obviously none of us will live long enough to participate in hundreds of years of history, but the point is that significant change does happen. There is always some generation present during tumultuous times.

Consider the airplane as an example of a life changer. The Wright Brothers flew the first plane in Kitty Hawk, North Carolina, in 1903. In 1969 we landed on the moon. Those two incredible changes took place within many people's lifetimes, and they were only about a short 65 years apart. During that time, however, the stock market went through major secular bull market advances of more than 200% and losses of 90%.

What should we do with this reality of change for the better and for the worse in regard to our investing strategy? Should we ignore it or try to take advantage of these things?

We no doubt feel disconnected from the Great Depression in America because that generation has nearly passed on. Yet there were people alive at that time who witnessed great changes that created both financial calamities and opportunities. The mistake we make is to disassociate ourselves from them and think it will never happen to us. It is always to someone else that disaster strikes. And once the disaster passes, some cavalierly suggest it was not really that bad, if we ignore the personal elements of age and circumstance. And perhaps there won't be great changes in our lives, but as I said in the Preface, I want the information here to be timeless, to be useful not only for today but also for tomorrow, for our children's children. If we are lucky enough to live in times of secular peace and prosperity without so much as a 20% stock market correction, we simply haven't yet lived long enough.

To emphasize this dichotomy between secular and cyclical markets further, I've included two charts. Figure 4.1 shows those secular

FIGURE 4.1   Secular Bear Market Losses from 1871 Through 2013

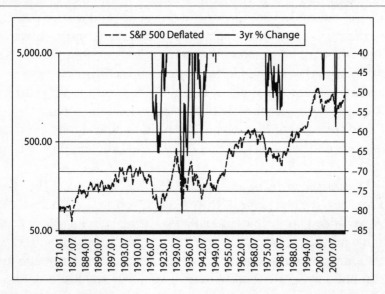

Source: Data from Standard & Poor's and Robert Shiller's website at http://irrationalexuberance.com.

bear market losses greater than 40%. Figure 4.2 shows all bear market losses greater than 20%. The prices are along the left scale, and the losses are along the right scale. Losses are different, but we should not be lulled into inaction by this. Try to place yourself at a time in the charts by your age.

In Figure 4.1, the cutoff to show losses is capped at −40% and worse. As you recall from Chapter 2, there have been four secular bear market periods over the last 120 years. You can see during those times that losses of more than 40% are common; they are the norm. During secular bull markets, you can also see that losses greater than 20% are very rare; they are typically capped at −25%. The two bull or bear secular markets really are two different beasts. They need to be identified if we hope to profit from them.

Figure 4.2 shows the declines on more of a cyclical basis. This change is also measured over three years, but as you can see also on the right scale, the number of times that losses exceeded 20% increased. The chart shows a significant difference in performance

FIGURE 4.2   All Bear Market Losses from 1871 Through 2013

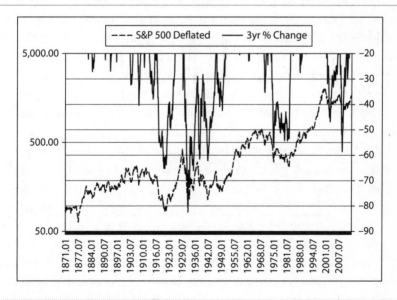

Source: Data from Standard & Poor's.

between secular bull and bear markets in terms of the number of 20% corrections. Look at the number in the 1920s and the 1950s and the 1990s in the secular bull markets: it shows nearly no corrections exceeding 25%. Compare that to the secular bear markets that followed. Again, as I mentioned, the point is to show there is a qualitative difference in how one should approach the two secular or cyclical markets. They are different, and so too should be our investment strategy.

Oh, to have the luck to buy at the bottom of a secular bear market when you are 40 years old, to accumulate during the great bull market run, and to have the luck to sell at the top of the secular bull market when you retire at age 65. Alas, it is no more than good luck and as such is unrepeatable. Timeless, instead, is what we want.

Their Response to Change and Uncertainty

The typical financial industry advice to the certainty of temporal loss in stocks is to diversify, to allocate your investment portfolio between different asset types like bonds. If you are more sophisticated or have a larger portfolio, you may also be advised to include foreign investments, inverse holdings, sectors, commodities, hedge funds, real estate, art, or other assets. We will look at these from a fund point of view in the next chapter, but the point is that the industry response to change and uncertainty is to diversify and yet to apparently exclude cash as one of those diversification assets.

For my part, I want to be clear that I understand the reason to diversify. Timing the market is much more difficult than remaining fully invested all of the time. In addition, we do age; the time to recover from market losses dwindles. Investing is inherently risky. There is no assurance of gain. There are unexpected disasters that impact the markets. My solution, however, is not to maintain the same potential for loss, albeit on a smaller proportion of your portfolio, by remaining fully invested, but rather to try to avoid the loss altogether by potentially using cash (the safest "company" and shortest "bond") as a diversification choice in both portions of the portfolio devoted to stocks and bonds. So, for my purposes, diversification is a real tool for both increasing overall portfolio gains and reducing portfolio losses. We will see the results of this approach in Chapter 6.

In addition to continuing to participate to the downside with the buy-and-hold strategy, there are four additional problems with the standard industry advice about buy-and-hold diversifying. One, the correlations between alternate investments are nearing 100%; the historic diversification advantage itself is disappearing. Two, bond yields as of 2013 had neared what may be their secular lows as shown in Chapter 3; this means that the potential upside offset to stock losses from a bond rally is not as large as it has been. Three, the upside return to the whole portfolio is capped to the degree of diversification. If the market doubles from its lows but your portfolio has only 60% in equities, the total portfolio upside is not as great. At secular bear market bottoms when there is that seismic wealth-creating shift to the secular bull market, we want to fully participate in the upside. Four, the standard industry advice continues to ignore the fundamental facts of personal circumstance and age that continue to affect us during bear markets. Again I ask, why sit tight and lose 50% or more of your portfolio in a bear market as the time to recover the loss because we age gets shorter and shorter?

The financial industry is recognizing that correlations are increasing. For example, the 2013 *Journal of Accounting and Finance* article "Asset Class Impacts on the 30-Year Efficient Frontier" by Matt Maher, Harry White, Phil Fry, and Matt Wilkerson concluded that, except for bonds, the long-term effectiveness of diversification across other asset classes (stocks, real estate, commodities, international markets, hedge funds, natural resources, and private equity) is doubtful. As the fund industry developed and exploited the different classes, the correlations have increased across different asset classes. Success breeds standardization; the peaks and valleys are leveled. Advantages are arbitraged away.

In essence, the implication of this increased correlation is that what is growing in importance in terms of not losing money is twofold: one, the ability to successfully time the markets and two, the ability to accurately allocate portfolios to the best fund managers. We've seen this example earlier about the huge spread between leaders and laggards, even in the same style.

The other problem, as I've mentioned, with this allocation advice apart from cash is that it ignores your age factor. It may take your lifetime for this recovery to happen, as happened to investors in the Great Depression. So, this solution, diversify, is really just a less than ideal mechanism for coping with change and loss. It is not the proactive transformation that I am advocating.

Further, while it is true that the risk of downside loss to the total portfolio is limited because of diversification, so too will be the upside. To the degree that your investments are not in stocks when the market is in a bull market, that is the amount you don't gain. For example, if you have $100,000 and 60% is in bonds, when the market doubles as it has from the bottom in 2009, your equity portion of the portfolio will have gained 100%, but only for 40%. The $40,000 is now $80,000, but had you been fully in stocks, your portfolio would be worth $200,000. That is a substantial difference. It begs us to find and implement market timing or asset allocation that works. This is not to say, of course, that timing will be perfect, but look at the give-up in terms of the portfolio's potential. We will look at timing more in Chapter 7.

As another example of this typical advice: if the recommended allocation of diversification is 60% in equities and 40% in bonds, we can subdivide the equity side, the 60%, and find that we might have 75% in domestic equities and 25% in foreign equities. If we drill down even further into the domestic portion, we might have 33% in large-cap funds,[1] 33% in mid-cap, and 34% in small-cap. And again if we drill down even further, we might have 50% in growth large-cap and 50% in value large-cap.

What about other styles, like real estate or gold? We might have some of that too. By the way, watch out for advisors who assemble your portfolio based on historic information without some mechanism for change or updates. In other words, while having a portion in real estate may have helped in the past, why should it help in the future? Think 2007.

On the bond side, of the 40%, we might have half in government bonds and half in corporates. Of the part in corporates, we might have 10% in high-yield or junk bond funds.

---

[1] *Large-cap* refers to "large capitalization," which is the sum of the company shares outstanding times its stock price. Well-known, very large companies, like Google, Caterpillar, Pfizer, and Walmart, are examples. Typically the large-cap measures in the billions. Small-cap is measured in the millions to hundreds of millions. Mid-cap ranges between the two.

Each of these allocations can be sliced and diced nearly ad infinitum. There is practically an ETF or mutual fund for any country in the world. It is the same with industries; there is an ETF for nearly every industry from solar to technology to consumer discretionary.

All of this brings up the next two questions.

First, how did we select our allocation and subdivisions in the first place? Why 60% stocks and 40% bonds and not 30% stocks and 70% bonds? Why use gold or real estate and not aerospace or technology in the portfolio? Is it advised simply because real estate worked well in the past? Why assume the trend will continue? If we determined the set allocation on the basis of a snapshot of a particular time period, are those parameters that existed at that time still present today? What about for tomorrow? Recall what was shown in the previous chapters on secular trends in stocks and bonds. The times change. Moreover, it was shown that the efficient frontier is far from fixed; it flip-flops over the decades. Thus 60% stocks and 40% bonds (60/40) may work sometimes, but 90/10 may be better at other times. It is misguided to allocate a portfolio based on 100 years of data for someone with a 10-year or even 30-year investment horizon. Even then, if the advice is to allocate 100% to stocks because you are 20 years old, it is still simply based on 100 years of data that the market is higher than it was 100 years ago. It ignores the long-term personal factor. It ignores the goal of compounding gains.

Second, and just as important, how do we select the managers to implement these allocations? If the buy-and-hold idea doesn't really apply in a commonsense way to investing generally, why would buy and hold apply to a single manager? Is it just because that manager has the lowest-cost fund? It strikes me as disingenuous to brag about low fees and in the same breath say, Yes, we lost half your money twice in the last decade during the 2000s. In other words, as we allocate investments into and out of stocks, bonds, and cash, we should do the same with the managers. It is implicit that what is working to create wealth at one time may not work at another time. It is clear that some managers do a better job in one period than over the next period. Actively selecting managers is also extremely important to the cohesive, long-term, proactive investment strategy.

Their Selecting Standards

The primary method investors have been taught to use to pick a fund is to look at past performance. The assumption is that a top performer, be it an active or passive manager, will continue to be a top performer. We now know differently. The passive or active fund may perform well for a period, but that good performance usually coincides with cyclical or secular bull or bear periods. Furthermore, another question is over what time frame is that "past performance" measured? Was it that full 15 years needed to start to separate the manager's skill from luck? Investors tend to chase hot funds and then fail to sell when they cool.

It is always a bit sobering and humbling when you stop and realize your decisions may be slightly more than colored by the secular times and circumstances in which you live. Do you hate real estate? Is there a reason for this besides the implosion in 2007? Do you love stocks? Is there a reason besides the climb from March 2009? We like to think of ourselves as the captains of our fate. We like to believe our logic is above our emotions. We want to think we are above the fray. A couple of examples may suffice to convince us otherwise, to show that the times do affect our investment approach.

Given history's impact on stock and bond prices, it really should not come as a surprise to find out your investment approach is thereby colored. We all know people, usually grandparents, who lived through the Depression and swore off stocks forever. We all know people who have made a fortune from investing (Buffett) while others went bankrupt (Long-Term Capital Management [LTCM]). Your mileage may differ. In addition to the times, other factors such as the environment, your age, experience, available time, and interests also impact your selecting decision. So, how do investors pick their funds?

◆ Popularity
◆ Expense ratio
◆ Manager name
◆ Performance
◆ Concept
◆ Other

Certainly we know of grandparents who would not touch a stock if it were the last investment on earth. These people physically survived the Great Depression but lost financially at the time by "buy-and-hold" advice. We also know of those who, at least for a while, day-traded back in the late 1990s, who thought themselves skillful as they bought and sold daily and seemingly printed money from stock trades. Do we know anyone today who still day trades like that? The three-year bear market wiped out years of gains for many.

As one who incorporates the word *timing* into my moniker, I can testify that timing itself goes into and out of favor depending on the times. In the secular bull market of the 1990s, when bear markets were more shallow, less broadly based, and quicker to recover, timing became viewed as a four-letter word. This dismissive attitude then met with the nearly unheard of three-year bear stock market from 2000 through 2003. As the 2000s continued to unfold, after a 13-year secular bear market in which two declines of roughly 50% occurred and now retirement looms closer by 13 years, timing—that is, capital preservation as well as growth—becomes much more important to these investors. By 2013, some indexes were still below those levels set in 2000. Thirteen years is a long time to take the risk of investing without making any money in the stock market. Risk and no reward, eh? Compounding is lost.

Don't think for a moment that the times impact only nonprofessional investors. It doesn't. If anything, it impacts the professionals even more. The pressure to outperform the indexes has grown substantially since the 1970s when the first index fund was created.[2] It has proven to be a formidable high-bar challenge for many to meet year in and year out. Thus we have the growth in assets in the index fund.

Humbling

Incidentally, this is the reason that historical returns that appear too good to be true, usually are. No one beats the market each and every year for 30 years. Managers who claim they do so are emphasizing skills that don't truly exist, that are outside norms of mere mortals.

---

[2] John C. Bogle of the Vanguard Group is generally credited with helping to create the first index fund.

Working in the investment market, whether in stocks, bonds, or commodities, I can share with you that it has to be one of the most humbling jobs there is. And if you don't humble yourself, you can be sure the market will do it for you shortly. So it was with interest I read about the Bond King, Bill Gross who at the time was with PIMCO, who asked himself in March 2013 in his monthly letter about whether or not he was a good investor.

Eh, what? This is the same guy with hundreds of millions under management with a great track record built over some 40 years. Was his career coming to an end, and was it time for some self-reflection, or what gives?

Gross's question was whether or not he was good because he really was good at what he did or whether he was good because of the times, the epoch, in which he invested. The bond winds have been at his back. To his point, we have been in a 30-year bull market in bonds (see Chapter 3). Was he a skillful investor, or did he succeed because of the luck of the winds from the secular trend of falling interest rates and therefore the rising bond prices by default?

To his credit, he was publicly asking the question. This by itself suggested a certain humbleness. To seriously ask the question, whether you're good or lucky at something, is to prima facie humble yourself; it really is what every manager must and should do regularly. History is littered with so-called great managers who did well for a period but who basically failed to keep asking the question over the span of their careers. It is no doubt why the Stock King, or more accurately the Oracle of Omaha, Warren Buffett, also conducts this self-appraisement, openly looking at his successes and his failures in his annual letter to shareholders. There's nothing like public humiliation to keep you on your toes.

When the market is rising, it is the easiest thing to do, to confuse your brains with the bull market. Has your fund or ETF been making money lately? If it has been making money, is it because of your smarts, because of your being good at the job, or is it simply the rising market?

The rising tide lifts all boats; when the tide goes out, we see who was swimming naked (Buffett). As we saw, it takes some 15 years before one is able to separate the lucky manager from the skillful manager. Those 15 years will include many cyclical bull and bear markets, and they may include the start and end of secular ones. And even then, it is still possible to play the fool who yet turns and says, Yep, 15 years, and I am invincible at what I do. Instead, stay humble, my friends.

We don't have to wait 15 years or longer to answer the question of whether it was luck or skill. We can simply plug in the fund's numbers, run the metrics to rank them on a risk-adjusted relative performance basis, and continue to monitor them. If the managers falter, we move on, leaving them to ponder whether they were unlucky or unskillful. There are excellent managers who do outperform the market for a while. My C-lect process understands this.

At the same time, let me briefly mention here again, as we saw in Chapter 1, that there is a huge spread between funds with the exact same objective, the exact same pool of investment choices, with nearly the exact same fees, but with widely different results. So, while it is admirable that Bill Gross has asked the humbling question of whether he was good or not as an investor, it is clear that compared to his peers, the answer is obvious. He was skillful. That the wind was at his back is also obvious: a fully invested position in a secular bull market by a smart manager is the way to invest to greatness. Just be aware that the times will change.

To be clear, while Bill Gross may question his investment acumen by wondering if he is simply a product of the times, it is obvious he is more than that. Yes, he had the wind at his back buying bonds, but so did all of the other bond managers of the last 30 years. But for every top 5% of managers, there are also the bottom 5% of managers using the same exact investment pool from which to draw their holdings. What we are trying to do in this book is provide the tools to help investors separate the two groups. Your lifestyle is at stake.

We could ask the same question about whether it was luck or skill or some combination of the two that propelled many other well-known managers to the top. Warren Buffett was a value investor working in the small-cap area. He began earnestly investing around the bottom of the secular bear market in the 1970s. How is his record in the past 15 years, about which he himself has said, it is harder to manage billions than millions? Peter Lynch, too, searched out small-cap stocks that were devastated in the 1970s and became bargains for the picking. Then there was Sir John Templeton searching out

Japanese stocks with P/E ratios around 3X. Michael Price was investing in bankruptcies before it was in vogue. These managers have great track records, but were they truly skillful, or were their successes really attributable to the secular trends and undervalued areas in which they operated? I would absolutely agree that surely there was skill.

Where are the big-name managers now? The world seems picked over. Inefficiencies have all but disappeared. The small-cap area now, unlike Lynch's time, has hundreds of investors, rather than just a few, looking there for gold. Furthermore, the secular trend has a much greater impact than we like to acknowledge. It is one thing to buy stocks when the average P/E ratio is around 6X, the way it was in the year 1982, versus buying when the P/E ratio is north of 20X, the way it was in the year 2000. Or when the book value is at 1X versus 5X. The possibility of success simply changes when one buys something that is cheap relative to either its assets (balance sheet) or its growth (income statement). Alternatively, stock picking in a rebuilding economy like the 1950s will be different from stock picking in a stagnated economy like the 1970s. The point is that the secular environment will make a huge difference in an investor's ability to make money, let alone to hold on to it. As Buffett also acknowledges, "Use market fluctuations to your advantage and seek a margin of safety."[3] Would anyone call him a market timer? But why not? According to Berkshire Hathaway's 13F filings, Buffett sells 80% of his holdings within two years, and about 30% are sold within six months.[4] Great investors admit the mistakes and errors they make in the course of buying and selling. Funds have their turnover ratios. I just call it what it is: market timing.

Being first has its advantages. Being early has its advantages. Having the secular wind at your back has its advantages. At some point, however, in investing, these things change as others come in, making bargains hard to find. Eventually price departs from value.

---

[3] Robert G. Hagstrom, *The Warren Buffett Way*, third edition, 2005.
[4] According to 13F filings analyzed from 1980 through 2006, as described in the paper *Overconfidence, Under-Reaction, and Warren Buffett's Investments* by John S. Hughes, Jing Liu, and Mingshan Zhang, Social Science Research Network (SSRN), 2010.

There is a term for this strategy as the market continues its upward advance until it completely disassociates from value: the greater fool strategy. You never want to be the last to buy. Instead, if the value has left the building, you always want some fool greater than you to buy the investment from you and take it off your hands. The last buyers of the tulip bulbs or baby beanie fads can relate. Incidentally, please note the term is "greater fool," as in there is a lesser fool who comes before, but who is a fool nonetheless.[5]

Now, given that the secular times do affect our investment decisions, we saw in the first three chapters my emphasis on the broad outlines of fund and stock and bond market history. These huge wealth-changing trends affect us today also. I emphasized the market history in order to provide perspective as we move through the rest of the book. In other words, were we in a rip-roaring bull market, you might be reading again about how to make millions by day-trading or by using other people's money in real estate. If we were in a depressing bear market in which we won't even open our brokerage house statements that come in the mail, you might be reading again about bonds or CDs or cash under the mattress. We don't need these things. What we need is perspective and insight and a proactive rotation strategy that recognizes the secular trends that influence our decision-making process. We need a way to invest with the managers doing the best today and a way to evolve as the times change.

So, unless you are in the money management industry, you have a day job or you are looking for one or you are retired from one. Let's take the first scenario first. You have a day job, and you might be an engineer, a clerk, a firefighter, a teacher, a doctor, or handyperson. You might be an employee or an employer. The one thing these jobs all have in common is that the individuals who fill them have relied on someone's expertise in helping them make the buy and sell

---

[5] It is with chagrin and a bit of embarrassment that I know this all too well as I stored stuff I was sure would keep going up in value. What value, right? It's like gold; is there a dividend, a P/E ratio, something by which to measure its value, or is the value simply in the eye of the beholder?

There was a *60 Minutes* exposé in 2013 about an artist who tried to sell some of his works for $40 each on the streets of New York. His other artwork was in museums and studios, and one of his pieces usually sold for around $40,000. When he tried selling it on the streets, he didn't sell all of it, even at $40.

decisions about what funds to own, what investments to make, and what allocations to maintain.

So, how did you pick the fund you've invested in? How did you pick your allocation between stocks, bonds, and cash? Maybe it was part of a 401(k) plan. Maybe you searched the Internet. Maybe you inherited it. If it was part of a retirement plan, then you have little control over the fund choices, unless you're the company's administrator. But even then, the retirement committee has to have some reason for choosing the fund group they did. What was it?

Isn't the best explanation for buying Fund ABC as opposed to Fund XYZ that you believe you will make more money with Fund ABC for the risk you are taking? Isn't it that the investment will in the future make you money given a certain level of risk? Isn't this really the bottom line? After all, who cares if Fund ABC charges 1/10 of 1% and made 2% net, while Fund XYZ charges 1% and made 5% net? Which is better? Or does it matter if a fund has $1 billion in assets versus another that has $100 million in assets, as long as the former is making you more money for the level of risk incurred?

Whether they are talking about passive or active funds, marketing materials are masters of manipulation. We know this. They appeal to emotion, rather than logic. They want you to picture yourself in a swimming pool by the beach being served your favorite beverage, while someone pampers your every whim and fancy. Or to picture yourself sailing the ocean in your yacht. Or to picture yourself in a mansion by the sea. Invest with me is the idea.

There is also the flip side to the greed pictures: the fear pitch.[6] Picture yourself in a breadline. Picture yourself under a pile of debt with no job prospects. Picture yourself in the poorhouse. You get the picture.

These emotions tug at our hearts every day of the week, and they are very useful in marketing. They are also used in the fund industry. To be fair, there is also the logic pitch that says, We have you covered. Do you want gold? We have a gold fund. Do you want technology? We have that too. Do you want a broad-based actively

---

[6] Please don't be offended by these terms, but they are accurate. They massage our emotions, and everyone has them.

managed fund? We have that too. Do you want an index fund? Yep, we have that too. They have it, but do we want it?

Are those aforementioned bullet points the reason to buy one fund over another? Sure, we want to be wealthy and avoid the breadlines. We want to provide a legacy for our children. We do not want to be broke, subsisting on the minimum government programs. None of those pitches, however, is to offer the solution of how to manage the managers in an unknowable, ever-changing world.

In the fund marketplace, there are leaders and laggards, and they change. Our job is to differentiate between them, invest with the leaders, and avoid the laggards, and do so year after year. I suppose the bottom-line question of whether it was skill or luck that propelled the manager to the top in the rankings really doesn't matter. What matters is recognizing that, for whatever reason, the leaders will change over time. Active will tend to do better than passive in secular bear markets. Passive will tend to do better in secular bull markets. How we identify and rotate with the leaders will be the subject of Chapter 6.

Timing

Investors diversify using cash, stocks, and bonds because they know there is risk of loss. In addition, they diversify between domestic and international funds and between market caps from large to small. They are assuming that there will not be 100% correlation between their diversified equity holdings. This assumption is being challenged, however, as the world becomes more interconnected. In the modern interrelated world, the correlation of market direction between the United States and Europe or Asia actually nears 100%. Perhaps 40 years ago, the correlation was much less. Don't make the mistake of thinking diversification among a number of assets that are in fact correlated will help avoid losses. It won't.

As an example of this, even a short 20 years ago, a trading strategy some people used to employ was to buy and sell international funds based on what the domestic market did on that day. If the U.S. market was up 2% in a day, the assumption was, because of correlation, that the international markets would also jump the next day. You could take advantage of this because the international funds were still priced at the previous day's closing prices. If the U.S. markets fell sharply, these investors sold international funds, which again, were still priced at the previous day's close. This worked for a while because the U.S. market was priced at that day's closing prices but the international funds were still priced at the previous day's prices.

Eventually the fund industry caught on to these sharpies that exploited this. The industry made some changes. The industry thought it was unfair to long-term holders for short-term traders to, in effect, make substantial money based on time zones. These companies decided to price in advance the international fund that day on the assumption it, too, would move in the same direction the following day. The net asset value thus became an estimate, not an actual number, but that's a different story. They also banned timers by instituting holding periods and imposing short-term redemption fees. Fair or not, the point is that it was a tacit agreement that correlations existed. Since then, correlation has grown even more. Success gets arbitraged away on Wall Street. Or it gets outlawed.

As briefly mentioned earlier, there is also the problem with using bonds as diversification to offset stock losses. Historically in a recession-induced stock bear market where GDP is falling because of a lack of demand, typically interest rates should also be falling. Bond prices move inversely to interest rates, so if rates fall, bond prices increase. This is to offset the drop in stock prices. Today, however, bonds have been in a 30-year secular bull market. Yields are substantially less than they were before. Shorter-term maturities are near zero percent. How much further can they fall? Will they fall enough to substantially offset stock losses?

Investors cannot avoid stock market losses by owning more stocks from different countries or industries. Nor can they avoid losses by using bonds, if bonds are at the end of their 30-year secular bull market. The only way to avoid loss is to use cash as an asset class. Take a look at Figure 4.3. It shows when during the last secular bear market in the 1970s that stocks fell and bonds fell (interest rates rose, this is noted as % on the chart on the right scale).

To take another example, we look backward and know now that some things rebounded from their steep losses in 2009, but we

FIGURE 4.3 Secular Bear Markets from 1966 Through 1982

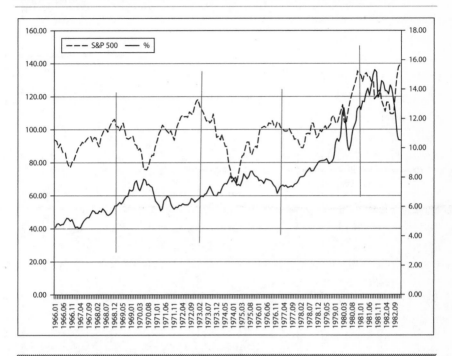

Source: Data from Standard & Poor's.

shouldn't make the additional mistake of thinking that all stocks rebounded. It always comes back, some say; but tell that to the citizens in Rome or to buggy-whip manufacturers or propeller plane techies or tech bubble babies from the year 2000. All things don't rebound necessarily. Some managers understand this. Some do not. Buy and hold or buy and diversify may not be the best answers to avoiding losses and maximizing gains.

Recall the efficient frontier[7] chart from Chapter 2, Figure 2.3. It is shown again here as Figure 4.4. This chart shows the efficient frontier by decade, which may or may not correlate to secular bull

---

[7] Again, the *efficient frontier* is the point, the ratio of stock and bond allocations in your portfolio, where the most return for the least risk is maximized.

FIGURE 4.4 The Efficient Frontier from Modern Portfolio Theory over Different Decades

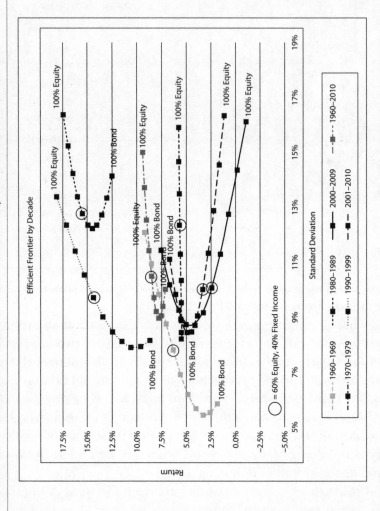

Source: Data from Rydex/SGI (now Guggenheim Partners). Copyright © Guggenheim Investments 2014 (guggenheiminvestments.com).

and bear markets, yet notice how the best investment mix changes by decade from emphasizing 100% bonds to 100% stocks. It shows the risk would be the same either way, but the returns are completely different.

Further, imagine how even more inefficient the frontier would look once it was correlated to actual secular bull and bear markets in stocks and bonds. The point is that one size does not fit all of the times, let alone all of the people.

Wouldn't it be far better to approach investing with the answer first to the question of what type of secular market are we currently in? This goes for stocks and bonds. Then invest accordingly. This is our point of view. The standard industry motto is to be fully invested all of the time and diversify if you don't like losses, but never with cash equivalents as one of those diversification choices.

The so-called efficient frontier where the least risk meets the most reward fluctuates over time. Truly the question about how to invest is best answered by identifying the kind of secular trend within which we currently operate. Maintaining a 60/40 diversification split based on a 100-year snapshot with all of its inner mutations of allocations is panning for fool's gold. It is not efficient, and it does not optimally reduce risk, nor does it optimize potential reward.

What is the alternative solution to this question about how to manage your money in terms of change? I suspect two answers.

One is cash. As developed in Chapter 3, cash is simply the shortest duration of a bond. If interest rates are rising, all bond prices are falling. The amount they are falling will vary by a number of factors, but if we keep everything else the same except for the bond's duration, the percentage decline will range from the greatest to the smallest based on duration. So it is for cash, which has the ultimate short duration of second to second. For our portfolios to actually travel along the efficient frontier, to truly capture the most return with the least risk, we are therefore forced to use cash from time to time.

If cash is the logical, ultimate safe, shortest-duration bond, how might this same idea apply relative to stocks? In other words, if bonds are in a bear market, we should use the safest bond, which is cash. If stocks are in a bear market, how might cash be viewed as the safest stock?

Think of cash as a company. It has a pristine balance sheet of whatever denomination the cash is. It is an asset with zero liability. It is fungible. It is liquid. It provides cash flow, measured as the interest it earns. It also has an intangible benefit called "peace of mind." The difference between a business and cash, however, is that cash won't decline in value. Businesses as measured by their stock prices will fluctuate. Cash is fairly well fixed. The point is simply that cash may be termed like a business along the valuation axis. It is the safest business.

Incidentally, this cash-as-company comparison is akin to that of Benjamin Graham who would look at a company's balance sheet to determine its value. He asked, What is the liquidation value? What is my margin of safety if I buy? If the company market cap (generally defined as the stock price times the shares outstanding plus debt) is $100, we can compare that to its book value or replacement cost or earnings potential. If the underlying assets less all liabilities are worth more than $100, then the stock is undervalued. If the assets less liabilities are worth less than the market price, then the price is too high. Thus the idea of using cash as an alternative store of value is present in this simple analysis. In other words, if we could liquidate a company and receive back our investment plus a profit, then that would be a better value than holding cash. If we can't, however, then cash is the better of the two "stocks" to buy as the alternative.

As investors, however, the problem with this analysis is that we don't have control to effect the liquidation or sale of the company. Management too often has a built-in incentive, called a "salary," to maintain the status quo. Thus there are investors who "rattle the cages" as shareholder activists attempt to close the gap between price and value. The point is that there is value in the stock, rather than holding cash. If the value weren't there, no amount of shaking the apple tree will get you an orange from it. This is where the secular trends and valuations are so important. The market fluctuates between cheap and expensive, just like the value of a business.

One last offsetting factor to consider when using cash as a "stock" is the idea that a company may grow. Cash is static, except for the interest it might earn. A company's earnings or dividends may increase over time such that its perceived value today becomes cheap compared to its potential.[8]

Any further discussion about individual stocks is beyond the scope of this fund book, but the point remains that cash is simply a very safe business that must be compared to other businesses. Along these lines of delineating value or growth stocks, for our part, we look at whatever is working for the fund manager. We don't particularly know how the manager defines these things. For some investors, a P/E ratio below 10 is cheap, but for others anything below 15 is cheap. For growth investors, it is the same thing—the definitions and requirements change from manager to manager. Thus 20X earnings might be cheap for a company growing at 50% annually. And as already shown, there is a wide spread among the performances of managers who are using the same stable of funds. There are also times when the market as a whole is far overpriced. It is during those times when the managers are still forced to buy and hold, but we who have cash as an alternate stock or bond are not.

Selecting the Right Manager Matters

This is point number 2 to emphasize, especially if the reader is unconvinced about treating cash as an investment alternative along the value line from a very risky stock/company to a pristine "stock/company" (cash). Let's say you still want to be fully invested. How should we proceed?

As we saw in Chapter 1, there is a huge spread in performance between the top and bottom funds that exists each year after year. The leader in any one period more than likely won't be the leader

---

[8] In the 2008 and 2009 debacle, we investigated the business development industry and bought some companies whose price was roughly half that of their net asset values. Five years later one of them that we still own is paying a dividend roughly equivalent to the price we paid. We really do like bear markets where values are outstanding.

in the next period. This applies to both the actively managed fund and the index. There is a time for both. So, with our selecting process, we make sure we are invested with the top funds (defined as those providing the most return for the risk taken), rather than the laggard funds. This helps us in two ways to answer the question of how to avoid loss, if we are fully invested always. One, the manager who is performing the best in a bear market will bubble to the top in our rankings based not only on performance but also on risk-adjusted performance. Two, in a bear market, what will happen is that the funds whose managers have raised cash will bubble to the top in performance rankings. They may still be losing, like the indexes or their peers, but because of their cash holdings, they will be losing less. So, whether you believe in active asset allocating (a.k.a. market timing) or not, it will still behoove you to proactively manage the managers in the selecting process. I will look more closely at my selecting process in Chapter 6.

Conclusion

In this chapter, we have been reminded that things change and that nothing is permanent. While it may seem farfetched to consider national change on a century-long basis, we have also seen that change on a personal basis is an often-ignored fact. It does no good to look at the 100-year chart that ends high if we ignore the fact that we are older or that substantial losses have been incurred. Emotions come into play. Would we actually hold during the period when our portfolio is down 50%? Moreover, it is simply misleading. Had we been taking their age-based allocation advice in the first place, we wouldn't have remained in that fully invested stock position as we got older.

We want to change the simple standard industry advice. We know full well that we age. We know our personal circumstances change. We know emotions affect the decision-making process. We know some managers are better than others. We know there are times when cash is the best place to invest. Given these facts, there is no reason to take a passive investment approach, a.k.a. buy and hold. There is no reason to employ strategies that may have us selling because of our age at precisely the time we should be accumulating. Likewise at the top, why buy because of our age, if we happen to be 30 instead of 60? What does our age have to do with the market? Instead, at signs of trouble, we want to move our assets into safety investments. When the worst becomes discounted, we may start buying again.

5

Uncertainty and Choice

IN THIS CHAPTER, WE WILL EXPLORE THE WAYS THE FUND INDUSTRY has reacted to sure uncertainty. We all know the market will fluctuate; it will go up and down. Some of us may also know those fluctuations may devastate a portfolio by up to 90% or take decades just to return to breakeven. Lastly, a few of us admit we do not know the future with perfect certainty. What do we do about these things?

One way the industry reacts is that it slices and dices the stock and bond markets into bite-sized palatable chunks to offer thousands of funds, as if more and more choices, each with a narrower and narrower focus, are somehow better than all-purpose, broad-based funds. Another way is that it reduces its fees and suspends its analytic stock picking and allocating activities, as if paying less is any solace after losing half your money in a bear market. The third and more recent way is to provide age-based allocation funds, as if one's age has anything whatsoever to do with the directions and values of the markets.

On the surface, these things may seem sensible. Who can argue against offering more choices, lower fees, and easy investing? But do they answer the real problem? What do we do about sure loss? How do we know which fund or which strategy to select? Why ignore our personal age and circumstance when assembling a portfolio? Or perhaps worse, why use an age to assemble a portfolio?

Here are two examples of one reaction to these things. Vanguard has its balanced Wellington Fund with 60% allocated to stocks and 40% allocated to bonds. It also has its Wellesley Fund with just the opposite allocation. Fidelity has seven offerings whose stock and bond allocations range from 85/15 to 20/80. They both have introduced a number of target-date funds. What is the point of having so many mutations of the stock and bond allocation relationship?

Perhaps the real reason for so many offerings is a bit more of a nod to the marketing department than to anything else. It is the attempt to always have a company fund in the top 10 funds list; it is name recognition. If stocks are hot, the 80/20 fund can be listed. If bonds are hot, the 20/80 fund can be listed. Out of hundreds of funds offered, having one in the top 10 funds list might give the impression that your fund company has some value to provide.

The fund industry is a profitable business. It helps to have funds in the top 10 list. More than that, however, part of the reason for this proliferation of choices stems from a couple of historical accusations against the industry and specifically against the active management side. One was known as *style drift* and the other was described as *closet indexing*. By looking at fund types and then entering the active-versus-passive debate, I will address these issues next and then talk about the directions in which the industry went to address them.

Style Drift

The accusation of style drift occurred when investors who thought they were investing in a particular kind of fund learned later to their chagrin that the fund's actual holdings identified it to be in a completely different and usually unexpected investment style. A famous example of this was Fidelity's Magellan Fund. People thought they were buying an all-purpose equity fund; they wanted a stock fund—Peter Lynch's, to be exact. But under new management with Jeffrey Vinik, the Magellan Fund became stuffed with bonds nearing 30% of its total assets. This was not just style drift from, say, small-cap to large-cap; rather, this was asset drift from equities to fixed income.

Of course, that asset drift problem also may arise when funds try to use market timing. When investors buy a stock fund, they expect some sort of stock market participation and generally at its fullest. The job of the portfolio manager is thus to be 100% invested in stocks, even if the market is going down. This is the reason it is up to the investor, not the manager, to take the approach we advocate of managing the manager.

Had Vinik's bet paid off, though, would anyone have complained? But if not Vinik, there would be other funds, and there were, who style drifted and asset drifted from their appointments. Style boxes thus became the norm, matching fund specifics to investment styles. If you are in one box, then you should not drift too far into another box. Management-by-box became the norm.

The fund's prospectus may be a boring read, but it is a read that will at least provide information on what an investor should expect when buying that fund. If the fund has a wide investment berth, and some funds still do, eschewing the one box for the whole field, then when the manager takes advantage of that, no one should be surprised.

For our part, we do not get riled up over this style drift issue. We continue to rank managers based on C, their risk-adjusted relative performance, without prejudging or faulting them. Let them do what they do best, it seems to me. We simply recognize that elements of luck, as well as some skill, may be driving the success. It may be, as Gross hinted, the secular shifts in the markets that do happen, that may drive performance, not the managers. As such, the bottom line is that we are prepared to sell when the fund underperforms, regardless of box or not.

In addition to asset drift, style drift also happened as funds invested in different sizes of companies than what the investors expected in the equity space. Style drift was actually much more of a problem for investors than asset drift. For example, investors may have thought they were buying a small-cap fund only to learn that it held primarily large-cap or mid-cap company stocks.

Frankly, drift is a difficult issue. If the fund manager bought lots of small-cap stocks that grew successfully over the years, the fund was successful and attracted new money. The new investors thought they too were getting small-cap stocks, but the reality may have been that the manager was forced to buy more mid-cap stocks. The fund was growing too large to continue operating in the micro- or small-cap sector. It happens. In addition, the universe of small-caps might have been redefined to include larger stocks. The number of funds will grow if an area becomes hot, thus shrinking the potential stock universe. Should the manager be forced to sell just because he had successfully bought companies that grew in size? The new buyers to the fund hadn't participated in the growth, so what should be done?

Open a new fund and close the old one became a common technique. This is another reason for the proliferation of funds. Nearly every manager will confirm that at some point, the increase in a fund's size will eventually limit its performance. Unfortunately, this doesn't prevent the fund company from opening a second fund with essentially the same objectives. Not much has been accomplished with this gambit.[1]

Closet Indexing

The next accusation to beset actively managed funds was that many funds were closet indexers but charging larger fees than passive index funds. These funds essentially mimicked the index they were supposed to try to beat. Better to fail in conformity than try to succeed as the outlier. The question arose, Why pay more in management fees to a closet index fund when investors could buy the index fund itself? You pay less in fees and have the certainty of knowing what you're buying were two powerful arguments active funds had to overcome; they still have to overcome this.

The fund industry's response to these issues was to broaden their fund choices, even duplicate certain ones, while narrowing the manager's focus. Gone were the days when a manager had much more freedom to buy and sell actively in any area of the market as he saw fit. There was to be much less style drift, let alone asset drift. Freedom was replaced by rigid rules to focus on asset class and style

---

[1] Morningstar did a study of closed funds in 2003. The company found that the funds closed due to outperformance, which had attracted too much new money. After three years of closure, however, 75% had dropped to the average in performance. What I recommend is to monitor the closed fund just as if it were still open. If it begins to underperform on a risk-adjusted relative performance (the C ranking), then we move on.

format and to decouple, if only a little, from the index, if you were an active manager.

These two problems led to two so-called solutions. One was the style box, and two was the expansion of types of funds even within the major division of active and passive approaches.

Style Boxes

One of the easiest ways for investors to divide the market into manageable chunks of thousands of funds is with the style box system. It's fairly well known. Growth or value is ranked on the vertical scale, while large- or small-cap runs across the horizontal. It really is an ingenious approach because it seems to say something important and useful. However, the reality is that we have much more work to do with it. ·

Besides, what good does it do, for example, to learn that Fund ABC is a large-cap value fund and it just lost 50% in the past year? How much information does the box really give us? Does it help to know how we lost money any more than that we did lose money? Or consider the upside: What good is it to learn that Fund XYZ is a small-cap growth fund if it just made 50% in the past year? What good is that information in terms of future performance? Will small-cap continue to do well? Will growth do well? Will the fund itself, whether active or passive, do well? Of what use is this information to our long-term financial well-being? Given the ongoing increase in correlations between styles, why is this important?

The answer of course is that the box speaks to our need for diversification in hopes that it will offset losses we know are coming. This is the industry's response to coping with losses. Diversify across the tick-tack-toe squares in the hopes that it will help your portfolio somehow. Unfortunately, correlations across styles and countries are increasing.

While I am talking about actual information that helps the decision-making process, I want to also mention the necessity of including capital gains and losses when looking at investment returns measured by yield.[2] High-yield funds, for example, may pay above

---

[2] I recall my parents talking about people they knew who had bought Mexican pesos in the early 1970s because the yields there were so much better than the CD yields

average yields, but this is not a promise that they will also achieve capital gains. They may lose and lose such that any positive dividend yield is more than negatively offset by capital losses. Total return is the metric to use. *Total return* equals dividends plus or minus capital gains or losses.

As well, when you are calculating your portfolio gains and losses, be sure to factor in whether you added or subtracted from your investment account.

In addition to the growth or value scale and the small-cap or large-cap scale, there is also the domestic or international scale upon which to practice diversification. Some funds focus on investing in the international markets. Like their domestic counterparts, these, too, may be actively managed, or they may adhere to an index. And like the domestic market, there is a proliferation of slicing and dicing the international markets both by country and by industry.

In avoiding style drift, fund companies grew the number of fund choices. At a certain level, this proliferation of funds reflects more of a slot-machine mentality, wherein there are a couple of big fund winners, and lots and lots of losers, each year. And next year, when you go back to the casino to your fund machine that was so good to you last year, you find that it does nothing but cost you—the one good fund is now lagging its index. Worse, when the market tumbles, that fund may also go down even more. There is no consistency in the advice; it does just seem like a matter of manager luck. If it weren't, we'd see the same managers on the pedestal as the years go by. It is a tough business to be sure.

Fund Types

Of all the choices the fund industry provides, one area in which the fund industry has added value, in my opinion, is with their inverse funds. These funds are designed to profit when the market declines. For example, if the S&P 500 Index declines 10%, an inverse S&P 500 Index fund should go up roughly 10%. These

---

at home. Mexico is our neighbor—what could go wrong? The only thing these investors didn't count on was the practically overnight devaluation of the peso relative to the dollar in 1976. The net result was to wipe out their juicy yields plus some.

FIGURE 5.1   Percentage Allocation Between Stocks and Bonds for a Lifestyle Fund

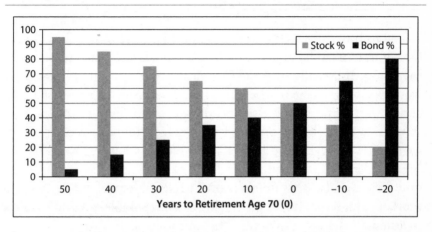

funds may be used to hedge a portfolio or to profit from declines. There is, however, a learning curve with these types of funds, but it is beyond the scope of this book.

After kudos comes criticism. *Lifestyle funds* are the industry answer to one-stop shopping based solely on an investor's age. These are also known as *target-date funds* or *age-based funds*. They are the industry's way of meeting retirement needs, offering a mixed combination of stocks and bonds that changes over time as you the shareholder near retirement age. The mix of stocks and bonds changes depending on the duration of time remaining to the target date. Figure 5.1 shows the way these funds work.

There is already $500 billion invested in these types of funds. The younger-aged investors dominate this category. According to Fidelity numbers,[3] nearly 75% of those aged 20 to 24 use this type of lifestyle fund for their 401(k) contributions. For those aged 30 to 34, nearly half use this type of fund. Vanguard reports similar numbers.

I will talk about various problems with these types of funds. For example, they do not solve for risk of loss. In fact, they may exacerbate the losses by requiring the fund to sell based simply on

---

[3] From a Fidelity survey published November 21, 2013.

the investor's age at precisely the wrong time (at the market bottom when value is widespread). They do not maximize gains and minimize losses. Let's go a little deeper.

First, I ask, Really? Has anyone anywhere ever heard it said that I need to buy this stock or sell this bond because of my age? On the face of it, a lifestyle, or age-based, asset allocation seems to be sound investing, but really, it isn't. It is simply a way to avoid making a value decision. Is the market cheap or expensive? An age-based allocation doesn't deal with risk and reward in absolute terms but only in relative terms based on something completely divorced from the markets! A lifestyle fund for a 20-year-old may have 95% stocks and 5% bonds. A lifestyle fund for a 70-year-old may have 15% stocks and 85% bonds. This doesn't solve the problem of stock losses or market valuations. It accepts the losses as inevitable, remaining fully invested all the way down into the unknowable future.

As we saw in Chapter 1, it will be all too inevitable that as the investor ages, the fund will sell at what amounts to be the worst of all times, at the bottom. In addition, it may be buying at the wrong time without regard to valuations. This is not a solution to the risk of investing.

Moreover, fund companies assemble lifestyle funds differently from each other. Buyer beware. The investor simply needs more information to be able to make a complete decision.

Some will argue this allocation point by saying that a 20-year-old might lose only $1,000 of her $2,000 in the 401(k), but I would reply it is still a 50% loss. If we're trying to compound that money, which is the argument in the first place (start early), it won't help us at all either in terms of the loss or the slippage of time it takes to come back to breakeven, let alone to earn a decent return.

While I am discussing this, I again want to be clear that I understand the principle behind the thinking. A 20-year-old does have another 40 years to recoup his money, while a 60-year-old who just lost 50% has what, until when, to recoup it? Is there some magic number called "That's it, the sum of my life, and it's over"? Is it retirement? As we know, life expectancy has gone up from age 70 in 1960 to age 79 today. Cancel the travel plans, honey, because I just lost half our money. Who wants to hear that? Yet how many investors follow the standard industry advice of buy and hold and diversify based on age. No, I just don't think a blanket age-based diversification is a viable solution to the risk of loss.[4]

A close cousin to the lifestyle fund, whose asset allocations between stocks and bonds change with your age, is the *hybrid fund*. These were the precursors to the lifestyle funds. Hybrid funds hold some relatively constant combination of stocks and bonds, such that with one purchase, investors receive that built-in diversification. So the 20- and the 70-year-olds will buy the same hybrid fund, and they will both receive the same allocation. It could be 50/50 or some other combination, but it won't usually change dramatically the way lifestyle funds do. It won't change its allocations based on an investor's age, but it may do so based on market valuations.

I would interject here that I find both groups interesting. We will look at what makes this so in Chapter 6.

I've briefly touched on specialized funds like those that are geared to specific sectors of the economy. They too may hold their place in the portfolio. Sectors will concentrate on one industry, like technology or utilities, or in one region of the world, like Sweden or Brazil. These funds are very limited in what they may invest in. The advantage is that when an industry or region is doing well, with one investment you know you are fully and immediately participating. There are no caps to the upside. Of course, the risk is higher also. There is no diversification. Again, we employ tools to help us select and time these industries and regions, which we will look at later.

Lastly, I will briefly mention another group of funds known as a *fund of funds*. These are funds that buy other funds. The problem is that they typically use only the funds in their sponsor's group. For example, T. Rowe Price has some funds of funds. They may invest only in other T. Rowe Price funds, which again, may or may not be

---

[4] I briefly mentioned this in a previous chapter, but it bears reiterating now. Historically, a 60% stock and 40% bond ratio was the standard diversification approach, but this standard was built over the years based on what may turn out to be more normal times. The idea was that when stocks declined, bonds would rally and thereby offset some of the stock declines. Today, however, after a 30-year secular bond bull market, how much further could bond yields fall (and prices rise) in order to offset a stock market decline? The safety net is deployed from much lower yields and/or prices, and it may not be the offset some count on. The solution, of course, is active asset allocation, a.k.a. market timing.

laggards or leaders against their peers. Other funds of funds may cast their nets wide and far. For our part, we treat them like all the others. Another problem is that they may have a second layer of fees. The first layer is the underlying fund, and the second layer is the fund of funds. We just ask on a risk-adjusted relative performance basis, how are they performing for me?

Active Versus Passive Funds

There are periods of underperformance and outperformance by both types of funds. This is important to note. I'm not aware of anyone or any strategy that succeeds 100% of the time in each and every year. This is okay. What really matters is the cumulative result.

To my thinking, it is not so much the fact that a proactive rotational allocation strategy may work better than buy and hold. Rather, to me it is the fact that the downside risk of loss is mitigated. Obviously, if we were to compare moving into and out of the market to the investor who employed buy and hold in 1929 and thereafter, I doubt there would be any question in that investor's mind about which approach to use.

We don't know the future. We don't know when the bear will end after some percentage of loss. In the worst case, it was about 90% back in the Great Depression. All we know is historic data. Everyone uses that and tries to discern how to profit therefrom. We can all see the market fluctuate, and we can see bands around which the turns from bull to bear and from bear to bull took place. The problem isn't that something is backtested; we all use history. The real question is whether the strategy will be duplicable in the future. Will the conditions in the future mimic the conditions in the past?

There are two more points to be made here. The first concerns the standard industry advice related to age and circumstance, and the second concerns the math of investing. If you lose 50%, you have to gain 100% just to return to breakeven. Irrational investors move the markets up and down in fits of greed and fear.

Take the simple industry idea of an investor who was 50 in the year 2000 with nearly $150,000 in her portfolio. The industry's advice is that she has another 15 years to invest, so she has time to recover any declines. At the bottom in 2003, she is now 53, and her portfolio is worth about half, or $75,000. What's the standard industry advice? She now has less time to recover from losses, she has aged, so she needs to sell some stock funds and buy bond funds. Precisely at the wrong time!

Let's assume, however, that her advisor just told her to hang in there. By 2007 she is back to about $150,000 again. See, I told you so, he might say. But then the next bear market begins, and by 2009 her portfolio is back to about $75,000 again. Now she is 60. This time he agrees with her that it is time to sell, that she just doesn't have the time left to recoup the losses. Sell at the bottom because of your age. And then the market recovers, but her portfolio can't because it's not fully invested in stocks as before.

So the buy-and-hold advice divorced from the reality of personal age and circumstance just falls flat when the facts of the real world in which we live and breathe are superimposed on the actual market data. Again, it is simply ridiculous to look at a 100-year chart and tell investors that even if they bought in 1929, things turned out well for them.

With this in mind, especially as it relates to the push into passive index investing, I will now look at the argument for and against passive or active funds.

Index funds have been offered as a solution to, for want of a better description, the lack of manager skill. More than that, however, is the fact that whatever advantages might be found in the markets are arbitraged away. But if one decides to use index funds only, to be the market, history is full of times when indexes fail miserably against their active managers during secular bull and bear markets. It is a false dichotomy. We may have seen that some 75% of active funds fail to beat the index, but that is not to say owning an index fund is an actual solution. The recent environment is a good example. Index funds, as we know, are back to about breakeven from their peaks in 2000. It is a misinterpretation of the data to pit active against index. Recall the stock market boom that peaked in 2000. Some industry-specific funds, like the Internet, doubled in 1999. The indexes themselves that had this industry as part of their makeup did better than other indexes. If one chased their hot performance without a sell strategy in place, it was a few short years later that the funds had given it all back, plus some. Buy in hope, and sell in despair. As we saw in Chapter 2, this includes the S&P 500 Index, the mother of all indexes, that gave back a decade of gains and took another decade to get it back, just to return to breakeven. And again, the investor is older with less time left to make it back. In the meantime, some actively managed funds have been making new highs for years.

There simply has to be a better conversation about this than the active or passive argument.

For us, the issue of making money is better framed not as pitting index against active but rather, how do we manage the managers, be they active or passive? How do we know what to buy and sell and when to buy and sell? There are times when active beats index and other times when index beats active. I suggest that we use both.

At its worst, we just need to realize that, based on studies about skill and luck, the fund industry has narrowed and defined itself into niches out of which comes performance almost solely based on luck, or to be more polite, based on nothing more than being in the right place at the right time. Great selecting because of the hot area, but can the manager repeat it? Not unless that style does well the next year. If your fund must invest in consumer staples and consumer staples are hot, then your fund should do well. If the index favors the large-cap growth and large-cap growth is "where it's at," then it will do well. No skill involved here either. It's not that the manager discerned that those stocks would do well for some reason but that he was already mandated by his prospectus to invest in them. His great numbers are based on his prospectus. If your fund must invest in technology or gold, then when those areas are hot, your fund too should be hot. Likewise, this is also generally true about the broader styles: if the small-cap area is booming, your small-cap fund should also do well.

Having said that, however, as we saw earlier in Chapter 1, even when the industry or style may be hot and all funds invested in that area should be doing well, there is still a wide variance in performance from year to year. There is in fact still an element of manager skill at work against peers. Thus, it is still incumbent upon the investor to pick the right fund whose assets are in the right place at the right time. We just need a mechanism to figure which fund manager is performing relatively better for the risk taken today.

Thus, the necessity of monitoring and ranking funds is still essential to achieve long-term success. Some managers will outperform their peers, even from the same specific objective and pool of stocks. It is a fascinating issue. They have the same pool of stocks, take the same risk, yet some funds will lead, and others will lag using that exact same pool of stocks from which to choose their fund's holdings.

All of these new fund choices mean our job of selecting is harder, not easier. In the allocation process, we have to account for personal investor circumstances like age and job security, picking some mix between stocks and bonds to try to approach the efficient frontier of the most return and the least risk, a frontier that shifts during secular markets. But in addition, we also have to pick the right stock and bond funds themselves.

If we want 70% in the stock market, it is not enough to place 70% of our portfolio with manager ABC, where ABC may be underperforming the remainder of his exact same peer group. We may pick a leading manager only to find out a year later that for some reason[5] the fund is now lagging its peers. What should be done? How long will we give the fund to recover?

If we respond by further slicing our 70% allocation into different styles, like commodities and real estate, we still have to answer the two main questions: Is my fund top ranked against its peers? And is this sector of the market moving up against the other sectors?

By this time, readers already know my basic answer to these questions. Rank the funds in some way. I do it by C, the risk-adjusted relative performance number. The details of this process will be shown in Chapter 6. For the rest of this chapter, we will look further into the industry response to the unknowable future, to sure losses, to style drift, to luck, and to diversification. And then we will drill down more specifically into the passive responses, which are also known as index funds; and we will then return to look into the actively managed funds. As we will find, both may be reasonable responses and might be used at different times. As we saw, the

---

[5] There are a variety of reasons a fund that was outperforming its peers is now lagging. Maybe the outperformance was a factor of luck and the tide has turned. Maybe the manager has changed. Maybe the investment committee has changed membership. Maybe the fund has too much money and the manager cannot redeploy it as well. This latter reason is the most frequent problem. If you can't be nimble, you can't jump over the candlestick (a form of charting).

secular trend as it reveals over- and undervaluations in stocks and bonds may be a better determinant of our answer than is the table of fund provisions.

The mission of the stock market investor may be summed up in a single sentence: it is to seek to profit therein by exploiting inefficiencies and unanticipated information wherever they exist. Capital flows then, they say, to the best usage. If a company is making wide profits from selling widgets, we can be sure more companies will enter that same space. Or, as we saw earlier, the company, if it is more of a monopoly, like railroads, raises its prices too much and government may intervene. The same is generally true of people. People flow to the best usage of their time and brains; they go to where they can make the most money. Wall Street has produced numerous millionaires. Over the years, and especially since the 1960s, it has attracted more and more of some of the smartest people. It is now full of sharp, competitive, motivated people with some of the best brains and newest technology and deepest pockets on the planet. They are all seeking to exploit price inefficiencies and information first. Paradoxically, its very success is one reason for its downfall in terms of providing superior, consistent, year-after-year returns. It is one reason index funds have grown in popularity over the last 30 years. If there are no inefficiencies left, then indexers have at least one point in their favor.

Moreover, Wall Street was once the land of the unchallenged. Knowing the right people was critical in profiting from the inside scoops. It was not what you knew but who you knew if you were to profit from being the first one to act on new or unknown-by-the-rest information to either buy or sell. This insider advantage has shrunk over the years as the Securities and Exchange Commission has been cracking down on some high-profile cases.[6]

---

[6] The last bastion of legal insider trading was in Congress. The show *60 Minutes* did an episode on this in November 2011. Congress then passed the STOCK Act in April 2012. They gutted it about a year later in that the reporting requirements were nixed by unanimous consent after 10 seconds of consideration in the Senate and 14 seconds in the House. With no way to track their trades, they are still in effect "permitted" to take advantage of their insider knowledge. For example, if the members of Congress know that a drug will be permitted, they may buy the company stock beforehand without repercussion. The poorest of the poor may go

It was also a game played against the novice who thought he could compete against built-in house advantages. Stock prices were once quoted in fractions of dollars, not in pennies. Spreads between bids and asks were once at least 0.125 and wider to buy and sell at the market. The change to pricing from fractions to decimals has reduced the house's take. Spreads between bids and asks has narrowed from 0.125 to 0.01 and even less for some. Some stocks trade in hundredths of a penny now. No longer is it as easy to make money by capturing the spread, by acting as a type of market maker yourself.

In addition to using bid-ask spreads, the industry frowned on the small outsider trying to also make the market by sitting on the bid or ask side. The brokerages wanted you to buy from them at the higher ask price and sell to them at the lower bid price. They wanted to capture the spread. They didn't want you to sit there with them or move in between their wide spread.

It didn't happen often, but I recall entering orders in the 1980s between the spread and my orders not getting filled as the market traded through my price. When I would call to complain, the brokerage's explanation always sounded just a shade away from making it up as you go along: "But we will try to do better next time." "There were orders ahead." "You didn't get your order in on time." "The market moved away regardless of what your time and sales report says." "Your time and sales tape is wrong." I heard all sorts of excuses over that time.

Over the years, all of these things slowly changed and improved, gradually leveling the playing field between institutions and individuals.

One warm sunny morning in downtown Dallas, I attended a company's shareholder meeting where I met the original SOES "bandit" Harvey Houtkin. SOES stands for Small Order Execution System. He was there for the same reason I was; we each had invested in the same public company because we were using similar tools to identify what we thought were undervalued micro-cap stocks. We believed at that time, unlike now, that this area of the stock market

---

to Washington and come out in the 1%. When did America start exempting the lawmakers from subjecting themselves to the same laws as everyone else?

was still inefficient. And so, we would routinely find companies trading for less than the value of their net assets like cash and real estate, thus valuing at times the profitable operating business for free. We had both found this intriguing little "cheap" company, and we were at this shareholder meeting because we wanted to hear more from the company's executives. We wanted to know, What will you do to close the spread between your company's price and its value? Your public company is not a private piggy bank, you know.

A few months later I met Houtkin for lunch in beautiful Boca Raton. We talked about his investment roots, and he described those tumultuous times after the crash of 1987 as "printing money." The investment climate had been slowly changing ever since Mayday in 1975 when trading commissions were deregulated. Commissions have dropped even more since then from more than $100 per trade to around $10 or less per trade today. There are times when trades are even free. At the time in the 1980s to hear Houtkin explain it, the big boys still slept at the switch of their trading machines, as they dreamed that their succulent "capture the spread" business would remain the same "as usual" for the next 30 years, just as it had for the previous 30. Bankers' hours they had and expected to maintain as entitlements. So what would happen is that the bids and asks would get out of kilter on the SOES. For example, Houtkin would buy 1,000 or fewer shares of a company at $60.125 (the out-of-kilter ask) and immediately sell them at $60.375 (the out-of-kilter bid). He'd get $250 credit less expenses posted to his account. Bang, bang, bang, all day long during those bankers' hours, day after day after day, he'd search for and make those sorts of trades as fast as he could find them and type. Printing money in what was basically riskless trades. Those days are long over.[7]

---

[7] After working at the large Wall Street firm, I joined a local broker-dealer. It was at this time that I started to look at the small-cap area of the stock market for inefficiencies. After meeting and talking with Harvey, I recall excitedly approaching their back-end trader who entered the trades and maintained their inventory. "We need to do this too," I said. "It's perfectly legal, and we can make a ton of money." Silly me for assuming that people think the way I do, wanting the most return with the least risk. Pooh-pooh, he intoned; not interested. I'm not sure if it was somehow beneath him or if he was worried about what his buddies at other firms would say. After all, this wasn't technical analysis, nor was it fundamental analysis,

Easy money easily won attracts competition. When you find gold, it is tough to keep your mouth shut. Even if you do keep quiet, it is tough to explain your lifestyle change. As others moved in, inefficiencies disappeared eventually. From those days, competition and computing power had grown by leaps and bounds over the last 30 years. Wall Street with its seemingly endless profits had attracted the best players. Use your brains, not your brawn. Electronics was shrinking the time between those getting information first and the rest of us. These exploitable inefficiencies had slowly, but inevitably disappeared. As a side note, this trend was also the beginning of the suggestion that the active manager's advantages had begun to shrink. Index funds, which essentially admit that there are no worthwhile inefficiencies any longer, began their ascent.

In the investing world, not to mention the rest of the world, being first holds a great advantage over being a latecomer.[8] Who had the fastest ships as they switched from sail to steam centuries ago? Using the SOES, this continued the same trend of who's first; the principle is identical. Be first and be fastest to gain the advantage. Today, this advantage is measured in milliseconds and millions of shares. The playing field has been leveled, if you take the fly-by approach. If you look at the microscopic view, however, you still find traders trying to take advantage of price differentials between exchanges, just as Houtkin did. They do it electronically, by computer now, rather than by hand, and over fiber networks, rather than through copper. Indeed, some are doing it near light speed with lasers. It is all the same idea, the same in-the-know, be first, profit principle. Exploit price differences of the same security in what are essentially

---

but it was as near to risk-free trading as ever existed since and then legally on Wall Street.

As an aside, I've long felt that Wall Street is the only place where investors routinely walk past $20 bills that those on the other side of the trade eagerly snag up. It's a strange juxtaposition, but perhaps the real reason the broker-dealer trader wouldn't participate in the SOES trades was because doing so went against his kind, the other traders at other firms from which he would handsomely profit day in and day out. How much better to nip a bit from the outsiders too uninformed to snag the money?

[8] The old saying is that "the early bird gets the worm." The sassy reply is that "the second mouse gets the cheese."

riskless trades. Stocks may trade on different exchanges and only for milliseconds is there a difference, but the price differential may be taken advantage of for fractions of a penny. Buy XYZ and sell XYZ faster than the next guy. If you multiply those fractions by the tens of millions of trades, the profits add up day in and day out. Bang, bang, bang. Regulators, however, have begun looking at this advantage as a form of front running.

Incidentally, there is a lot of whining and hand-wringing about these things, as if they are unfair. I imagine the same thing happened when the first steamship plied the waters. Those who owned and those who leased the sailing ships were in for some lean times. The hare did win the race. What is important for us to recognize here is that Wall Street is a business. It is not a social gathering, and there are no socialist ideas. Frankly, though, it is the only place where the public all too often steps across a $20 bill without thought, while the sharks are greedily exploiting any remaining pockets of ignorance. I want the playing field as level as the next investor does.

So index funds emerged 20 years ago as computing power grew. Thus a wider base of skilled players slowly and steadily entered into the scene and smoothed out the relative differences between valuations and anomalies and inefficiencies. Institutional trading grew from 20% to near 90% of the stock volume. The huge management fees active managers charged cut returns year after year, but to what end? The skill differences between active and passive managers did not expand to justify the costs. Everyone now had fiber networks. Everyone had the same news feeds. Everyone had real-time quotes. Everyone was scouring the market for any tidbit of advantage.

Except for those who engaged in illegal trading activities,[9] it seemed no one had an edge. The active managers' performance could no longer justify the fees they charged. Active institutional managers didn't compete with the market any longer. They were the market. It is tough to beat yourself.

---

[9] Those trading first on news in milliseconds and scalping hundredths of a penny are considered legal. I suspect this, too, will change in order to level the field even further. They will disseminate the news in a different way to take away the speed advantage. After all, this is no different from the olden days when the steamship captain had the advantage over the sailor. Competitive advantages have a way of disappearing as they are found illegal or otherwise.

The reality of investing today is that it has taken on the appearance of operating as a commodity business[10] now. Why should I pay you more for the same product and service I can get from someone else for less?

The book *Winning the Loser's Game,* by Charles D. Ellis, noted how the performance differences between active and passive managers was shrinking, even back in the 1960s and 1970s. Again, why pay more in fees for less performance advantage?

Many investors are very familiar with the studies that show passive fund management (index funds) outperforming active fund management. Vanguard has championed this. Over any 20-year period, the S&P 500 Index outperforms more than two-thirds of the active funds.[11]

Today there is about $1.3 trillion invested in index funds. CalPERS[12] is one of the latest and largest institutions to apparently change what they are doing; they are moving from an active approach to a passive approach. Other high-profile investors, like Warren Buffett[13] and Charles Schwab,[14] are recommending index funds.

As can be seen, they have a strong argument. All things being equal, you will be better off paying less in fees with a buy-and-hold approach. The reality is, however, that not all things are equal. As

---

[10] A commodity business is selling something that is essentially the same from vendor to vendor. It is like selling an ounce of gold: it should be priced exactly the same from vendor to vendor. Why would anyone pay more to someone for the exact same commodity? So too with the money management business and index funds: why should someone pay more for the exact same index fund as another?

 Of course, if the gold is shaped into a ring, then the commodity is no longer a commodity. A higher price will be charged. So too with the fund business, but the active fund has a high hurdle over which to jump to justify its existence. Either that, or one counts on the slot-machine mentality to prevail.

[11] Lipper Leaders and Vanguard Funds routinely publish this statistic showing the majority of index managers outperforming active managers over various time frames from 1 to 20 years.

[12] CalPERS is the California Public Employees' Retirement System. It is the second largest in the United States, behind the federal pension system, and it is the sixth largest in the world. They had 1.7 million employees and an investment portfolio of $260 billion as of June 30, 2013.

[13] See page 20 of Warren Buffett's 2013 Annual Report.

[14] 2014 Schwab Center for Financial Research.

you will see, we don't advocate this approach. We don't want to hold the laggards. There are times, like the last 14 years, that active management outperforms passive funds. Much of the relative performance depends on the secular trends. And it all depends on your selection process when you bought the fund in the first place.

For this chapter, suffice to say many institutions and individuals are embracing the passive management strategy. It is based on the recognition that the investment playing field has all but been perfectly leveled by now, that historical inefficiencies upon which active managers made their names do not clearly exist any longer, and that management costs account for the bulk difference in performance.

As just discussed, some say that persuasive arguments for utilizing active fund management are all but disappearing. This is because previously known market inefficiencies are in fact disappearing, whether it is in price differentials or news feeds or fund styles like micro-caps or emerging markets. Institutions dominate the trading activity; again, it is tough to beat yourself. Active managers, however, press on and try to beat the market index in a variety of ways, but essentially they still try to exploit stock market price inefficiencies. They try to find undervalued stocks whose assets are mispriced or growth stocks that have more potential than expected. But with the growth of Wall Street, those stock market inefficiencies dwindle steadily year after year. It is just a matter of time, the indexers say, before the active managers consistently underperform the passive index managers by upward of 90% each year.

There may have been a time when inefficiencies in the stock market were widespread. In fact, some of the grand old names of fund management can trace their beginnings to investing in inefficiencies. Peter Lynch of Fidelity sought out small-caps before the idea of breaking the market into its components was even thought out. Sir John Templeton of the now Franklin/Templeton Funds sought out international stocks and found them trading at 3X earnings.[15]

---

[15] Sir John Templeton is perhaps best known for his order to buy every stock on the NYSE and AMEX below $1 per share. This was at the time that Hitler appeared to be winning the war. I should point out again here that most investors still think that war is bullish for stocks. It is not. The opposite is the truth, unless you buy at the absolute worst time. See Chapter 2.

Michael Price would investigate bankruptcies for pricing inefficiencies. Warren Buffett also traces his beginnings to the small-cap market's inefficiencies and specifically to the then unknown insurance company GEICO. T. Rowe Price once bought growth companies whose P/E ratios were less than half their growth rates.

Today's active manager has a much different milieu in which to invest. Global markets are the norm. Small-cap is its own category with billions already invested there and hundreds of eyes investigating. Active management trying to exploit those inefficiencies based on ineptitudes and ignorance—its very success sowed the seeds of its demise. There was a time when it was possible to take advantage of an uneven playing field. Wall Street was bigger, had deeper pockets, was more connected, faster, and smarter than its competitors called "the public." One by one, however, over the years, the playing field was smoothed by regulation, education, openness, and competition.

As the playing field leveled out, making it more and more difficult for active managers to outperform consistently the indexes, we've seen other active managers who had runs, made names for themselves, and then flamed out. Their disasters stoke the arguments of the indexers against the active managers. Each exploited a niche as he or she rose to fame and fortune, but the niches no longer so clearly and so deeply exist. Inefficiency exploited for too long ends as an efficient market. It's just the nature of the game.

Out of this leveling came creativity, though in different ways. In addition to the proliferation of mutual funds, the exchange-traded fund (ETF) market grew and developed. With better technology, it is possible to price an index with hundreds of stocks on a second-to-second basis. Commissions are down. Trading volumes are up. BlackRock, using the name iShares, is the dominant player in ETFs. There are other providers like Schwab, Vanguard, State Street, or Guggenheim for nearly 50 in total who offer hundreds of ETF choices.

There is one more point to be made here. We have also discovered over the years that active managers will beat passive indexes, but this is not to say that it is the same active manager who is outperforming year after year. To take advantage of this development requires a change in thinking from the old-fashioned buy-and-hold/forget strategy to evolve with the leaders by following the Comets: the leading risk-adjusted relative performance funds. We will review this strategy even more in Chapter 6.

Lastly, in defense of active management versus index management is the ongoing recognition that the stock market has a thing called "value" around which investors, including institutions, buy and sell. This is different from a manager's ability to outperform the market in any one year or even over multiple years. Paying attention to value is recognizing that there are simply times to be extremely cautious, bordering on being completely out of stocks because there is no value in being extremely aggressive or being 100% or more invested in stocks because there is value.

Conclusion

We track both passive index and actively managed funds, and we suggest you do the same. There is a time for both or one or the other. We recognize that managers, like comets, come into and out of prominence. We also understand that the market itself, even at its most efficient, recognizes that once the market is overvalued, they—the fully invested active or passive funds—will all go down. It will provide you no solace to think you saved 1% in annual fees in your passive management portfolio if you lose 90% in a Great Depression bear market.

6

C-lecting Strategies

WE'VE SEEN THAT THE FINANCIAL INDUSTRY'S TYPICAL RESPONSE TO risk of loss is to tell you three things. Diversify between stocks and bonds, and remain fully invested. Don't use cash as an asset class. Don't shift your allocations between stocks and bonds based on value or trends but only on your age. But the truth is that no one knows the future. Your age has nothing to do with market values or future success. There will be fluctuations in prices. Nonetheless, diversification properly used is a valuable tool.

To be clear, a static diversification between stocks and bonds typically creates an inverse relationship between the stocks and bonds. You can't have one positive result without the other negative impact. One, diversification should help reduce the risk of loss, but in so doing, two, it also reduces your potential for gain on the upside. The point is that a standard 60/40 diversification allocation does not answer the question of what to invest in or whether even that 60/40 split is the best one to have today. Why not shift the percentages based on what is taking place recently, rather than on a market capitalization snapshot from the 1950s? It does not tell us how to make the most money with the least amount of risk. Plus, as we saw, the efficient frontier that measures those stock and bond relationships does change over the decades. We have a method that addresses the standard shortfalls.

Furthermore, diversification alone does not answer the question of what to buy—of how to select the top active or passive funds. It does not recognize that leaders and laggards change over time. If you select a poor fund, be it active or passive, your gains really will be capped to the upside in a bull market, and you'll still participate to the downside in a bear market. It is one thing to say that you need to put 60% of your assets into stock funds and 40% into bond funds. It is a whole different thing to say that you should put 60% into these specific stock funds where the reality is that their leadership will eventually change and you will need to be ready to reallocate as markets change.

We've seen how many of the mighty managers have fallen, both in the active world and in the passive world. Buy and hold and diversify as a strategy really is not the proactive answer to the investment question we are looking for.

For us, the answers to the two questions about selecting and timing are really very simple. One, use cash as an asset class for potential diversification purposes. In this way, when stocks or bonds are falling, we can move into the safety of cash. We also find this principle at work with fund managers. The managers who use defensive tools will rise to the top in performance ranks during high-risk periods. We may switch to them as the times warrant. When the markets are rallying, we can move to a 100% participation level in the funds whose managers are outperforming the markets. Two, invest with the fund leaders and avoid the laggards in both the active and passive worlds, knowing that they will change over the years.

I need to emphasize this additional point about the use of cash as an alternative: it may be external to your portfolio (the common usage) or internal to a fund; that is, a fund manager may take defensive measures at times. What this means, as we measure C, the risk-adjusted relative performance of funds, when we enter a bear market, is that the manager who raises cash internally or takes other defensive actions in her fund will bubble up to the top in the performance rankings. So, whether we actively sell funds and buy cash equivalents or whether we remain fully invested and hold the new fund leaders that internally have taken various defensive measures, the principle is the same. Cash is being used (externally by us or internally to the fund) to safeguard results.

In this chapter and the next, we will drill down into these two selection and timing themes. One, which funds are doing the best in the current environment? Two, where are we in the secular cycle, which influences our timing decisions? In sum, with this two-pronged approach, we advocate the process of managing the managers. We seek to employ the idea of managing the managers within the very long term cycles, rather than buying and holding and forgetting and then making changes because of age only. This means we will asset allocate between stocks, bonds, and cash. It also means we will change the fund manager as necessary. We measure these things monthly while knowing we may make potential changes on a two- or three-month basis. This time frame is needed so as to avoid brokerage firms' short-term redemption charges.

It really is a radical idea to approach money managers as the money manager yourself, as a mega manager, a manager of managers. This idea for individual investors is similar to, but not identical to, how some institutions approach investment management.

For fund managers, the prospectus is the rule of the land. They must follow the prospectus, regardless of market or industry influences. It usually means the fund will not raise cash, but it will remain fully invested all the way down in a bear market. This also means they have to invest in industry areas that may be out of favor. In the examples to follow, we will see the impact of these two forces. As proactive manage-the-manager investors, however, we don't have to do either.

Can't you hear the howls of protest against us? I have over the years. They say, I am the manager, not you. My fund charges less than everyone else. I have the skills, not luck. I have outperformed for X number of years. I have billions under management. I have years of college and advanced degrees; what was your degree in? But the truth is that it is your money. Take control of it. And remember, there are lots of mediocre managers managing billions of dollars whose marketing skills are top-notch. In the investment world, as in any aspect of life, managers are not all above average. You surely can't make it worse by providing some proactive oversight to them. Vote with your pocketbook. I'll show you how.

The reason they can't all be above average, above the market, as we saw, is that they are the market. This is one reason why index funds have become popular. If you can't beat them, become them. To be fair, passive index funds may have one built-in advantage over active funds: it is their lower fees. To the same performance degree that an active fund charges, say, 1.5%, but an index fund charges 0.10%, that cost difference accrues to your benefit over time.

One drawback to index funds is drawdowns in bear markets. As they follow their prospectus, they will be fully invested all the way to the bottom. Why watch your portfolio drop 30% or worse? In the next chapter we will explore ways to approach timing.

Another problem for diversification (besides losing money and capping the upside and holding laggard funds) is, Why hold funds in out-of-favor industries or styles? As a recent example of this, take the international fund XXX that has lost 50% year over year, yet it still has $500 million under management. Why do investors stick with it? Diversification? Avoiding loss? Making money? Holding the best fund? Low cost? It boggles the mind.

Is it really a conscious choice to lose and keep losing money? There really is no reason to doubt that over the very long term, say, the next 100 years, the domestic and international stock markets will be higher than they are today. If America remains great for the next 100 years, as it has the past 100, businesses will grow; hence, so, too, will its stock market increase. I also have no doubt that the indexes will lose more than 50% a few times along the way. Why guess at this? Why not do something about it?

Even if investors have to have diversification, they should at least have a way to attempt to stay with the leaders in that style that is providing diversification. In Chapter 1, we saw that the difference between the top funds and worst funds is a chasm that will not close year after year. Here is a table contrasting top and bottom ETF funds over recent years. These are the average returns of the five best and five worst ETFs:

Year	Best	Worst
2013	77.6%	−53.2%
2012	52.6	−33.8
2011	17.4	−48.8

Selecting the right funds matters to your financial goals. What are the ways to select funds? There are a number of rating services available to the public, and they use a variety of approaches and metrics. For my part, I look at a set period of returns also. I don't mean to be obtuse, but I also do not want to provide proprietary information because I want it to continue to work well in the future for you. If my work provides you an advantage, I don't want it arbitraged away, as other strategies have been.

If we ask 100 people what they want from their investing, most will say something to the effect that they want to make money and not lose it. To refine this explanation, we could rephrase it to say, just as the financial industry says: we want to make the most return with the least risk.[1] That is, after all, the modeling behind the idea of the efficient frontier. It is the point on the curve where more return is made only with increased risk. It is also the point where for the risk incurred, you are being compensated.

Before we proceed further, I want to give a quick quiz on the mathematics of investing that will bring home the importance of investing with the leaders and trying not to lose it. Nearly half of the investing public will give the wrong answer to this question. In the example of a portfolio's losing 50% in the first year and then gaining 50% the following year, where is the portfolio's value at the end of year 2? Have I made money, lost money, or returned to breakeven in this example?[2]

In addition to the mathematics of investing, we must also keep in mind the human factors of investing like circumstance and age.

---

[1] If one invests in stocks or bonds, there is the risk of loss. It is unavoidable. Among other things, there have been in the past and will be in the future what are called Black Swan events, like terrorist attacks. The market may drop overnight, and you cannot do anything about it until the next day. The good news is these are few and far between, and historically the market returns to where it had been.

[2] The answer to the question is that my portfolio will still be net down. Let's say you invest $1,000. You lose 50% by year end. Now your portfolio is worth $500 (50% of $1,000). In year 2, you gain 50%. Your portfolio is now worth $750 (50% of $500 [$250] plus the $500 you began the year with). In sum after two years, your portfolio is still down 25% from its original value ($1,000 originally, $750 after two years). Mathematics, and the human elements of age, circumstance, and emotions are why bear markets are so devastating to investor wealth creation and retention.

In the example above, the human question is whether I remained fully invested for those two years, considering that in year 1, I lost 50% of my retirement money. Would I really be there for the recovery? Studies, as we've seen, have shown investors performing worse than the results of their funds. Why? Investors often buy and sell at the wrong times. Everyone resolves to "stick to it," to remain fully invested, but the reality is that the advice to buy and hold in the first place is simply wrong. Bear markets are nearly always worse than expected. It is very hard to watch your portfolio lose half and not react by selling. Besides, doing nothing ignores the reality of our makeup, and of age and circumstance.

When you consider your own investment account, another factor that must not be ignored when calculating performance is your contributions and withdrawals. You must separate out your contributions in order to calculate your real gains. Over a four-year cycle in the example above of the market's losing 50% and gaining 50%, if you find, however, that your account is up from the start value at the end of the period, the math doesn't lie: the gains would be attributable only from or because of your contributions. It wasn't something your manager accomplished for you.

This is not to say that we should avoid investing. We shouldn't. All I'm suggesting, again, is to approach investing differently. After all, investing carries risk. What the rules are saying, however, is to avoid permanent loss. This would involve our avoiding stocks in a bubble or our buying companies whose products and methods we do not understand or our ignoring where the market is in its secular trend or our neglecting to consider various valuation measures that we looked at in Chapter 2. It will take years to ever get back to breakeven after suffering a 50% loss because it will require a gain of 100%. In the meantime, as we've seen, personal age and circumstance keep marching on.

Selecting Based on Past Performance

Throughout this book, I've been contrasting the standard industry advice of buy and hold or the new mantra buy and sell based on your age with my approach to actively managing the managers. Before I drill down further into this, I want to amplify this comparison a little more.

There are numerous advisors, fund companies, newsletter writers, and columnists who assemble portfolios based solely on a static past performance. The most typical allocation advice derived from that is the 60% stocks and 40% bonds portfolio. In that mix, some will substitute 5% to 10% in real estate or commodities. Some will further subdivide the 60% into domestic and international funds and then subdivide it further into small-cap, large-cap, and value funds. Some will do the same with the 40% allocation to bonds, buying some variety of high-yield, international, inflation-protected, short-end, and long-end bond fund combinations. The idea is to end up with some portfolio today that provided the past historic allocations that produced above market gains. Sounds great, right? There are two problems with this type of stagnant approach to assembling a portfolio based on past performance.

One is my by now familiar refrain that this advice does not tell us which specific active or passive fund to buy. As we've seen, there are times for both passive and active funds. There is a chasm in performance between the top and bottom funds in the same style or industry. For example, they might recommend 10% of your portfolio be invested in real estate funds. Which one? Why one index fund over another? Why not an active fund? There is simply no recognition of the fact that fund performances are not equal, even from among funds picking from the same stable of stocks, as we saw way back in Chapter 1.

Two, which is the main problem, is that the allocation advice is based solely on a stationary past performance, as if past conditions will be similar to future conditions. In turn, this problem encompasses three problems. One, the circumstances under which the "best" allocation is assembled may or may not repeat in the future. Think real estate funds. Just because it may have done well for years doesn't mean it will continue to do well. Think Great Depression or Great Recession. Two, the time frame during which the "best" allocation is assembled may or may not be suitable for your personal situation. Your mileage will vary. As we have already seen, the efficient frontier of the traditional 60/40 split is built on a snapshot from the 1950s. The reality is that no one truly benefits directly from that long 100-year horizon. Three, the efficient frontier, as we've seen, actually shifts over time. It is a mistake to take even a 50-year snapshot of the "best allocation" and say, Here, do this, too, for the next 50 years. After all, some static combination of investments had to work the "best." Will the same assemblage still work the "best" in the future? It is doubtful, and you won't know until 50 years pass, but there are lives and billions riding on the bet they're telling you to make today.

At this point, someone may ask if the backtesting I perform doesn't suffer from the same pitfalls. The answer is not at all for three reasons.

One, I am not using static historic backtested information upon which to preset some inert future fixed allocation ratio.

Two, if Fund ABC is a top fund in one time frame, it may be because the manager has 90% stocks and 10% bonds. In a different time frame, Fund XYZ is a top fund because the manager has 10% stocks and 90% cash. My backtesting is to see whether the rotation strategy based on C works or not in picking the best funds as the years go by. In other words, I am testing a strategy to see if the strategy itself works. The allocation decision is not fixed; it is a continuous rotational process.

Three, if we agree that the concept of the efficient frontier is true and accurate as a measure of a way to optimize a portfolio's risk and reward, then I am using something that recognizes this in real time. In other words, we find that the best funds one year won't necessarily be the best funds the following year. It is the same with the combination of assets. The allocation that worked well in the past six months may not be the best combination for the next six months, let alone the next six years. Odds are they won't be. Just because Fund XYZ did well in the secular bull market, it is not to say that Fund XYZ or the underlying industries will do well in the secular bear market. We also find that sometimes passive beats active funds and vice versa. And we find that in a bear market, funds with the lowest fees drop just as much as funds with the higher fees. And lastly, we find the efficient frontier shifting over the decades. My approach takes all of these various factors into account.

Having said all of that, my strategy obviously will require more time and effort to implement than a portfolio based on a fixed allocation that gets rebalanced once a year or every five years, like "age based" funds, into the same choices. They don't call them "lazy portfolios" for nothing. After all, we need to continuously answer the questions: Which funds will we use? Who is making money today? On the other hand, the reader has to decide whether the results justify that monthly or weekly or daily commitment. Let's look further at results.

Selecting Based on Most Return and Least Risk

For this chapter, we want to explain the process we use to identify the top fund picks based on risk-adjusted relative performance. As long as we are taking the risk of investing, why shouldn't we try to identify and stay with the leaders? What we want are the top funds as measured by C, the risk-adjusted relative performance number.

Different investor services, of course, use a variety of tools to answer the same question about which fund to buy and hold. For us, we have to have a way to measure the spot on the ever-changing efficient frontier where everyone longs to gather: at that point where the portfolio achieves the most return for the least risk. So this is really to ask a three-part question. How do you measure return, and how do you measure risk, and then how do you put the two ideas together?

People have measured risk in a number of ways, like standard deviation and beta. *Standard deviation* measures the amount of variation around an average. If the variation is low, it means that there is less dispersion around the mean; it has less volatility. A higher deviation means data points are spread widely. So, for example, a portfolio fully invested in stocks will have a larger standard deviation than a portfolio half in stocks and half in cash because cash has a lower standard deviation than stocks. *Beta* is another measurement of risk. It describes an asset's return as compared to a benchmark. The benchmark might be the S&P 500 with a beta of 1. A beta of 1.2 would mean that the asset should fluctuate by 20% more than the benchmark.

For my part, I wanted something more simple and intuitive and applicable across asset classes. So I measure risk as volatility, or *V*. The volatility is the total return over any period. We could measure it daily, weekly, monthly, quarterly, yearly, or longer. The idea behind this is that it provides us a way to measure risk across all asset classes. What I mean is this. A money market fund that remains at a net asset value of $1.00 will have a V of 0; it doesn't fluctuate. That doesn't mean it can't break the buck in the future; like any measure, it just measures what has happened. A short-term bond fund that fluctuates in value might have a V of 0.2. The S&P 500 (large-cap) might have a V around 3. The Russell 2000 (small-cap) might have a V around 4. Typically small-caps are perceived as more risky than large-caps. Small-caps will fluctuate more up and down as measured by V. The point is that V will measure the same thing across all asset classes such that one number will tell you what to expect from your various investments and how they compare with each other. The table below shows a variety of V rankings as of December 31, 2013:

World Growth Index	2.7
Dow Jones Industrials	2.6
S&P 500	2.7
Russell 2000	3.2
Dow Jones World	2.4
Dow Jones Precious Metals	7.3
Dow Jones Bonds	1.0
Long-term bonds	2.0
High-yield bonds	2.2
Bonds world	1.4

To be clear, this V rating changes in real time. It will change with the market changes, as Figure 6.1 shows for SPY. SPY is the exchange-traded fund (ETF) that attempts to mimic the returns of the S&P 500 before expenses. The SPY scale is on the left. The V scale is on the right. This is the period from 2005 through 2013.

One inference to draw from Figure 6.1 is clear: as V increases, the commensurate return must increase to make it worth your while to remain invested with a particular fund. As you can see, if V is increasing, it means risk is increasing. This means the relative performance return must increase in a down market (perform relatively better than the index) or it must increase in an up market (perform relatively better than the market) to compensate for the increased volatility (risk). As such, you can understand why top and bottom funds will change over time. This also means there are times when a fund may be increasing, but because its V rating may also be increasing, its C rating drops. We will explore this further after discussing returns when combining these two concepts into the C rating.

FIGURE 6.1 V Changes with Market Changes for SPY from 2005 Through 2013

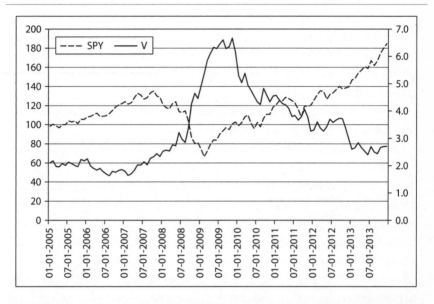

Source: Data for SPY from State Street Global Markets and data for V from the *No-Load Mutual Fund Selections & Timing Newsletter.*

The second part of the selection equation is about return. This is measured in the same way by nearly everyone. Return is capital gains or losses plus any dividends. It is the total return to be exact. This, too, may be measured over a variety of time periods. For example, if a fund begins the year at $10.00 and ends the year at $12.00, then the return is 20% [(12 − 10)/10]. If it pays dividends, these, too, should be accounted for to give you accurate return information.

This absolute return provides some information, but not much. If a fund gained 20% in a year, then how do we know if this was good or bad? So the next step we use in figuring out which fund to select is to compare its return against an index. We call this relative performance comparison CS. The idea here is to begin to find those funds whose returns are better than the market's return. For example, if your fund is up 20%, you might think this is great, until you find out the market is up 30%. It works the same way on the downside. If the market declines 20% and your fund declines only 10%, you may be dissatisfied, but your fund has still outperformed the market. The idea with CS is to try to identify, before risk is taken into account, which managers could be adding skill to the relative performance equation.

On the other hand, if in contrast, the market is up 30% and your fund is up 50%, is that a fund to buy? Like risk, return by itself doesn't tell us much either. I will speak more on combining the two measures shortly.

This now raises the question about which index to use to compare relative performance. For stocks, some will use the S&P 500, while others use the Wilshire 5000, and still others will try for more sophistication and find a comparable, specific index to use against what the fund's prospectus says is its market. There is a comparable index for nearly any fund. For my purposes, this is simply obscuring the question of whether I want to invest in that industry or sector in the first place. Take gold, for example. Of what use is it to say I have the best gold fund because it lost only 40%, while the gold index lost 50%? Have we learned anything just because the fund outperformed its index? So, for my purposes, I now use what I call the World Growth Index (WGI).

This index is made up of 20% in each of five ETFs. The ETFs are EEM (this is the iShares MSCI Emerging Markets ETF, which is made up of large- and mid-capitalization emerging market equities); EFA (this is the iShares MSCI EAFE ETF, which is composed of large-and mid-capitalization developed market equities from Europe, Australia, the Far East, excluding the United States and Canada); IWM (this is the iShares Russell 2000 ETF that seeks to track an index composed of small-capitalization U.S. equities); QQQ (which is the INVESCO PowerShares QQQ that tracks the Nasdaq 100, which is 100 of the largest domestic and international nonfinancial companies listed on Nasdaq); and SPY (which is the SPDR ETF that seeks to correspond generally to the S&P 500 Index, before expenses). Capital gains and dividends are reinvested. It partly answers the diversification questions by investing in ETFs that track domestic and international companies in a variety of market caps ranging from small to mega.

Figure 6.2 compares the WGI and SPY.

With the WGI, we now have something broad and liquid and real (net of internal fees) against which to compare all of the funds

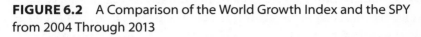

FIGURE 6.2   A Comparison of the World Growth Index and the SPY from 2004 Through 2013

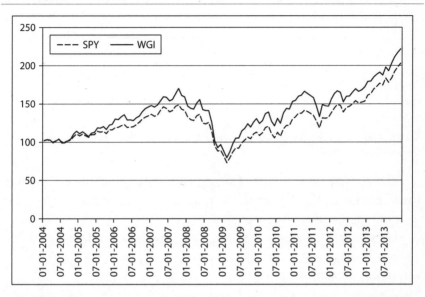

Source: Data for SPY from State Street Global Markets and data for WGI from the *No-Load Mutual Fund Selections & Timing Newsletter.*

we track from sector to industry, from passive to active, from domestic to international, from large to small, from growth to value. We have, as it were, leveled the performance playing field. If the WGI is up 10% and a fund is up 12%, the fund has outperformed by 20%. If the WGI is down 10% and a fund is down 5%, the fund has still outperformed.

As mentioned, though, returns do not exist in a vacuum. The next question is then, what was the risk the manager incurred when making its return? This leads to some initial observations. Remember, we want the fund providing the most return and the least risk. So, for my purposes, I adjust the relative performance return by the risk taken. This makes intuitive sense. For example, an index fund whose risk was 3 that returned 12% is better than an active fund whose risk was 4 that also returned 12%. Of course, if the active fund returned 20% with a V of 4, that could be worth investing with too. If the active fund matched the index's return, but did so with half the risk, then again that, too, garners a better C rank. The following is a table to give further insight into this process. The data is from the *No-Load Mutual Fund Selections & Timing Newsletter* on December 31, 2013, from the Hybrid Class. C is the final number:

	V	CS	C
Fund A	1.9	66	34.2
Fund B	2.1	61	29.7
Fund C	0.9	24	28.3

Source: Data from the *No-Load Mutual Fund Selections & Timing Newsletter* on December 31, 2013.

The relative performance CS adjusted for the volatility V gives us the C ranking. The higher the C ranking, the greater the return per unit of risk the fund has provided.

These three results will change as new data becomes available. Thus it is not a static selection methodology, but rather a proactive rotational allocation strategy.

Selecting Mutual Funds

For years, I approached mutual fund selecting with the same C approach. I will describe this traditional approach next, but then I will describe how I have begun to apply the same approach directly to subgroups like hybrids or small-caps, to specific fund families like Vanguard or Fidelity, and to 401(k) plans. Examples of each application are shown.

In the *No-Load Mutual Fund Selections & Timing Newsletter*, my monthly letter, we track about 800 funds. As mentioned, I rank them all by C. Where do we define the top-ranked funds? There has to be a line somewhere. Traditionally we drew it at 5%. That top 5% was our buy list.

We are not hyper traders, buying and selling the portfolio each month, as if activity adds up to something. I've run backtests on this and actually there are times when less activity is better than monthly adjustments. There are also times when yearly adjustments are too infrequent to achieve the goal of most return and least risk. We continue to hold the fund as long as it remains in the top 20%, which means it has 5 Comets, the top 5%, and next 15% or 4 Comets. So we buy from the top 5% and hold as long as it's in the top 20%.

Incidentally, I use the metaphor Comets, or C, to describe what I do because I want the metaphor to match reality. Comets, unlike stars, come into and out of prominence, just like funds. That's the reality.

The next group of the 800 is composed of 60% of the funds tracked, and it is the lower 15%. And the worst group is the bottom 5%.

As mentioned, for some 20 years, this has been the strategy. And it has worked well, along with market timing, to try to capture most of the advances and avoid most of the declines. Thus the *Hulbert Financial Digest* ranks my newsletter number 1 over 20 years for risk-adjusted performance through December 31, 2013.

Having had this past success with the C approach on mutual funds, I began to apply the same strategy to ETFs. I then reopened some old research I had done on a sector rotation strategy for Fidelity Sector Funds. These successful results prompted further research from looking at the whole 800 fund database into applying the strategy on fund style subsets. I began with the hybrid style, also known as *balanced funds*. Hybrids, as you may know, invest in varying percentages among stocks, bonds, and cash from domestic to international and large- to small-caps. Unlike most stock and bond funds, some hybrids have wider latitude in their objectives. To be sure, some must follow a standard allocation, but some have the freedom to truly manage the portfolio in the way the manager sees best. This was the perfect first style application for C. Details are shown below. In turn, with this success, I began to apply C to other style subgroups like small-caps, large-caps, value, and internationals, as well as to the bond funds. From there I applied it to specific fund families, like Vanguard, Fidelity, and T. Rowe Price. Lastly, I looked at specific 401(k) plans to see if this manage-the-managers by C would work there also. Again, details are shown below.

C-lecting in Styles

To be clear, the C strategy is essentially using the same methodology to analyze the specific styles that we apply to the 800 funds. The only difference is the application. How does this change affect results? Figure 6.3 compares the new application of C on the hybrid style to the SPY and to the Growth Portfolio in my monthly letter.

FIGURE 6.3 C-lect 2 Hybrid as Compared to the SPY and to the MAAP Growth Portfolio, Year-End Values, from 2000 Through June 2013

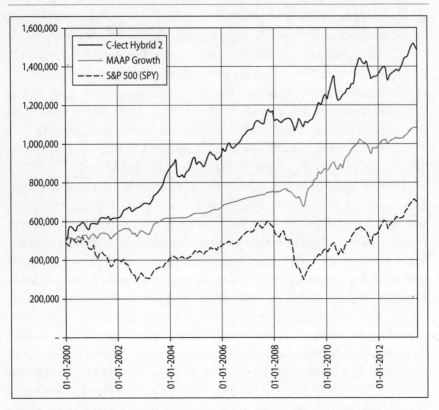

Source: Data for SPY from State Street Global Markets and data for MAAP Growth and C-lect 2 Hybrid from the *No-Load Mutual Fund Selections & Timing Newsletter.*

It is always an interesting question that managers get daily: What have you done lately for me? Where do you go when you are already number 1? The only thing to do is to top what you already accomplished. The C-lect 2 Hybrid strategy based on C would do this. Over the period from January 1, 2000, through June 30, 2013, the new C-lect 2 Hybrid leads the whole pack. My Growth Portfolio outperformed the SPY, and the C-lect 2 Hybrid outperformed the Growth Portfolio.

To clarify further this strategy on hybrids, there is no outside market timing added. The C-lect model in this example takes care of market timing. As mentioned before, the funds that raise cash or take defensive action in a bear market bubble up to the top of performance; they rise in the C ranks to be owned. As the market turns from bear to bull, the fully invested funds holding the strongest sectors bubble up to the top in performance. We thus sell the laggards and buy the leaders over the months. It is a strategy to stay as close as possible to the ideal point of the efficient frontier wherein we make the most return with the least risk.

I want to mention a couple of items in Figure 6.3 for your consideration as a way to emphasize the points I've been making throughout this book. First, after the bubble burst in 2000, the SPY dropped about 50% over the following three years. But note how the C-lect 2 Hybrid, by using C, continued to rise. It rotated away from balanced funds primarily using stocks to those using more bonds. My newsletter portfolios also rose due to a combination of market timing and top fund style selecting.

After the bottom in 2003, all portfolios rose strongly again until 2007. Even by then, however, the SPY could not make up for the previous severe bear market losses. It is simply the mathematics of investing and compounding. This point is so important. Please don't just read over it and move on. If you lose 50%, it takes a gain of 100% just to return to breakeven. Again, we age during that time, and the time left to recover subsequent losses is narrowed. Starting in 2007, the SPY again lost about 50% in the next bear market. Since then it has recovered, but because of taking defensive actions, like using cash, all portfolios are even more substantially higher. The point is this: if your strategy avoids the bear market and participates in the bull market, then is there a case to be made that the market will ever catch up? The mathematics says it is nigh impossible. In this example right now, the market as measured by SPY would need to gain about 250% more to reach where the C-lect 2 Hybrid result is.

Please note the sharp drop in the C-lect Hybrid in 2011 and in 2012. It has since recovered. This period was marked by quick changes in Congress as they wrestled with the "fiscal cliff," sequestration, and other issues. The point is that the C-lect strategy may or may not outperform the market in any one year or even stretch of years. But because it is based on a solid foundation, like the efficient frontier concept and manager streaks and performance reversion to the mean, it should outperform over many years. Our goal is to stay with the leaders and avoid the laggards as measured by C.

Lastly, again, this is a 14-year period wherein the personal factors of age and circumstance must also be taken into account when figuring which strategy would be the best.

C-lecting in Hybrids

Figure 6.4 pulls out the C-lect 2 Hybrid and compares it only against another hybrid: the Vanguard Wellington (VWELX). Hybrid funds use a combination of stocks and bonds.

FIGURE 6.4   C-lect 2 Hybrid as Compared to the Vanguard Wellington (VWELX), Month-End Values, from 1993 Through June 2013

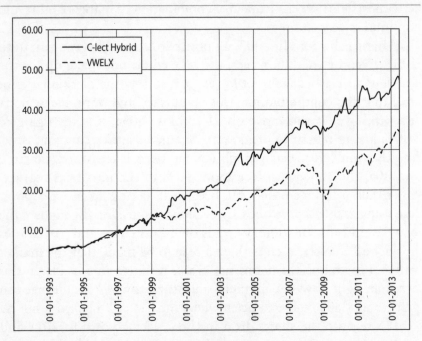

Source: Data for VWELX from www.InvestorsFastTrack.com and data for C-lect 2 Hybrid from the *No-Load Mutual Fund Selections & Timing Newsletter.*

The 35 hybrid funds chosen for inclusion in this backtesting based on C are some of the no-load funds in our newsletter database that have been around the longest. The 35 categories also included two ETFs: SPY (based on mimicking the S&P 500 before expenses) and AGG (based on mimicking the aggregate bond index before expenses). The data includes dividends and capital gains. Prices are adjusted for dividends and capital gains. The data is from Investors FastTrack. There are no fees or commissions or taxes accounted for. Funds are held for more than 90 days to avoid most brokerages' short-term redemption charges.[3] Funds considered may have been closed to new investors. Not all funds were available for the whole period.

One point before moving onto other subgroups, notwithstanding my earlier comments about trying to decide whether your manager has luck or skill. Clearly there are managers who do a superb job at what they do in certain environments. C attempts to pinpoint them. As long as their C ranking warrants it, we remain invested with them. This next section will bring out this point further.

In addition to C-lecting hybrids, we are also providing information on picking the top funds in the other styles. We rank small-cap funds, large-cap funds, value funds, international funds, and many other styles.

C-lecting in Families

We may use the same C-lect strategy on specific fund companies. For example, we use this on Fidelity Sector funds as a rotation strategy. We may also use this on T. Rowe Price funds or Vanguard funds or Guggenheim Rydex funds or any of the other hundreds of fund families. Moreover, we can use the same proven C-lect strategy on any group of funds like a 401(k).

Figure 6.5 is the result of using the C-lect strategy by buying 2 Vanguard funds that are leaders out of 35 Vanguard funds. As you can see, using a fund simply because it may be the low-cost provider

---

[3] Discount brokers like Schwab and E*TRADE require investors to hold a fund more than 90 days to avoid the brokerage short-term redemption fee. There are other brokerages with shorter or longer periods. In addition, some funds will impose a redemption fee if you sell their fund before their short-term holding period expires. For example, some funds have a 7-day or 180-day holding period.

FIGURE 6.5 A Comparison of the Vanguard 500 Index Fund Investor Class (VFINX) and C-lect 2 Vanguard from 1992 Through 2013

Source: Data for VFINX from www.InvestorsFastTrack.com and data for C-lect 2 Vanguard from the *No-Load Mutual Fund Selections & Timing Newsletter.*

does not necessarily produce superior returns. What matters most over time is staying with the leaders, while avoiding the laggards. In the following example, we used the Vanguard 500 Index Fund Investor Class with the ticker symbol VFINX as the comparison benchmark. VFINX attempts to mimic the S&P 500 Index before expenses.

Over the period shown from December 31, 1992, through June 28, 2013, the VFINX gained 438%. Using the C-lect strategy on the 35 Vanguard funds from the Vanguard family, the C-lect portfolio gained 1,242%. The strategy picked the top 2 funds out of 35 and held them for at least three months. During that period, no single Vanguard fund out of the 35 achieved a greater return. The point is, sure, go ahead and use low-cost funds, but stay with the leaders while you do so. This is what is more important. And to my earlier comment, clearly there are managers who produce superior returns. The plan is to proactively "hire" them and to "fire" them.

C-lecting ETFs

In addition to mutual funds, we also use this C strategy with ETFs. Our goal is the same—that is, to buy the risk-adjusted relative strength leaders. We apply the same parameters, although over different time periods.

Figure 6.6 shows the backtested results of picking the top 5 ETFs out of a basket of 35. Like the fund data above, these ETFs were used because they had been around the longest. Dividends are included. Commission costs to buy and sell are excluded. The C-lect 5 strategy more than tripled, while the SPY index gained about 50% over the same period.

Please note that there is again no outside timing employed with this selecting strategy. It, too, was fully and always invested. As with

FIGURE 6.6   A Comparison of the SPY and C-lect 5 ETFs from 2000 Through 2013

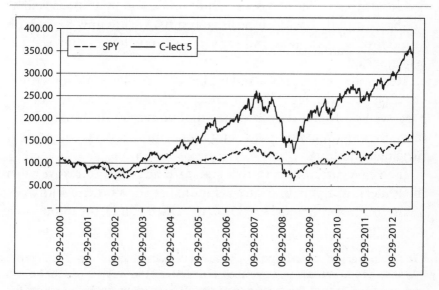

Source: Data for SPY from www.InvestorsFastTrack.com and C-lect 5 data from the *No-Load Mutual Fund Selections & Timing Newsletter.*

the mutual fund selection strategy shown above, the point is to show that picking ETFs by C was also a strategy that outperformed the index, which is SPY in this example.

Lastly, it is important to again note that all backtested results are not real time results but simulated results. There is no guarantee that future market action will be similar to or comparable with past history under which the results were generated.[4] The difference is that we are not taking a snapshot of history upon which to build an identical picture today that may or may not be viable in the future. Instead, we are proving a strategy of rotating through those managers who understand the market the best as measured by C as it changes in real time.

C-lecting in a 401(k)

It was a short step from applying C to fund styles and to fund families to the lightbulb switch when we asked, Will this work with 401(k) plans? We asked members of our *No-Load Mutual Fund Selections & Timing Newsletter* family to provide us ticker symbols of their company's 401(k) funds. We wanted to test whether this same C-lect approach would work on a smaller basket of diversified funds that included stocks, bonds, cash, and hybrids, as well as age-based funds. Based on positive results, we are now beginning to monitor 401(k) plans and rank their funds by C at www.401k Selections.com.

Remember, the typical standard industry advice is buy something based on your age, regardless of underlying values or trends. For our part, we ask, What does the fact that you're 60 or 30 have anything to do with making or losing money in the market? Nothing. Absolutely nothing.

The easy alternative to this standard advice is to evolve with the leaders using my C strategy. Figure 6.7 shows the results from doing so in 20 different 401(k) plans. Once you factor in ongoing

---

[4] This is one reason why picking stocks based on backtested results is so difficult. As soon as you actually try to employ your system, the very act of your buying or selling will change the measured results. The gap down or the gap up or the volume or whatever indicator one uses will be different in real time.

The difference between stocks and mutual funds or ETFs is that the net asset value is fixed by the market, not by your buying and selling of the fund.

contributions and perhaps a company match, clearly America will be ready to retire by avoiding the bear markets, participating in the bull markets, and evolving with the fund leaders. See Appendix D for more information about this.

The chart in Figure 6.7 shows the C-lect strategy in action over the last 20½ years from January 1, 1993, through June 30, 2013. It shows the best 401(k) plan and the worst 401(k) plan and the average of the 20 401(k) plans that we tested. It also shows the results of "buying and holding" the Vanguard Wellington Fund Investor Shares (VWELX), which is a typical balanced fund, and the S&P 500 as measured by SPY. Each of the five "positions" started at

FIGURE 6.7   A Comparison of the C-lect 401(k) Strategy, Vanguard Wellington (VWELX), and SPY from 1993 Through June 2013

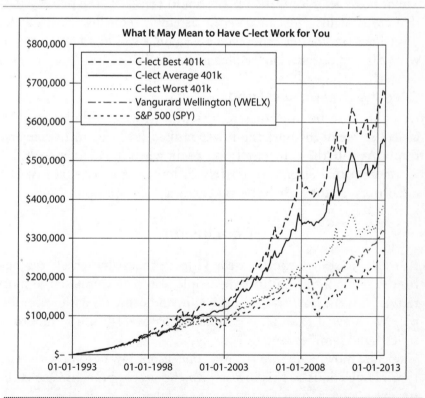

Source: Data for SPY and VWELX from www.InvestorsFastTrack.com and data for C-lect 401(k) strategy from the *No-Load Mutual Fund Selections & Timing Newsletter.*

$0.00. A contribution of $500 per month was made into each "position." You can see the end results on the chart.

There are a couple of takeaways to note. The C-lect proactive rotational allocation strategy on 401(k) plans outperformed traditional buy-and-hold investments in a balanced fund and the market as measured by SPY. There was a wide difference, however, in the ending results between the best 401(k) plan and the worst 401(k) plan. The same C-lect strategy was applied. The same $500 per month contribution was made. We assumed at least a two-month holding period before rotating out of a position. The difference is attributable to a combination of three things. One is cost—the lower the better. Two is diversification—the wider the better. Three is the fund. As you know by now, there is a wide difference in performance between funds picking their holdings from the same "stable" of stocks. To the extent possible, your 401(k) plan should consist of the better funds that are available. We can also help assemble these lower cost, wider diversified, and better fund choices. Again, I would refer you to our www.401kSelections.com site for more details.

C-lecting the Weakest Funds

In addition to buying the strongest funds, we could also use this C-lect strategy to short the lower-ranked ETFs or to use inverse funds. As you know, inverse funds profit when the market declines.

Shorting ETFs is a completely different strategy that involves other risks, and it really is beyond the scope of this book.

Conclusion

In this chapter we explored the C-lect process by which we pick funds. We took our guiding principle of trying to make the most return with the least risk, quantified it, and came up with a C number. We showed examples of ranking the overall funds, subgroup styles, fund families, and 401(k)s by C.

Before moving on into the full conclusion, I want to raise the two typical objections to this invest-with-the-best approach. One is the turnover issue, and two is the buy-high fallacy.

Many worry about generating too many short-term capital gains from the invest-with-the-best approach. What a problem, right? We try not to let the tax tail wag the investment dog. Nonetheless, turn-over for tax considerations may not be too great. It depends on the market trends. For the C-lect process, it averaged from three to four trades per year. Some trades were long-term (more than one year) and some were short-term. In a tax-deferred account like an individual retirement account (IRA) or 401(k), the question of long-term or short-term gains and losses is not a factor.

Some also question this strategy because they think it is momentum based. Thus they fear they will buy this new fund high and may eventually sell it low. Hopefully, by now, no reader still believes this fallacy. The fact is, in a bull market, nearly all funds are going up, not just the leaders, but even the laggards. If you buy any of them, you could still be "buying high," doing exactly what is feared. The key difference is that our C rank is based on a fund's risk as well as its reward. This proactive rotational allocation strategy is designed to avoid momentum that eventually stalls. The technical term for this is "reversion to the mean." Recall that the C, the Comet metaphor, recognizes this potential problem as funds, like comets, come into and out of prominence; so we instead move from leader to leader.

To be clear, there are, however, some services that do employ a momentum-only approach. We are not one of those services. Again, our approach is different in that we adjust the fund's performance numbers by its risk. And we look at relative performance; we do not look at absolute, stand-alone performance. We want the top risk-adjusted relative performing funds.

Keep in mind that we do try to sell high in terms of the stock market, in others' greed. We don't wait for the typical give-up at the bear market lows after already losing more than 40% of our money to sell. We also in turn try to buy low. No, the objection some people raise about the selecting strategy (buying a fund high) is really a misplaced market timing question. Easy to confuse the two, but it shouldn't be done.

We also make what we call "lateral trades." *Lateral trades* are sells and buys of roughly the same dollar amount from one laggard fund into a leader fund. We are just trying to make our money work harder—harder in the sense that we want the risk-adjusted relative performance leaders.

Recall that the leader fund could be leading because of some combination of better performance or lesser risk. So it is not the case that we necessarily buy high. We could be buying lower risk. In any event, a lateral trade is simply to keep the same amount of capital at work. We are taking the risk of loss when we invest, and we should try to invest with the leading funds. We've seen in the examples in this chapter that it matters.

We looked at how we manage the managers. We looked at our selecting strategies that are based on C: the risk-adjusted relative performance number. This applies both to mutual funds and ETFs. It really is a simple, intuitive approach to defining the funds with which we want to invest our hard-earned money.

In the next chapter we will explore some timing strategies.

7

Avoiding Losses and Capturing Gains

IN THE LAST CHAPTER WE LOOKED AT THE C-LECTING METHOD WE use to pick individual mutual funds and ETFs in fund styles, fund families, and 401(k) plans. In this chapter we look at timing strategies. The reason I use C as a timing or an allocating strategy is simple: we know we don't like to lose hard-earned money.

Incidentally, my not wanting to lose money has been true throughout my career. Even when I first began and had only a couple hundred bucks to rub together, I still did not like to lose. We know we don't know the future, but we are aware of history, be it measured in single years, in decades, or in centuries. To be fully invested always is to assume that everything will eventually work out, except when it doesn't, and that does happen every once in a while. We know that nearly all funds, unless they are specifically designed as inverse funds,[1] will more than likely remain fully invested during down markets and thus will lose us money. Lastly, we are age aware: we know we age, and we want to be young enough and healthy

---

[1] We covered the meaning of *inverse funds* in Chapter 5. Suffice to say here that inverse funds should profit when the market goes down.

enough to enjoy the fruits of our labors. For these reasons, we asset allocate, we manage the managers, and we use cash as an asset class.

We saw the importance of this in the previous chapters about the mathematics of investing. Study Figure 7.1 carefully. This chart idea is from Crestmont Research.

As you can see, the mathematics of investing is one reason why the first rule of investing is this: don't lose it. And the second is this: don't forget the first rule. Even a loss of 40% in a normal bear market will require a subsequent gain of 67% just to return to breakeven. If that whole loss-and-gain cycle runs a normal four to five years, it becomes a very expensive proposition to buy and hold and ignore. Compounded gains are lost. While an investor's portfolio may end up five years later in this example from where she was previously, when we account for circumstance, emotions, and age, the period

FIGURE 7.1   Getting Back to Breakeven: Why Not Losing Is More Important Than Winning

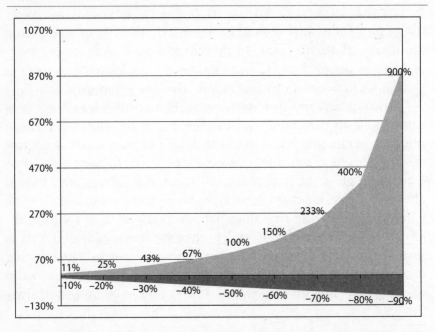

Source: Figure adapted from Crestmont Research. Copyright © 2014 www.CrestmontResearch.com.

has a far more negative impact on the investor than the financial numbers alone suggest.

Before moving on, let's look at a couple of myths about timing and propose alternatives.

In the first place, timing is not about being perfect in the buys and sells, about picking the exact tops and bottoms. No one has a crystal ball, and no one knows the future. In fact, if your advisor has a perfect-looking record, you can be sure there is something perfectly wrong. No one beats the market each and every year. It is the cumulative record of capturing most of the gains and avoiding most of the losses while investing with the fund leaders that will help you come out on top and reach your goals. So timing is not about perfection, about buying at the precise bottom and selling at the exact top. Never happens. It is, however, about capturing most of the gains and avoiding most of the losses.

That said, in the second place, it is also not about selling at the bottom in a panic of fearing further losses, nor is it about buying at the top in a worry of missing out on further gains. Reacting in fear or greed is just another way of saying that the trend is going to continue, and for no other reason I need to either get in or get out. Numerous studies have shown that, investor resolve to the contrary, reacting emotionally is in fact what many do. They buy at the top and sell at the bottom. Instead, we do try to act contrarily by selling at the top and reentering at the bottom. This is difficult to do because it will be acting differently from and going against the crowd. If you attend a cocktail party and everyone is talking about day trading and the sky's the limit and retiring in a few years at age 55, it's pretty difficult to wade in and say you're out of the market, that it is over-bought and overvalued and can go nowhere but down. Once the laughter subsides, you can mumble "Just kidding" and hope for the best. A few years later you're back at the party, and everyone is in a doom-and-gloom mood, saying, "We've seen our best days. Get out your survival gear. The country's insolvent, and the neighbors are buying farms and installing bunkers." It's also pretty difficult at that point to say you're fully invested again, that our best days lie ahead. And to not ask, "By the way, what's the address, just in case."

In the third place, timing won't prevent all losses. There are, as discussed soon, Black Swan events. These, by their very definition, are unknowable in advance. Anytime you invest, you have the risk of loss. We do, however, still try to avoid the main moves down and capture the main moves up. We might be early or late in this.

In the fourth place, there are no set rules about what timing must mean. Some use a fully invested and/or a fully on the sidelines approach to timing. Some move in increments in and out of the markets. Some use timing for a portion of their account, while keeping another part of their account fully invested at all times. Recall from the last chapter on C-lecting that there is a sense that the selecting process by C is a form of timing. The leaders in bull and bear markets are either taking full advantage of the gains or avoiding the losses. This shows up in the rankings. There are times when cash is providing the most return with the least risk. Remember that chart (Figure 2.3) that shows the efficient frontier changes over the decades.

In the fifth place, and also last but certainly not least because this point is very important: even if one completely eschews market timing, it is still of the utmost necessity to select and stay with the top C-rated funds as identified by their risk-adjusted relative performance numbers. We clearly saw this in the last chapter in a variety of applications.

It seems obvious to me that a manager's job is to make money. It is not to lose it. So why do they remain fully invested during bear markets? There are two typical industry answers and one buried answer.

The buried answer is that the fees are higher in stocks funds than in money market funds. Check out their prospectus. As examples, the average management fees from the largest money market funds average about 0.24% annually. Management fees from the largest stock funds average about 0.57%. That is about twice as much. Add in the commissions from trading the stocks and bonds in the fund of perhaps at least 0.15%[2] versus near zero in a money market fund, and one can begin to understand the financial motivation, right or wrong. Of course, there are managers who rise above the importance of receiving bonuses and paychecks, but for our purposes, we simply look at the numbers to explain this rather than try to divine their motivations.

---

[2] Greenwich Associates, March 12, 2003, presentation to House Committee on Financial Services.

The first typical industry answer is that, as we have already agreed upon, no one knows the future. Correct, and that's why investors tend to sell precisely at the bottoms because we have no assurance that stocks or bonds will rebound, let alone make a profit for us, within our lifetimes. The second typical industry answer is that market timing is impossible. To respond to this objection, we have to separate the answers of passive managers from those of active managers.

What's funny is that they all time the market every day as they time their stock and bond buys and sells. No one will ever say, "I bought an overvalued stock that I believed would decline in price." Never. Active managers always say, "I sold something because I wanted to buy something else because that alternative provided more upside potential." This is exactly what market timing admits to. If we substitute cash as a stock, its trading symbol is SAFETY, and just as we substituted cash for bonds in Chapter 3, we can easily respond to these objections. Like a manager who says, "I sold ABC Stock and bought XYZ Stock," we say, "I sold stocks and bought another stock called SAFETY [CDs or money markets or cash] because the upside of SAFETY, however negligible it may be, is far better than the potential downside risk of loss from holding the stocks I just sold." So the reality is that managers already employ a form of market timing every day as they buy and sell. They just never take the next logical step, for whatever their reason.

Passive managers, on the other hand, invest 100% of their funds' assets in order to mimic an index. Stocks may trade at 50X earnings with a recession heading their way, but they are fully invested and will remain so. Market timing is also a four-letter word to them. The question is, Did they become passive managers because of market timing per se or because of the track record of active managers? The answer is that they made this decision to be passive managers not necessarily because of failed market timing but because of failed active management. I say "failed," but as already mentioned, the reality is that the investment field is near perfectly leveled, and opportunities have been arbitraged away. So it's a comparison of apples to oranges to contrast passive management with asset allocation (market timing). Who wants to say, "I lost 40% when the market lost 40%"? Passive managers do because most active managers, according to historic averages, will be saying that they lost more than 40%.

To be honest, there is no doubt that market timing is difficult, just as is stock picking or fund picking. Difficulty, however, is not a sufficient reason to give up on it. The reason not to give up is related to mathematics primarily, but also to the human part, such as sleeping well at night. Thus, recognizing personal age and circumstance also enters the equation. If a portfolio loses 50%, it must gain 100% just to return to breakeven. Add in the time factor for that sequence of loss and gain, and the result is typically unacceptable to most people in their fifties, sixties, seventies, and eighties. Frankly, the work I have looked at on secular bear markets practically guarantees that if you can come close to successfully timing the ins and outs, you will end up far better off than the buy-and-hold investors. The mathematics simply nearly guarantees it. The fully invested strategy can never regain those losses compared to a portfolio that missed them and got back in later.

The astute reader may have noticed that I substitute the phrase *asset allocation* for *market timing*. The reason is simple: *asset allocation* is a nod to the reality of market declines, to the unknown future. It is a recognition that the efficient frontier shifts over the decades. We assume the market can lose 50%, and it does from time to time, so how do we avoid those losses? The standard response is to diversify. Use bonds, real estate, hedge funds, or other things to offset the inevitable. In all of this, the implicit acknowledgment is that market timing per se is impossible, but we will do a form of it anyway. We will time the market by simply not participating in it. However, this standardized approach may not be very effective for three reasons. As we saw earlier, a passive 60/40 asset allocation is not the true and accurate efficient frontier over time frames shorter than 100 years. While it limits your loss to just the portion in stocks on the downside, it also limits your gains of the same stocks on the upside. Inefficient, ineffective, and insufficient are the problems. What's the solution? With those caveats, admissions, and knowledge, let's move on and explore the world of market timing.

The computer has been one of the great equalizers of society in terms of providing everyone access to most of the same information. Remember that knowledge is power.[3] Practically anyone from the

---

[3] Knowledge itself is power, wrote Sir Francis Bacon.

poorest to the richest person may own a computer. If you don't have one, you may borrow one at your local library. With one, everyone may log on to the Internet and find troves of informational treasure with which to assess historic investment ideas and test new ideas. The problem, of course, is to separate the useful from the useless information. As we begin this chapter, I will briefly mention some issues to be aware of, and then we will delve into some tools that I use.

I have already pointed out two issues to watch out for. The first was the amount of time required to compile a track record in order to separate the managers with skill from those with luck; it takes roughly 15 years. The second was to watch out for lists of stock recommendations without some anchoring device like a portfolio with a finite amount of money within which the recommendations operate. Without a set amount of capital, there is simply no way to truly calculate actual returns.

A third issue to watch out for is success. Investing really is a humbling experience. Just when you think you or your favorite system or guru or advisor has it all figured out, things change. This is why the C-lect method shown in the previous chapter is so attractive. History is littered with once great managers and approaches. C-lect takes this into account with a rotational allocation strategy. Now let's take this a step further and look at a couple of strategies that were once great but don't really work well any longer. I already mentioned the CalPERS effect. Here is another.

The Dogs of the Dow[4] is a perfect example of these issues. One, it had been around for more than 15 years; its success appeared to result from skill, not luck. It made intuitive sense to buy out-of-favor blue chips. Two, it was conducted within a set portfolio so that actual allocations could be made between various stocks. The returns were real. It was skill, real, and so it was successful. All of these factors then led to its eventual demise. At the point when its popularity prevailed, the strategy began to fail. Investors began to anticipate the buyers and so positioned themselves ahead of time. The trouble was those were the buyers; they had already bought. So

---

[4] The Dogs of the Dow strategy is buying the 10 of the 30 companies in the Dow Jones Industrial Average stocks each year that have the highest yields. You hold them for a year and then rebalance. It is essentially a value approach.

the strategy began to fail as the arbitragers entered the picture. The skill, if there was any, was arbitraged away. All sorts of permutations, like buy the worst except for the worst of the worst, were suggested. It was easy with the computer to backtest a variety of strategies built on the original premise. Watch out for optimizations; after all, there's always something that has to work the best over a certain time period, as we saw with the standard 60% stock and 40% bond allocation.

Unfortunately for investors, there are numerous examples from which to pick that show an advisor or system whose returns, as it turned out, were based on luck rather than skill.

This third issue, one of success, is why I mentioned "some" tools—that is, "some" information will be discussed, rather than all. It won't do any of us any good in our investing lives to reveal every timing tool we use or how we assemble them. Some of the market timing tools I use are proprietary. They are simply not in the public domain and for good reason. We want them to continue to work well past my demise.

With these things in mind, let's look at some market timing tools.

Moving Averages

One well-known tool that is popular is moving averages. We already saw one example of this in Chapter 1. Moving averages smooth, or as the name describes, average, the preceding prices over some number of days, weeks, or months. For example, a 10-day moving average averages the current and previous 9 days' prices together to get the moving average price. Buy and sell signals ensue when today's prices close above or below the moving average. Figure 7.2 is an example of trading SPY (the S&P 500 ETF) shares using a simple moving average versus buying and holding SPY shares.

As you can see, the moving average did what it was designed to do. It captured the main moves up and avoided the main moves down. Because of the mathematics of losing, wherein if you lose 50%, you must gain 100% just to return to breakeven, timing outperforms buy and hold over this period. In fact, if one thinks there will never be any more bear markets and the timing will continue successfully, then the spread between the two series will do nothing

FIGURE 7.2 Trading SPY Shares Using a Simple Moving Average Versus Buying and Holding SPY Shares

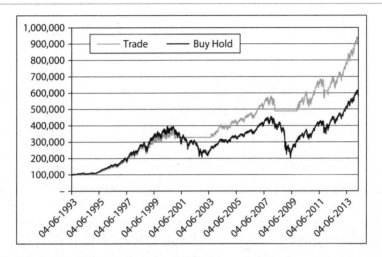

Source: Data for Buy Hold is SPY from State Street Global Markets and data for Trade is from the *No-Load Mutual Fund Selections & Timing Newsletter.*

but continue to widen. With these parameters, a buy-and-hold approach will never overtake the timing strategy, unless the market enters a prolonged period of years of whipsaws, which I speak about next.

Using moving averages is a very simple approach to timing, but it can also be very effective if the moving average calculations are designed properly. Years ago when I first looked at moving averages, I saw two big problems. The first problem was the frequent huge lag between the actual top or bottom and when the price closed above or below the moving average to signal a buy or sell. There was a large give-up of potential profit before an actual signal ensued. The second problem was a good-news-and-bad-news situation. The good news was that moving averages kept you in for much of the move up and got you out for much of the move down. The bad news was there might be whipsaws when there was no trend. Whipsaws are quick (within days or weeks or months) moves to get back in or sell back out from the previous signal, as shown in Figure 7.3.

FIGURE 7.3   Whipsaw

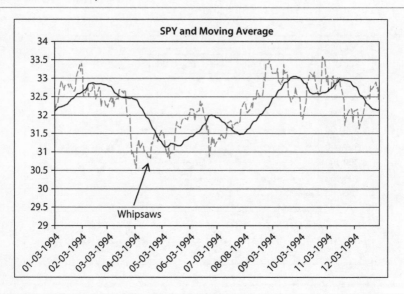

Source: Data from State Street Global Markets.

Before moving on, I want to mention that more recently I have reassessed moving averages, and I've decided that the whipsaw issue really isn't the problem we have been led to think it is. Whipsaws seem to be part of the past advertising messages that have said it was too costly, too time-consuming, too restrictive, too taxable, and too frequent for it to make sense to use moving averages. Today, of course, these issues really don't affect us. We can make trades for $10 or $5 and in some cases, for free. We can use tax-deferred accounts like 401(k)s. While some fund companies still do frown on very active buying and selling of their funds, others do not.

So the old advertising message was that moving averages weren't really too useful because whipsaws were bad and therefore investors should reject them in particular and market timing in general. Hang on during the losses because there is nothing you can do about them except diversify, which really does not address the issue. Instead, the new message I propose is to ask whether whipsaws may be considered positive. You might ask, "Positive in what way?"

To answer that question, we have to look at the purpose of using moving averages. As I've mentioned, I had the wrong ideas about them. In reality, they are not designed to get you in at the top or out at the bottom. What they are designed to do is to have you capture most of the main move up and avoid most of the main move down. This is shown in Figure 7.2.

You see, when the market starts down, no one knows how far down it will go. That is the truth. So we just sell. Likewise, when the market starts back up, no one knows how far the advance will carry. We just buy. Of course, it's not quite that simple, but that is the principle. No one knows the future. When we put age and circumstance into the equation, the decision to switch from risk to no risk is a no-brainer.

With that principle firmly in mind, let's look again at whipsaws. If the moving average is meaningful at all, it will have you on the right side of the main moves. The moving average is doing its job. What about whipsaws? For example, if you were invested for 12 months, and then you got a sell signal for a month, and then another buy signal was triggered, what was the point of selling? It is at least very irritating.

We simply don't know the future. The moving average is designed to avoid disaster and capture most of the up move, as we saw in Figure 7.2. The whipsaw is simply a reaction to this reality of not knowing. What should happen, however, is that in the well-designed moving average with the inevitable whipsaw, the sell and subsequent buy should be nonetheless fairly close to each other in price. It is the same on the other side: in the buy and subsequent sell, if it is a whipsaw, the prices should be close to each other. If they are, then the moving average has done its job.

Lastly, with moving averages, I want us to employ some of the aforementioned factors in our decision making. One is the human condition, and two is the human time. This should be interesting and useful.

On the bottom of a chart, rather than insert the date—let's say it was from 1999 through 2004—let's insert your age. Of course this will vary from investor to investor, but I want to bring the point home as best I can. So in 1999, let's assume the reader is 55. In the year 2004, she is now 60.

The next things to notice about this time frame are the human factors that arose like recessions, job losses, bills to pay—these events of life that are real and that tug at us as the market rises and falls. It is easy to hope our emotions are above it, and maybe they are, but the reality is that people do lose their jobs. They do have to use their investment account or retirement account to help meet obligations. Make it personal. Should we buy and ignore, or should we take a proactive approach?

In addition to these two factors is the third one mentioned earlier. We simply do not know the future.

Incidentally, investors modify moving averages in a couple of ways. They may weight them. They may use exponential moving averages. Others may also use some combination of moving averages, like a 50-day and 200-day crossover that is known in the press as the *death cross*. It really doesn't mean much because it is too popular. All of these things may be backtested to see which does the best on the assumption that it will continue to do the best. As already mentioned, however, once something becomes so well ingrained, so well known, it loses its forecasting abilities because people begin to anticipate the signals and act prior to their triggers. It is arbitraged away. Again, it's a tough business.

I should also reiterate at this point that there is no magical indicator that works all the time. As we saw in Chapter 2, stocks move in secular trends. The moving average, among other things we look at, may be used to identify them.

Just as we wouldn't try to saw some wood with a hammer, neither do we ask a moving average to pick a market's exact top or bottom. The moving average's job is to capture the main trend.

If we want to try to pick exact tops and bottoms, then we will need a different tool.

Divergences

Divergences are in a different class of indicators from moving averages. Divergences are designed to get you in closer to the bottom and out closer to the top.

A divergence is when one index diverges from the behavior of another index. If one index makes a new high, then the other indexes should too. If they don't, this could be a sell signal. Likewise, when an index hits a new low, if it is unaccompanied by other indexes, then this is a potential buy signal.

The Dow Theory is a respected, well-known investment approach that utilizes divergences between the Dow Industrials and Transports to determine the market's main trend up and down. For example, if the Dow Industrials moves to a new high but the Transportation Index does not, then that would signal a negative divergence. This means the stock market is vulnerable to a correction at best and a new bear market with a decline of at least 20% at worst.

The trouble with divergences is that they may continue in force for long periods of time before the market moves in the direction it is "supposed" to.

So, like moving averages, divergences may or may not be useful as standalone indicators. More information may be required before making a buy or sell decision.

Incidentally, it was an analysis of the Dow Theory record back in the 1940s that helped lay the groundwork for the random walk and rational investor theories—that is, the efficient market hypothesis. The author of the first study decided market timing didn't work. Subsequent analysis of the theory by others suggests otherwise. It is interesting to note that had the initial author concluded differently, market timing may have become more fashionable.

Sentiment

Like moving averages and divergences, investor sentiment is also in a separate class of technical indicators called *contrary indicators*. This indicator moves opposite to the market; it is contrary. If investors are too bullish, this indicator is bearish. People who are bullish are already invested. They expect the market to move higher, and thus they've bought; they are bullish. If this is true, who is left to buy? When this indicator reaches extreme levels, the market then rolls over and declines.

Likewise at market bottoms when investors are bearish. They have already sold. They are fearful, waiting for further declines. But this may be a positive sign. Who is left to sell? Perhaps all of the bad news is discounted and has already been acted upon. As a contrary indicator, this would be bullish.

Perhaps the best-known indicator in this area is provided by Investors Intelligence. Each week they poll advisors as to whether they are bullish or bearish or neutral on stocks. Action may be taken contrarily. Figure 7.4 shows the history of one of their indicators, the percentage of advisors who are bullish.

There are a couple of takeaways from this indicator. Clearly, advisors are just as prone to emotion as institutions and individuals. They grow bearish at the bottoms and bullish at the tops. As you can see in the figure, whenever the percentage of bulls drops below 40%, it is signaling that the worst may be over. But in major bear markets, as occurred in 2008, that number can shrink further before the final bottom is found.

Lastly, students of market history are well aware of the magazine cover indicator as a contrary sentiment indicator. Equities are dead, screamed *Newsweek* back in the 1970s around the lows.

The point with sentiment is to read the news as the media outlets react to the market such that you react accordingly, contrarily. If the market is up and the headlines keep talking doom and gloom, it is a

FIGURE 7.4   Investors Intelligence Bulls from 2008 Through 2014

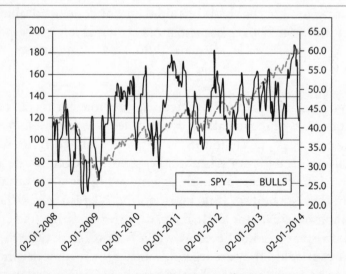

Source: Data for SPY from State Street Global Markets and Bull data from Investors Intelligence. Copyright © InvestorsIntelligence.com.

good sign that the market will continue to rally. On the other hand, if the market has been going down and the headlines keep screaming fear and panic, then from a contrary point of view, you know the market may be nearing its lows.

As mentioned in the secular stock market review in Chapter 2, right now, three prominent well-known advisors declared the death of equities in 2012 and 2013. This was surely a contrarily very positive long-term sign for stocks that heralded the ongoing rally. When those same or other prominent advisors pound the table that equities are the only place to be and that stock market timing is dead, then you know the top may be near.

Overbought or Oversold

This indicator is normally measured by the rates at which prices are changing. I use these indicators in two ways. The first way is as an overbought indicator within the confines of a bubble-defining move. The second way is as an oversold indicator within the confines of bear market movements. As you might discern, overbought indicators do not work very well in identifying cyclical bull market tops.

It is at this point that we need to be aware that markets may move from overbought to more overbought and vice versa. Take a look at Figure 7.5, which shows a bubble top in gold bullion as priced at its London morning fix (GOLD AM). It is characterized by the fact that the rate of price increases is itself increasing. This trend leads to the eventual bubble burst. See the fanlike sequence of lines drawn from the lows in 1976 to the spike higher in 1980. It is an exponential increase; and it is an unsustainable rise.

This same principle can be found across various investments and throughout time. Just name it:

+ Tulips
+ Farmland
+ Gold
+ Housing
+ Stocks
+ Bitcoins
+ Commodities

FIGURE 7.5 An Example of a Market Moving from Overbought to More Overbought

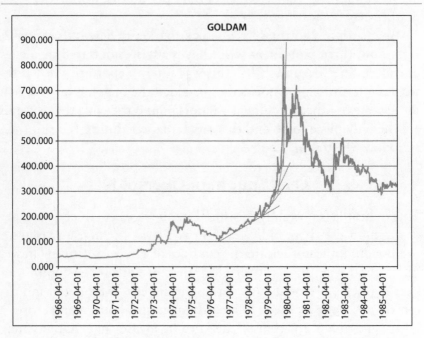

Source: Data from St. Louis Federal Reserve (FRED) Gold Fixing Price, 10:30 a.m. London time in London Bullion Market, based in U.S. dollars.

As you can see, this information is useful to keep you out of harm's way. This is a measure showing the rate of change increasing at a greater rate of change. It is a sign of a blowoff, a bubble top, a terminal move. It does not matter if it is measuring the price of soup or nuts or stocks. It is a sign to get out because when the bubble bursts, the downside plunge will be fast and furious. Hell has no fury than the greater fool stuck holding the bag.[5]

Incidentally, after the bubble bursts, the asset price will nearly always eventually fall to where it was prior to when the "silliness" began, to where the rate of change began to climb from normal to accelerated.

While overbought indicators are not too useful, except for the occasional blowoff top, oversold indicators work fairly well. This is

---

[5] To paraphrase William Congreve (1670 to 1729).

because exhaustion sets in more cleanly, faster, and more acutely than the overbought condition.

Fundamentals

Fundamentals are measurements that relate to the valuation of companies and the economy. These values are then related to the price of the company's stock. The comparison between the two will tell us whether stocks are expensive or cheap. As we saw in Chapter 2, this valuation will vary widely over the decades. The market is anything but rational. These relationships yield information like price-to-earnings ratios, book values, and dividend yields. For the economy, it is information like the gross domestic product, help-wanted index, and manufacturing shipments and inventories. These things help us determine whether the market as a whole is cheap or expensive or somewhere in between. They are not really precise timing indicators. The market can be expensive longer than you think. It can also move cheaper than you think. As Lord John Maynard Keynes once said, the market may stay irrational longer than you can remain solvent. For example, take a look at Figure 7.6.

This chart shows the nominal (not inflation-adjusted) S&P 500 Index and its P/E ratio. As you can see, whenever the P/E ratio is below 10, it is generally a low-risk time to accumulate stocks. In addition, notice how the P/E ratio stays below 12 for an extended period of time when the market is rallying, leaving the secular bear market as it moves into the next secular bull market. This is attributable to the E (earnings part of the ratio). The price is going up, but the earnings are growing fast enough to keep the ratio at a fairly low valuation. This is what was evident at the three previous secular bear market bottoms, but this is what was missing in the current rally from 2009.

Conversely, when the P/E ratio is above 20, the market is in a higher-risk zone.

These fundamental ideas may also be applied to the market as a whole. As we've seen, the cyclically adjusted price-to-earnings (CAPE) ratio is one way to measure whether the stock market as a whole is cheap or expensive.

At best, fundamentals are a way to help us determine where we are in the secular cycle. See Chapters 2 and 3 for more details.

FIGURE 7.6 The Nominal (Not Inflation-Adjusted) S&P 500 Index and Its P/E Ratio from 1871 Through 2012

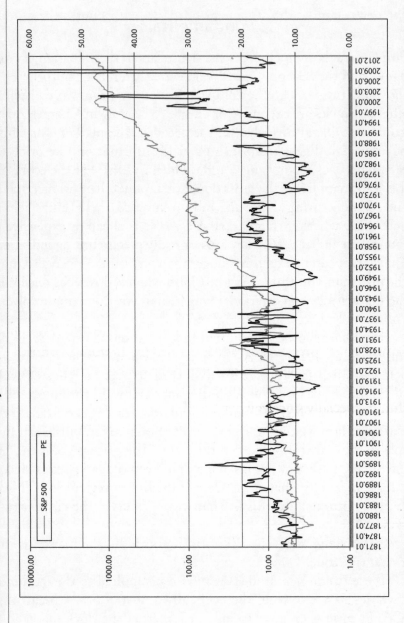

Source: Data from Standard & Poor's and Robert Shiller's website at http://irrationalexuberance.com.

News

As a last tool in the investment arsenal, I want to speak more about the news. Unlike the aforementioned tools, this indicator is much harder to quantify, codify, track, and ascertain as to its bullish or bearish impact. Nonetheless, it is useful for what it is.

One guiding principle in understanding the news and its market impact is that the market does not like uncertainty. Uncertainty is a cause of sell-offs. The resolution of that uncertainty is a cause for rallies.

Not all the news is bad of course, and it doesn't have to be used to trigger sell-offs. Some of it is positive for stocks, to be used as buying information, especially if there was a problem that had sent the market into a bear market and that problem gets resolved. Once the news turns, stocks should too. One thing to monitor for this resolution: when the bad news comes out, watch and see whether the market continues to move lower, or was the news discounted? It would be discounted if the news that came out was bad and the market did not decline further. The second thing to watch is when the law changes as regards a particular problem. For example, this happened in 2009 when the accounting guidelines changed that said banks could use their judgment to mark asset values to the market. This was a huge positive for the market. In fact, it defined the bottom and turn.

Of course, some news interpretations are born from 30 years of practicing the art of investing. Experience has to count for something, especially since you can't really quantify other people's behavior. My goal, however, is to help the reader make investing more of a science by quantifying these things. For example, asking whether the stock or bond or index price is above or below the moving average will yield a simple answer. This can be followed as a trading strategy. Quantifying is not as easy with reading the headline news. But if you want to get in and out closer to tops and bottoms, try monitoring the news and the market's reactions to the news, rather than watching only moving averages. Watch for tax law or accounting changes, as well as congressional budget deals that will help or hamper certain industries and the stocks therein.

The news story, as noted in Chapter 1 and above, about the House Financial Services Committee's pressuring the Financial Accounting Standards Board (FASB) to ease their fair value rules in

March 2009 is a good example of an indicator that marked the bottom of the bear market. For those who could artfully read the times, the panicky terror of potential nationwide bank and brokerage and insurance company insolvency was over.

Another point with reading the news is that the market discounts the future. Once it is done discounting the known future, the news, it stops moving in the direction it was moving in before the information was distributed or known. The well-known phrase "Buy on the rumor and sell on the news" comes to mind. But again, this is an art, not a science.

Black Swans

One other thing about investing that we need to be aware of is the fact of exogenous risks. These by their very definition are unknowable and unforeseeable. These are Black Swan events. This is one good reason to diversify, to have your overall financial house in shape, because they do happen.

Black Swan events were named after something that actually took place from the Dutch explorations in the 1700s. True story. Everyone, at that time, knew that all swans were white. A Dutch explorer in Australia, however, discovered a black swan. Imagine the uproar, the fallout: the feather markets, the hat markets, and the fashion industries were turned upside down. Imagine you were a merchant who had just stocked your shelves with white-feathered hats for the holidays. Oops. There fly away that year's sales.

So Black Swan events are unanticipated, unknowable events that rarely happen. When they do happen, the consequences are swift, sharp, and typically negative.

To be clear, Black Swan diversification is not diversification to mitigate losses from bear markets. We try to anticipate bear markets as they develop. We use cash as an asset class. We rotate with the fund leaders. We may try this by looking at the moving averages, for example. We can search the news for fundamental changes. Black Swan events, however, are random events that range from pleasant, like a new discovery, to disaster, like terrorist attacks. The totally unexpected happens, and fear causes the market to drop. There is nothing you can do about it. Once it is past, however, the market typically recovers and often moves higher than where it was prior to the disaster. So, on a personal level, to be prepared for Black Swans is to have things like debt under control and a savings account, such that bank or market shutdowns are manageable. Buffett would say to buy a stock as if the market will close for five years. Templeton's holding period would be about five years. Black Swan events happen, but they shouldn't fundamentally shake our analysis.

Other

There are all sorts of other strategies that investors use to try to allocate between stocks, bonds, and cash. The Internet, maybe even your mailbox, is filled with opinions and supposed ground-floor opportunities. I would caution that they all will sound very appealing, very rational, and usually, very of the moment. "Of the moment" is to say what is hot now. They want action immediately. For example, when solar energy was new and exciting, various proponents sprang up extolling its benefits as a long-term solution to the energy crisis. The industry went up. IPOs came out. Newsletter editors were saying, "I found XYZ Solar that went from $1 to $100 in two days, and here's another one just like it." Save your money. Save yourself some grief. As we saw, we know it takes at least 10 years and really more than 15 in order to qualify as a skillful investor, rather than a lucky one. Gray hair is not for nothing in this industry.

History is littered with what seemed like accurate and reasonable investment ideas and strategies. Fibonacci numbers and wave counts became the rage for a while based on a supposed prediction of the 1987 crash before it happened. Subsequent to that, based on the same "analysis," there were predictions for the market to return to 600. It was all luck. Cycle investing according to the sun, stars, and moon was the rage for a while, until the eclipse. It too cycled out of favor as investors lost. Even value or fundamentals lost favor as the market kept soaring in 2000.

The Nifty Nineties of index investing went sideways during the "lost decade" of the 2000s. Ten years is too long to take the risk of investing without any of the reward.

I get this type of information all the time because I'm in the business. I simply throw it where it belongs without paying too much attention.

So, as one way of approaching alternative strategies—this "other" information category—can we ignore all of the systems and advisors that have not yet passed their fifteenth birthday? Even if they have a good one- or two-year record, the question is always, How will they do in the next bull or bear market?

Lastly, let me also mention, as a caveat, the entertainment factor, for want of a better description, we find among various advisors and Internet sites. The mundane and plodding are often overlooked for the bright and shiny.[6] Some companies are very good at repackaging what is common and selling it as useful. It is akin to building a record on advertising, rather than on quantified results. But there are some websites that provide useful information very well. Please don't confuse the fact that they are entertaining or that their political or religious views might match yours or that their spin and polish is impressive with a promise of your investment success. Like everyone else, we suggest comparing their results against their peers and determining from the numbers the best places to invest. As a matter of fact, this is what we do. Rank the managers with the recognition that things change; then buy the leaders and avoid the laggards. Repeat the next week or month or quarter or year.

Timing Results

All of these timing strategies are alternatives to the industry advice as to how to avoid the risk of loss, which is to use a fixed diversification. From a portfolio point of view, diversification reduces loss simply because you have less invested in an asset. This is also to say that you will have less invested in the asset when it is increasing in value. There is always some trade-off using the standard industry diversification strategy.

On the loss side, for example, if your portfolio is invested 100% in stocks and stocks are down 30%, your portfolio drops 30% (assuming all other things are equal). If your portfolio is 60% in stocks and 40% in bonds and stocks drop 30%, while bonds are unchanged, your portfolio declines 18%. On a relative performance

---

[6] One of my summer jaunts during my college years was to explore for gold. The experienced miners said, "Don't fall for the shiny stuff; that is fool's gold. The real gold is dull." Even with that nugget of advice, I failed to find any. Probably just as well.

portfolio basis, you have reduced your loss, but you haven't reduced your risk per se. Your portion at risk remained at a loss of 30%.

On the gain side, for example, when the market jumps 30% and your portfolio is 100% in stocks, you gain 30%. If you are 60% in stocks and 40% in bonds, your portfolio gains 18% (30% of 60%).

In these examples, diversification did not prevent either the absolute or relative loss, and it did cap your gains.

As I have suggested throughout this book, to actually manage the risk, we must be proactive by actively allocating the portfolio between stocks and bonds and cash according to a viable selecting or allocating strategy. Again, the industry advice is to consider only stocks and bonds. For our purposes, as mentioned earlier, we simply need to think of cash differently and as an actual company or bond.

Thus, for bonds, as shown in the following table, we compare cash by looking at it as simply an ultra-short-term bond. Cash "matures" daily, even second to second, without risk of default.[7] For stocks, in comparison, it is the ultimate no-risk "company" with a pristine balance sheet consisting of the asset value of the dollar and no liability and a "cash flow" of the interest earned on the dollar:

Cash and Bond Duration

Daily	Monthly	Yearly	Up to 5 Years	Beyond 5 Years
Cash	CD	T-bill	Note	Bond

The table below compares cash to stock (company) P/E ratios. Rather than comparing cash to a single company in this example, I will compare it to the market on a value basis—that is, CAPE in this example—but more will be shown shortly:

Lowest Risk	Low	Medium	Greater	Very High
Cash	P/E <5	P/E >5 <15	P/E >15	P/E >20

---

[7] Given congressional histrionics in 2011 and 2012, like the rating companies, I also wonder whether America's cash (its T-bill supply) will remain truly riskless forever, at least on an absolute basis. On a relative basis, if Congress "defaulted" on our debt, I suspect one would still want cash with the assumption that the politicians would eventually figure it out.

One thing to notice in those two tables and throughout the rest of this chapter is that one's age or circumstance is not apparent in the equations. It is far beyond the scope of this book to delve into personal finance, but my assumption here is that readers will have their personal debt and job income under control. In other words, if you don't have a savings account, if you can't pay your bills on time, or if your job is not secure, then investing in stocks may not be for you. Likewise, with the age factor. There have been times when the market will decline further, even though it was "cheap" to begin with. We have to, and do, keep these things in mind. So having a cash alternative at any age is good advice. The difference here is that our cash allocation will wax and wane depending on the market's value and other factors.

With that in mind, the question is whether timing or asset allocation between stocks and bonds and cash can successfully be done or not. But even if it can't be done, make no mistake that diversification hasn't truly solved the problem of loss either.

Stop Losses

No one or strategy is perfect. Everyone makes mistakes. And there are the rare insiders who commit fraud, who cook the books. It happens to large and small. The market does its best to humble you. We do our best, but the market is constantly digesting new information. So we need a way to deal with the unknown. Some don't acknowledge these things in their buy-and-hold pitch. We, however, may use stop losses.

Stop losses are designed to get you out of the market with a predetermined level of loss. Some use 10%, others use 5%, others something else. This again is active management of your portfolio.

Combinations

In the end, the best approach to timing is to agree that there is no single accurate indicator. Rather, a combination of factors should be employed, along with the stop loss. For example, we could use trend factors and valuation factors to come up with these results. We could add in sentiment measures. We could also mix in other technical factors. Figure 7.7 shows one testing strategy to pick the areas

FIGURE 7.7 A Testing Strategy for Picking the Areas of Market Tops

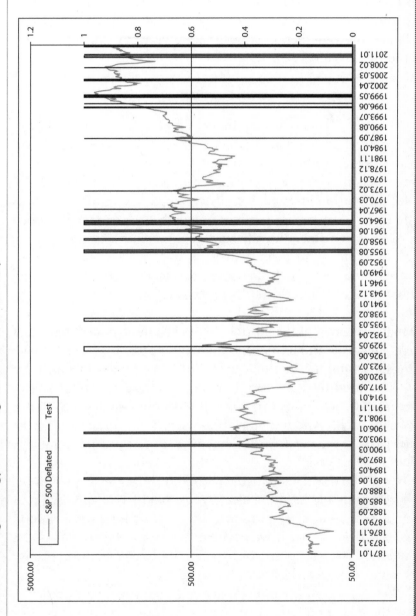

Source: S&P data from Standard & Poor's and Robert Shiller's website at http://irrationalexuberance.com and Test data from the *No-Load Mutual Fund Selections & Timing Newsletter.*

of market tops. The strategy is a combination of technical (rate-of-change) and fundamental factors (CAPE). As you can see, the latest reading (October 2013) is one of caution. But as you can also see, the period leading to the bubble top in 2000 was one of caution, yet stocks continued higher for about another year. It was the same way prior to the crash in 1929.

Conclusion

Let's be honest. There is no easy answer as to how to deal with the certainty of stock and bond market losses. The industry recommendation to diversify isn't the final answer; it doesn't even approximate the best answer. Yes, diversification may limit the loss of the whole portfolio, but for the portion invested, it really accomplishes nothing. If stocks are down 50%, your stock portfolio will probably be down that much too. At the same time, diversification caps the upside to your portfolio. If stocks are up 50%, it is only your stock portion that will probably also climb about 50%. Standard financial industry diversification is simply moving from the 50-foot seesaw to the 20-foot seesaw. The swings are less, but it's still on the same playground of up and down. The highs and lows of the portfolio should be more muted, but losses remain inevitable and unmanaged and uncapped.

So something besides diversification must be used to mitigate risk. In a bond bear market, I advocate selling the longer-term, lower-rated bond and buying the shortest-term bond, which is also known as "cash." And in a stock bear market, I advocate selling the riskier parts of the portfolio and buying the most pristine company, which is called "cash."

Even if the timing isn't perfect, and no timing strategy will be, the portfolio should be ahead of a buy-and-hold/forget approach over a complete market cycle of four to five years. Moreover, it should be even further ahead if we measure it against the secular cycles of decades. I suggest continuous portfolio management using active asset allocation between stocks, bonds, and cash.

When we add in the human factors of age and circumstance, it makes the solution of using cash as an asset class even more clear as a necessary choice to achieve successful portfolio management. We know things change over the decades and centuries. The mistake to avoid is thinking that since we didn't experience the Great Depression and since we see the market higher today than it was in the past, then we should always be fully invested in equities in that portion of our portfolio.

So we know that the market has a thing called "value" around which it moves from undervalued to overvalued. We know it moves in trends. We know it moves through secular cycles. We also know we need to stay with the ever-evolving fund leaders and avoid the fund laggards.

We also know that what works today will change in the future. Sharp-eyed readers will note that the old 200-day moving average does not work as well as the 300-day moving average. Things change. It is the fool who does not stay humble or rests on his laurels.

Lastly, I would again mention that the C-lect approach may be used as a "timing tool." As part of the pool of funds to rank, we may use a money market fund. Like with any stock or bond fund that may be ranked by C, so, too, can the money market fund be ranked against the market and adjusted for its risk. When stocks are declining, to get the most return for the risk taken, the money market funds bubble to the top in performance by C.

In the end, a market approach that successfully navigates in both bull and bear markets will do three things:

◆ Capture the main up move
◆ Avoid the main down move
◆ Employ stop losses both to buy in and to sell out for when things go wrong

We will assemble all of this information about timing and selecting in the final chapter.

8

Some Assembly Required

TO PARAPHRASE LORD JOHN MAYNARD KEYNES, WHEN THE FACTS are brought forth, I change my mind; what do you do? It is a succinct saying to prod us to change our former ways when we have new information. There was no error or mistake that we made in the past about which we have to now force ourselves to find a justification to maintain. Rather, we know it was a judgment call based on the best available information we had at the time. Today, however, I hope this book has provided you with fresh information upon which to base new decisions for your financial future. The fault is not in the past. But there would be fault now in continuing to operate on the old, outdated, incorrect assumptions. So let's review three key pieces of new information and some investing factors, and then we'll drill into the specifics of assembling a portfolio that is based on C-lecting the top risk-adjusted relative performance fund leaders over time.

One of the key pieces of new information we have learned is that the efficient frontier (EF), far from being fixed, actually changes and shifts over the decades. The outdated 60% equity and 40% bond fixed allocation was essentially based on the world of the 1950s. It was supposed to be a snapshot, not a never-changing movie. Waving the snapshot in the wind does not change anything. The fact is that the cusp of the frontier where return is maximized and risk is minimized shifts and changes.

With that in mind, the second key we found was that buy and hold simply cannot and does not keep your portfolio on the edge of the efficient frontier. It is impossible because buy and hold is fixed, but as we saw, the efficient frontier changes. The industry then pulls out a 100-year chart and says, "Don't worry about it. See. Even if you bought at the top in 1929, you'd be ahead 50 years later." This is advice divorced from the reality of personal age and circumstance. It does not come close to our goal of maximizing return and minimizing risk. Most bear markets result from economic dislocations. Recessions are common, and you have no control over them. Nor do you have much control over losing your job. But you do have some control over keeping or losing your wealth.

A third new key piece of information is that the standard industry advice regarding ways to diversify may not be the best for you. For example, the diversification idea of age-based investing or target-date fund investing simply has nothing to do with the stock or bond market results. At their 10:00 appointment, they might advise the person who is 30 years old to buy 100% stocks because that is the place to be. At their 11:00 appointment, they might advise the person who is 60 to lighten up on stocks because that is the thing to do. The reality is that your age does not matter to your investing success. Your age simply has nothing to do with market valuation.

What do we propose to do about this outdated advice on which so many rely? We suggest three things.

One, to reach this goal of staying on the cusp of the leading edge of the efficient frontier where return is maximized and risk is minimized, we have to employ a strategy of measuring it and implementing it in real time on an ongoing basis. By its very definition, the tool we have been using for some 20 years, the C-lect strategy, does this. C is the risk-adjusted relative performance number. Each month we rank the fund database as a whole, the fund styles (hybrid, small-cap, international, and so on), the families (Fidelity, Vanguard, T. Rowe Price, American Century, Janus, and more), and the 401(k) plans (just like yours) to arrive at the current leaders. And then each month, after meeting the required minimum holding period, we may rotate through the leaders. We sell the laggards and buy the leaders, as the efficient frontier wanes and waxes through secular and cyclical bull and bear markets in equity and fixed-income investments.

Two, along this line, we have learned that the markets move in secular cycles whose very natures also shift and change. There are discernible differences between the two. Secular bear markets are different. Secular bull markets are different. Knowing which type of market we are in will help in the investment decision-making process.

Three, another key piece of information we have learned is that not all funds are created equal. The manager matters. Each and every year there is a huge spread between the leaders and the laggards. How do we pick them? Past performance alone is not the sole criterion. Manager name alone is not the sole criterion. Cost alone is not the sole criterion. We saw an example of employing the C-lect strategy on the supposed low-cost provider Vanguard. What improves performance the most over the long term is C: striving to stay on the cusp of the efficient frontier where return is maximized and risk is minimized over time. To be clear, there are times to use passive managers, as well as active managers. However, the manager's name or affiliations, like his past results, do not guarantee future results. To be sure, some managers will have spectacular runs; other managers will bring up the rear. And there will be many others who fit in between. Furthermore, they shift and change over the years. We have created a means of identifying the leaders and investing with them as they come into and out of prominences: we use C, the risk-adjusted relative performance number.

To sum up, we learned that the efficient frontier shifts and changes over the years. We learned that diversification really has nothing to do with your age, but rather should shift with market values and trends. And we learned that performance varies widely among funds, even between the ones focused on the same investment style. The solution that deals with each of these keys is C.

We will look more closely at the application of this C-lution on portfolios. But let's turn first to some other important factors.

Investing Factors

There are several factors to apply to our analysis of investments: the rule of 72, compounding, math realities, age realities, circumstance realities, and inflation realities.

Rule of 72

The rule of 72 is a handy way to determine how many years it will take to double your money given a set rate of return. For example, if you make an average 8% annual return, it will take 9 years to double your money (72 divided by 8 is 9). If you just lost 50% of your money in the last bear market, it will now take you 18 more years to double your original investment at the same average of 8%.

There goes early retirement. There goes compounding. The point, already made, is that sitting through bear market losses is devastating to your creating and keeping wealth. There has to be a better way than buy and hold.

Compounding

Compounding builds on that rule of 72 idea. It tells you that your interest earned is also earning interest for you. You've probably heard of the golden goose fairy tale? Like most tales, the idea behind the children's fable is simple, yet profound. Don't kill the golden goose because it is producing something unique for you. In your life, it could be your investment portfolio, or it could be your job. Be the best employee ever. Be the best boss. Arrive early. Stay late. Don't work on personal things on the company's time. Your job is paying you, like the golden goose. So don't kill it. Don't get fired.

Compounding thus extends to your investment principal, your nest egg. Your nest egg is the thing paying you. It might be a total of $10,000 in a CD at 1%, which pays $100 per year. That $100 would be what you can spend or reinvest, but to compound it, you'll need to save all or some of it. You reinvest $10,100. Even worse than spending all the $100, however, would be to spend some of the $10,000. That would be killing the golden goose or at least plucking some of its feathers.

Now, there is a line between frugal and foolish. Foolish would be to never enjoy your retirement life, never pluck out a feather or two of principal to take a vacation or repair the home or help the grandkids in college. The point, however, should be clear: don't kill the goose.

At the same time, the tale can also work in a positive way. I'm not a goose farmer, but I suspect like any animal or relationship, the more it is properly tended and cared for, the more it produces. Likewise, it is the same with your portfolio. The more attention it is given and added to, the more it should grow and thus produce for you. This book should provide you some tools with which to accomplish that.

Unfortunately it is not until retiring that most investors truly begin to consider this idea that their portfolio will produce their spendable income; it will replace their earned income. Only then do some invest the time to become educated and comfortable with investing principles. Instead of waiting to learn these things after retirement, learn them as you accumulate. Treat your portfolio as if you had to live off of it now. For example, if this idea is followed, you will try not to lose half of it now in a bear market, any more than you would during your retirement years. Don't sell at the bottom. Avoid buying at the tops. Consider the market's value. In your 401(k), invest with the top funds as ranked by their C number. If you do this, it may turn out that you can retire with more and earlier than you otherwise have been told.

Math Reality

The reality of math is simple. If you lose 50% of your capital, you must make 100% just to return to breakeven. This whole sequence of loss and recovery may take years while you are moving ever closer to retirement. When a decline starts, no one knows how far the bear will continue. This is why we use the C-lect approach to proactive rotational allocation. This is why we use stop losses. This is why we use the selection process to stay with the leaders. This is why we use cash or the fund manager who uses cash as an asset class.

Will it be a typical cyclical bear market in a secular bull market bear loss where it drops 25%? Or will it be a cyclical bear market in a secular bear market disaster where it might drop upward of 50% or worse? No one knows. In addition, no one knows how long it will take to recover from the loss. In the meantime, you've aged, while your bills continue to come in. Compounding is lost. The rule of 72 is extended. Why sit through this certainty of loss?

Age Reality

Underneath the reality of math and compounding, of bull and bear markets, of secular and cycle trends is the just as real human factor of aging. I don't want to be morbid, but obviously each year that goes by brings each of us closer to our death. The average age of death in the year 2011 in America was 76 for men and 81 for women.

Let's put this point in perspective. Let's consider the amount of time over which the most recent bear and bull stock market cycled from its starting point to its bottom and back to its starting point. That would be the horizontal axis. The vertical axis is the portfolio value. I daresay most of us think about the vertical but rarely about the horizontal and its implication for each of us personally, until we are already into our retirement years.

Let's say you entered 2007 with $500,000 in your stock account. Maybe you held some bonds too in a separate account. By the time the bottom of the bear showed up in March 2009, your stock account would probably have been worth about $250,000. This assumes a passive buy-and-hold index approach. It would not have been until 2013 that the market and your stock account made it back to pre-bear market levels. Add up the time. Seven years would have elapsed. What does that mean? If you were 60 entering 2007, you were 67 in 2013. If you were 50 entering 2007, you were 57 in 2013. The math is easy to apply to your own age, but the meaning, not so much, eh? But let me touch on a couple of things to be aware of if you take the standard industry advice on investing:

♦ The time to recover from the next big loss is narrowed.
♦ The time to retirement is shrunk.
♦ The compounding factor is reduced.
♦ The rule of 72 is crimped.

Circumstance Reality

It is interesting to find out that in the Great Depression, unemployment touched 25% of the workforce. When I was younger looking at the drawn faces of people in breadlines in the school books, I was always under the impression it went north of 50%. The pictures of the unemployed in breadlines without hope are haunting. Yet, what were the other 75% of the workforce doing?

It is said that the retailers who would sell their merchandise at losses, would then have the necessary capital to rebuild their inventory at even lower prices with the latest and greatest goods. They were the ones to stay in business. The lesson was to take the early fast loss in order to reinvest for the future recovery at lower prices.

The economy eventually recovered, but what of the human element? Jobs are lost in a recession, yet living goes on in the form of house payments, car payments, college tuition, or any other myriad expenses. Again, how much better off would you be if you sold near the top with your nest egg nearly fully intact as the market began its plunge?

Inflation Reality

Inflation is the rise in prices. A common example is the price of postage that has gone from $0.03 in 1920 to $0.49 in 2015. What this means is that it takes more money to maintain the same standard of living as before. This has been one of the problems with the recovery in the 2000s. Middle America's income is stagnant, even as prices have increased. If over the last 10 years you have been making $50,000 a year, which is about the median income, and you have been spending $45,000 a year, but prices have increased 10% over those 10 years, you are now unable to afford the same things as before. This also makes it tough to get ahead.

The second point is that inflation affects those on a fixed income, such as retirees. Sure, social security adjusts the check for inflation, but typically it is not a full compensation for inflation.

All of this is to suggest that we must maintain the growth part of our portfolios, even into our retirement years. But with the standard buy-and-hold mentality or the age-based allocation advice, this will be a nigh impossibility to implement. Active asset allocation that manages the managers is the only approach that tries to avoid losses, to pick the top managers, and to avoid sitting through the declines. Active asset allocation then tries to reenter at lower prices as the market begins its next bull advance.

New Information

The point is simply to reinforce what we learned earlier and the necessity of applying its lessons. The markets move in cycles. We don't have to suffer the losses to our capital and to our time. There are managers who try to avoid these losses. There are managers who outperform their peers. We try to find them, invest with them, and be ready to move funds elsewhere when they begin to underperform.

Successful investing—that is, creating and retaining wealth over the years from your investments—is not an easy task. It requires a proven strategy and the discipline to follow it. How easy is it to sell when everyone is talking about how easy it is to make money in the stock market? How easy is it to buy when everyone is talking about how much money was lost in the stock market? "Buy stocks?" they ask. "I can't even open my brokerage statement."

We know investing is fraught with pitfalls, curveballs, and blind-sides. Just when you might think you have it all figured out, what it is becomes popular, and it becomes a trap, like the well-publicized Dogs of the Dow strategy. The advantage is arbitraged away as investors try to anticipate the actions of other investors. The great indicator that had been working to signal buys and sells moves to a new extreme to the upside or downside and fails, as investors saw in 1982 at the great secular shift. We get whipsawed buying and selling and buying right back. Or the market "crashes" without warning as it did in 1987. There are Black Swan events, and by their definition, they are simply not know-able in advance. The market's foremost job is to keep the investor hum-ble. Rarely is anything clear. Investing is an art as well as a science.

For our part, recall our primary guiding principle from Chapter 1. We strive to make the most return with the least risk. It sounds simple enough; it's quite intuitive; it makes sense. Everyone in fact basically agrees with the goal. Indeed, the whole idea of a fixed allocation (60% stocks and 40% bonds) is based upon it. But, as we have seen, the efficient frontier is far from fixed.

Truth be told, not everyone really and ultimately has this same goal to make the most return with the least risk. We know that the fund managers' goals are not necessarily our goals. The brokers' goals are not necessarily our goals. As such, when the market moves into over-valued territory where the risk of loss is very high, they may not suggest any changes. When the market moves into undervalued territory where the risk of loss is very low, they still may not suggest any meaningful changes. So what do we do about it instead? We use these strategies:

+ Managing the managers (selecting)
+ Valuing the market (timing)
+ Allocating the portfolio

Since we know and believe these things, it is the reason we strive to invest at the efficient frontier where we provide the most return and least risk. Let's review three of the key points (secular trend timing, manager selecting, and portfolio allocating) from this book and then look at what we might do to change old habits as we implement this time-tested strategy.

In Chapters 2 and 3, the first foundation I laid was to show that both stock and bond markets move in broad, fairly well defined secular trends both up and down. Each phase has unique characteristics that we may use to help us define the type of market we are in. The primary takeaway is that fund managers in one market may or may not be suitable for the other market. The successful strategy in one market may not work in the other.

The alternative to this is that if you are a buy-and-hold investor, your future investment returns will be greatly determined by when you invest relative to where the secular bull or bear markets are in their phases. Excluding the market change from 2000, according to one source, if you bought at the bottom of the previous four secular bear markets in stocks, your average bull market gain was 810%.[1] But if you bought at the previous five secular tops, your average bear market loss was −14%.[2] This fact cannot be emphasized enough. According to another source, Robert Shiller's *Irrational Exuberance* estimates that buying when the CAPE ratio is the cheapest yields the subsequent 10-year returns average of 16.1%, while buying when the CAPE ratio is the most expensive yields −3.3%.[3] Talk about luck versus skill. With the wind at your back, your compounding wealth boat goes faster. Oh to be so lucky to buy in at the bottom of the secular bear market and to sell at the top of the secular bull market.

For some fund managers, secular trends are the source of falling for the phrase about not confusing brains with a bull market. The point of this historic information is to show that timing based on secular trends will beat a simple buy and hold over these long-term times. In other words, being fully invested in the secular bear wherein you lose 50% to 90% of your money is simply a wealth

---

[1] *Source:* CrestmontResearch.com. Average bull and bear market returns for Dow Jones Industrial Average.
[2] Ibid.
[3] Robert Shiller, *Irrational Exuberance*, 2006. Returns are for illustration only. An investor cannot invest directly in an index.

near-killer. The mathematics of investing shows the necessity of making 100% after losing 50% of your portfolio, just to return to break-even over many years. Compounding vanishes during this time.

I recognize that this is an incredible claim to many, but a simple timing model employed over the decades will show that avoiding losses is more important than capturing gains. We saw it throughout this book. Nearly every great manager will also tell you the same thing. Not losing is more important than winning.

C-lecting Managers

We saw that not all fund managers are created equal. Some perform better than others. And those who do perform better aren't necessarily the same as those who might perform better the following year or in the next secular market. That is the reality. Fees, names, and past performance really do not predict future relative performance among funds. Even within the same stock fund style, there is a great return range between the top 5% and worst 5%. It behooves you, therefore, to try to invest with the leaders and avoid the laggards, but how?

To pick funds, some use questionable forecasting tools like past performance, internal expenses, fund size, or management names. The tool we use to determine with whom to invest is C. As we have learned, C is the risk-adjusted relative performance number. C rankings show us the funds that are providing better performance per unit of risk taken. This, too, is why we practice a dynamic, proactive allocation process to invest with the leaders and avoid the laggards. It changes.

As also mentioned, we use cash (money market funds) as a fund choice. Everyone agrees with the point that clearly there are times when cash provides the most return for the risk taken. The point is that we also employ C as a timing tool to answer the question when.

Portfolio Assembling

We also explored why it is that the standard industry age-based asset allocation advice simply doesn't work well in the real world. It could have you buying at secular tops when stocks are expensive or selling at secular bottoms when stocks are cheap. The fact is, no one's age is related to potential returns or market valuations. It is just a silly recipe to try to reduce risk with a simple investment formula based on a long-term snapshot of past market returns and capitalizations that may or may not be appropriate in today's investing climate or to your personal situation. We saw that the efficient frontier shifts and changes over the decades. Your personal age is completely unrelated to potential investment returns, and furthermore, the age-related advice ignores the very fact of what it purports to accomplish—that is, it fails to take into account your age and circumstance. In other words, in a recession-induced bear market or a secular bear market, your age and circumstance must be taken into account in the first place in order for you to avoid doing nothing as the market itself does nothing but decline. We've reviewed these periods in Chapters 2 and 3.

As you age, that standard industry advice then may tell you to sell or lower your equity percentages at precisely the wrong time. Indeed, when the 30-year-old walks in, the typical financial advisors will tell him to buy, and when the 60-year-old walks in, those same advisors will tell her to sell. Eh, what? What happened to the idea of making the most return for the risk? Moreover, with buy-and-hold losses intact over the years, you lose the huge advantage from compounding gains that otherwise would accrue to you through the years, especially if you start saving in your twenties. We can summarize the standard investment industry advice this way: it ignores age and circumstance; it fails to address fund manager selection; and it overlooks market valuations within the secular cycles. Thus the typical asset allocation advice does not work to maximize your investment results with the least risk. We, to the contrary, advocate a proactive investment strategy that accounts for the real world of age and circumstance and the secular cycles.

What is this proactive investment strategy? As mentioned, it is two pronged:

+ Managing the managers (selecting)
+ Valuing the market (timing)

Managing the Managers

Take a proactive approach by investing with the leading mutual funds and ETFs on a risk-adjusted relative performance basis. We identify them by C. Buy and hold the leaders, while avoiding the laggards. Repeat this exercise monthly.

We have seen that there is a wide variance between the top 5% and bottom 5% of the fund managers who have been given the same stable of stocks from which to choose and the same objectives relating thereto. We must have a selecting strategy to stay with the leaders and avoid the laggards over time. We have seen that it is not enough to simply invest passively, as some people have over the last 15 years and who are just now getting back above breakeven. What a loss of time in which to compound the gains! Besides, from the year 2000 to 2008, the typical financial advisors' advice based on age was to sell at the bottom—that is, to lighten up at the exact time to be buying when value was again present. There are times to use passive index funds rather than actively managed funds and vice versa. But both types of funds have this in common: they will move up and down with the markets. Using a passive over an active investing strategy does not guarantee that losses will be avoided.

We have also seen that some funds are substantially more volatile and risky than others, yet they end up with the same performance. This too is to be avoided by using C. It is like driving in August one sunny day from one side of Texas to the other in a car with air-conditioning versus one without. They both get you to your destination, but one does it with far more comfort.

Valuing the Market

Recognize that the market moves from expensive to cheap and back again. Use the timing tools mentioned in the previous chapter. They are updated on our websites www.SelectionsAndTiming.com and www.401kSelections.com.

History shows us how impermanent the world really is, if we just back up and stretch our view over centuries to look at the forest rather than the trees. We know nations rise and fall with regularity like a centenarian's birthday cake soufflé that will continue to rise in an oven until the oven door is slammed. But, as actors in the forest chopping our way through the trees of life, the rise and fall of nations is not obvious to us on a day-to-day basis. We easily make the mistake of confusing our time on its stage as the end all, be all. That is the error of human nature to take a parochial and narrow time frame of reference based only on our own lives or even more narrowly, our investing lives from roughly age 25 to age 85, without considering the herd and how its behavior moves with and without us on the earth.

Whether we live in boom times or depression times, we tend toward this mistake of thinking the circumstances around us will never change and will always be the same. Today is like yesterday, and tomorrow will be like today. It is a mistake to think stock prices are necessarily set by rational people. They are not. The market swings from cheap to dear and back again. Will the stock market recover from its 50% loss in 2008 from the financial implosion? In hindsight, it has, thanks basically to an accounting rules change. Yet, we can look back on this loss and recovery and forget that the losses are more than numbers on a screen. When the bear starts, we have no idea how far the market will fall. Will it be 20% or 50% or 90%? How much better off would you be to take action early rather than find out later that it is falling more than you expected, as it always does? There is the human emotional toll to market losses of losing half your nest egg just as retirement nears. There are job losses, which lead some to forced selling in order to meet obligations. There are margin calls, which lead to more forced selling to stop the losses from compounding. And not to forget, we are older when the market finally recovers.

The reality is the stock market and bond market move in fairly well defined secular bull and bear market trends. The path is not always straight up or down. Some people have likened investing to a roller-coaster ride. But unlike a roller coaster, there is no safety net. So we try not only to identify these cycles but to profit from them. We saw these cycles in Chapters 2 and 3, and they last anywhere from 5 to 30 years in a variety of markets. Market timing or asset allocation will definitely improve performance numbers, when used correctly and when measured over a full market cycle.

All of these facts should lead us to make some new decisions. For example, I was giving a workshop presentation in 2012, and in the question-and-answer section, a person asked what he should do with his S&P 500 Index fund. He said he had been lured in with all the hype back in 2000 that low-cost indexing was the best and only way to invest. Since then, 12 years later, he was still underwater; he still had a loss in his cheap index fund. In a sense, he got what he paid for.

He knew after my presentation that many actively managed funds were hitting all-time highs, but his index fund was still badly lagging. To be sure, it may have led the pack up to 2000, but it wasn't doing so any longer. Basically his question boiled down to two concerns. He was afraid if he sold that the market would soar on up without him. He was also not sure about what to use for the replacement fund.

Twelve years is a long time to be invested, to take the risk of investing, and in fact to lose 40% to 50% not only once but twice over the period, and still end up receiving no compensation for taking the risk. There's no compounding there. He was older, closer to retirement, wondering if there wasn't a better way. In fact, it was long past time—not to sell out in righteous disgust and swear off stocks forever but rather to make some well-planned lateral investment moves into leaders that were providing better returns for the risk. A lateral move is one where you don't add to or subtract from your current investment. If the current value of your investment is $20,000, then you sell that holding, take the loss (or gain), and reinvest the same $20,000 in a different fund. All you are trying to do is invest with the idea of making some money with a fund that is outperforming on a risk-adjusted relative basis, rather than waiting to get back to breakeven before actually doing something constructive about it. Sell the laggard and buy the leader.

Of course, the real problem behind this lagging performance was buying into what has been termed the "hype" of index funds, the repackaged Nifty Fifty, in the first place, as the market soared to its secular bull market peak in 2000. Again, it wasn't the fact that the index funds were so efficient or rational or low cost (just look at their subsequent secular bear market history), but rather that they just happened to be invested in the right investment fund style in the 1990s that was soaring, which at the time of that peak was large-cap growth and technology. Many portfolios got lost in that forest and wandered for years thereafter.

Once this was understood, his question naturally was, Which new fund to buy? Maybe it is another low-cost index fund, or maybe it is an active fund. We just have to run the database numbers to find the risk-adjusted relative strength leaders for today. The fund industry does a fantastic marketing job with the goal of retaining your investment. After reading this book, you know what my answer would be. Follow the Comet, the C, which is the risk-adjusted relative performance. But this answer is not a one-time stand-alone solution; if it were, we would end up in the same place as the index fundholder: we would be taking the risk but not necessarily receiving the compensation. Instead, to be effective, one has to continue to monitor the leaders and laggards each month and evolve with them.

Think of it this way: if you actually bonk your head every couple of years or if you even worry about bonking your head, you can pick from any number of painkillers to help afterward. Or you can step back and decide that maybe a new strategy is called for that will attempt to avoid the pain in the first place. Which fund should I buy? What about the market? How do I decide to invest? Whom can I trust? Who has my best interests at heart?

Here is a three-step suggestion to help you get started on a proactive manage-the-managers and value-the-market strategy:

1. Make a list of the funds you own in your personal accounts or that are available in your company's retirement plan, like a 401(k).
2. Find the rankings for your funds on our website www.SelectionsAndTiming.com or www.401kSelections.com.
3. Hold your leaders. Sell the laggards and replace them with more leaders. Repeat.

Please note a couple of things with this general advice. It does not in any form or fashion take into account an investor's personal situation. For example, you might have a short-term loss in a laggard fund, and to maximize the benefit, the loss needs to be taken soon. Other investors might have a laggard fund that will still produce a long-term capital gain in a few weeks; they might want to hold on in order to capture that tax benefit. Laggard doesn't necessarily mean it loses money. In our methodology, it simply means that for the risk taken, the reward isn't there. One should also be wary of buying a fund before it makes a capital gains distribution.[4] Only you know your personal situation.

---

[4] Typically funds will distribute capital gains in the fall of each year prior to year-end. If you buy before the distribution, you will owe taxes on that distribution. In effect you will be paying the taxes, but you didn't reap the capital gains. You want to buy after the distribution.

The next thing to note is that taking these steps is partially making lateral moves if you remain in the same investment style. You are selling one investment and buying another with the same amount of capital. With a lateral move, you don't need to worry about selling out at what might be the bottom or buying at what might be the market top. All we are trying to do is move the money you already have at risk in the market to a fund whose manager is producing results commensurate with the risk. You already are accepting the market risk; let's just try to improve the return element.

Lastly, this is an active asset allocation approach that works over time. It is not buy and hold and then hope for the best after doing it once. It is not age based. It is a commitment, not to a fund per se but to a strategy of striving to invest at the cusp of the efficient frontier where the risk-adjusted relative performance leaders rotate over the decades. Leaders today will eventually become laggards, be they active or passive funds. It is simply the nature of the game. If it starts to downpour, it doesn't do any good to turn your wipers on once and then off again, or worse yet, keep driving with the top down.

Let's begin to put all of this together. As we saw in Chapter 6, we employ C ratings on mutual funds, ETFs, fund styles, fund families, and 401(k) plan funds. Our goal is to rotate with the leaders as the efficient frontier where return is maximized and risk is minimized shifts over the decades. As you might imagine, there are numerous ways to begin to assemble portfolios to meet your own personal tolerances of risk and goals for reward, but I will provide a few suggestions.

Think of it this way. We all participate in the race called investing. Whether we are just starting out with a new job and saving in a 401(k) or we are inheriting some money, we all use funds that invest for us. In essence, they are actually the ones running the race and they are "carrying" us. The question then is what's the best way for us to participate? Should we employ a sprinter for the long run? Should we use a low-cost runner? Should we use a big-name runner? Or should we view the process as a "relay race," knowing we can actually use any of them from time to time? We can manage the managers, instructing them to pass the baton of our money as we deem it necessary and prudent.

The financial industry has done its best to convince us that the sprinters' approach is the best. It is the one-fact approach to investing. It may have only the lowest fees. It may have only a well-known name. It may have only won the race in the last calendar year or possibly for the last 10 years. But, what about tomorrow? Do those facts really help us maximize return and minimize risk?

We now know some things too. We know there are some sprinters who do well in one period, but not in all periods. We know there is a wide variance in performance among sprinters every year. We know the low-cost sprinter is simply ignoring the fact of bear markets when the markets may decline 50% or worse. We know it is simply a matter of time before the leader turns into a laggard. To put this in more technical terms, we know three things that drive our C-lect process:

- We know the efficient frontier changes over the decades.
- We know funds do have streaks.
- We know those streaks end as the reversion to the mean takes over.

All I am suggesting is to use runners, use those funds that are on streaks, but when their C rank drops, implying that their "reversion to the mean" is beginning, then leave the tiring fund sprinter and buy the new fund that may just be starting on its streak as measured by C. Think of investing in terms of a relay race whereby you invest your money in the ever-changing leaders.

We saw this philosophy in action in Chapter 6. We saw that I apply C to mutual funds, to exchange-traded funds (ETF), to fund styles, to fund families, to retirement plans like 401(k) plans. Do you have 15 minutes a month to employ this relay-race strategy? Each month my newsletters are published with the funds' updated C rankings. Stay with the leaders and avoid the laggards.

I will now give a few suggestions on assembling the information, but keep in mind there are numerous ways to do this. In the first example, I take a 50/50 percentage approach, but it could just as easily be 70/30 or 30/70. This allocation decision depends on your personal situation that only you know.

The main idea with this is to "know thyself." Be brutally honest. How much of your nest egg are you truly willing to lose? This is where diversification is important. Take a look at Figure 8.1. It compares the S&P 500 as measured by the ETF SPY (SPY) and a typical balanced 60% equity and 40% bond fund as measured by the Vanguard Wellington Fund Investor Class (VWELX) with the C-lect 2 Hybrid strategy and C-lect 5 Fidelity strategy. The "2" and

FIGURE 8.1 Comparing SPY and Vanguard Wellington Fund Investor Class (VWELX) with the C-lect 2 Hybrid and C-lect 5 Fidelity, December 1992 Through July 2013

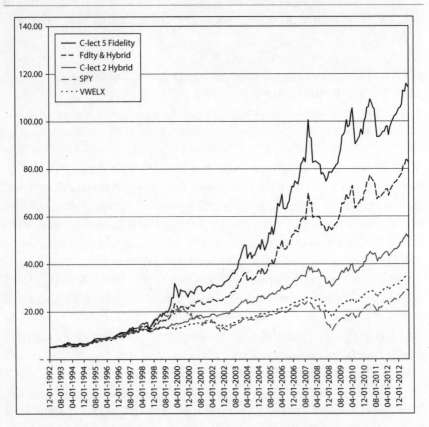

Source: Data for SPY and VWELX from www.InvestorsFastTrack.com and data for C-lect strategy from the *No-Load Mutual Fund Selections & Timing Newsletter.*

"5" in the C-lect strategy refers to the number of funds held during the backtest.

As you can see, the C-lect strategy of staying with the leaders and avoiding the laggards beat the markets as measured by SPY and VWELX. See some details in the following table. Please note this compares the C-lect strategy only. Portfolios were fully invested always per the C rankings. No money market funds were used.

Strategy	Average Annual Return	2000–2003 Bear	2007–2009 Bear
C-lect 5 Fidelity	16.1%	−34.4%	−49.2%
C-lect 2 Hybrid	11.6	29.9	−21.7
50% Fidelity and 50% Hybrid	14.3	−19.5	−40.6
SPY	8.6	−35.6	−50.8
VWELX	9.5	12.7	−32.5

As any great investor will tell you, always consider the bear market as well as the bull market when deciding on what to do. The takeaway here is to look at those bear market losses and decide if those are palatable. That average annual gain of 16.1% looks great, but to achieve that meant sitting through a decline of 49.2%. Granted this annual gain is substantially better than buying a low-cost index fund that declined 50.8% and gained only 8.6% over the same period, but would you sit through that bear market in order to "be there" when the market recovered?

The alternative is to consider using the lower-risk Hybrid strategy or a combination of the two. With a 50% combination in the Hybrid style and Fidelity fund family, it's drawdown in the bear market was 21.7%, but it still greatly outperformed the markets over the same time frame. This is a winning combination of more return and less risk.

The 50% split is only a suggestion of one approach of many to bring this information into personal usage. Figure 8.2 shows the raw returns for all the fund styles we track. The best style was mid-cap, followed closely by the aggressive style. The worst style was the contrary one. All 11 styles are compared against Vanguard Wellington Fund Investor Shares (VWELX). With 11 styles, there are numerous combinations that may be employed.

Lastly, I will comment again upon using C-lect in a 401(k) plan. The C-lect strategy does not require any plan changes. C-lect uses your existing funds in your specific plan. But having tested 20 different plans, I can tell you there is a wide performance spread between 401(k) plans with good funds and those with bad funds. The top quartile returned about 15.1%, while the bottom quartile returned about 11.3%. Using the C-lect approach in those plans in the bottom

FIGURE 8.2 Comparing 11 Fund Styles by C-lect Against the Vanguard Wellington Fund Investor Shares (VWELX), January 2003 Through June 2013

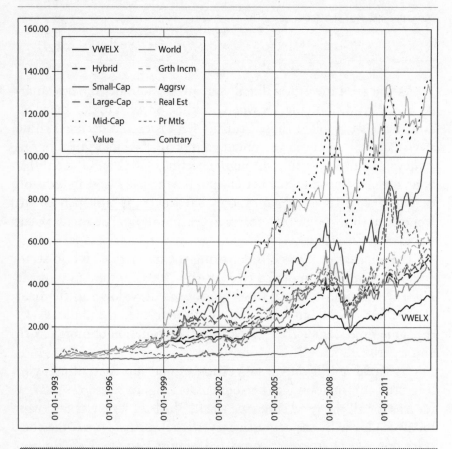

Source: Data for VWELX from www.InvestorsFastTrack.com and data for C-lect fund families from the *No-Load Mutual Fund Selections & Timing Newsletter.*

quartile still outperformed the buy and hold over the test period, and that nearly 4% per year difference compounding over 20 or 30 or 40 years to your retirement would mean hundreds of thousands of dollars difference to your retirement nest egg. Take a look at Figure 8.3 that shows results over the 20½-year test period from January 1, 1993, through June 30, 2013.

Contributing $500 per month over the 20½-year test period in SPY gained the least at $268,000. The combination stock and bond

FIGURE 8.3 Based on a Contribution of $500 per Month over 20½ Years, a Comparison of SPY and VWELX to C-lect 401(k) Strategy on Plans in the Bottom and Top Quartiles of 20 Tested Plans

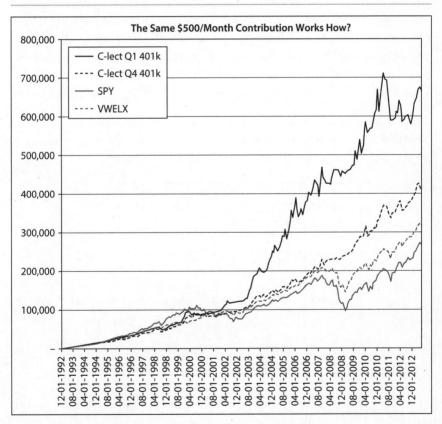

Source: Data for SPY and VWELX from www.InvestorsFastTrack.com and data for C-lect 401(k) from the *No-Load Mutual Fund Selections & Timing Newsletter.*

fund VWELX gained $319,000. Using C-lect gained the most. A plan in the bottom quartile (Q4) of the 20 tested plans gained $408,000. A plan in the top quartile (Q1) gained $666,000. So, for about 15 minutes a month of your time to make changes, the C-lect 401(k) approach could help your same dollar contribution work harder.

But for the most benefit, I suggest three things for retirement plans. One is to have fund choices that are leaders in their styles. Two is to have funds that provide a wide diversification. Three is to have low costs in your plan. Then you can let C-lect do the rest. We can help in these areas.

So, it is critical to realize we are in a race, but not just any race. It is a marathon, not a sprint. We can and must use multiple managers to help us reach our goals.

Lastly, take a look at Figure 8.4 which shows results over the period from January 1, 1993, through December 31, 2014, in a top quartile 401(k) plan we tested. It has wide diversification and low-cost funds.

The chart compares the same $500 per month contribution from January 1, 1993, through December 31, 2014, in three choices. The

FIGURE 8.4   Based on a Contribution of $500 per Month over 22 Years, a Comparison of SPY and VWELX to C-lect 401(k) Strategy

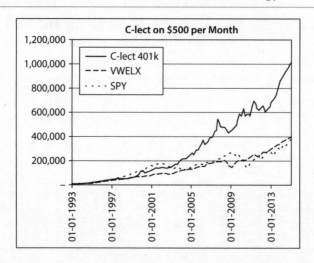

Source: Data for SPY and VWELX from www.InvestorsFastTrack.com and data for C-lect 401(k) from the *No-Load Mutual Fund Selections & Timing Newsletter.*

first is the S&P 500 as measured by SPY. This grew to $370,000. The second is the Vanguard Wellington Fund Investor Shares (VWELX). This grew to $391,000. The third is the C-lect strategy on the plan's funds (C-lect 401k). This grew to $1,002,000. It did so on the same $500 per month over the 22 years.

There is no assurance that the next 22 years will be similar to the last 22 years. But since we're in a relay race, let's not use the tools of a solo sprinter but rather use the tools of marathon runners.

What to Do Now

Let's circle back to the beginning. What would help us achieve wealth and hang on to it over the years and decades? We've seen that a buy-and-hold strategy really doesn't work well. At its basic level, it ignores many variables, like personal age and circumstances and the impact of world events on valuations. There have been times when a fully invested portfolio declined nearly 90%. More recently since the year 2000, we've witnessed two bear markets that scalped 50% from stock indexes each time. It took nearly 14 years for some indexes to return to breakeven, let alone to make a profit. The NASDAQ index is just now clearing its previous high set in 2000. There has to be a better way to create and retain wealth than accepting the standard financial industry advice of buy and hold.

It has been a great ride for this country and its citizens from 1875 to now. Will the next 140 years be as prosperous? No one knows. We certainly hope so, but the historic realities based on the growth and decline of other countries suggest that it may not be so smooth a trend upward. For our part, we plan to continue using what works. Manage the managers by buying the top funds and avoiding the laggards based on their C rankings. Move into and out of the stock market based on valuations.

Here's the bottom line for what to do about creating and retaining wealth over the years.

Fund Selecting

The formulas I use to arrive at C are proprietary. The idea behind it is not. It is the nature of investing, of the Modern Portfolio

Theory and efficient frontier to try to provide the most return with the least risk. You may find current recommendations in our newsletter or on our websites (www.SelectionsAndTiming.com or www.401kSelections.com).

Market Timing

It is the same with market timing. I have provided enough information in this book to show that considering value is a consistent way to measure the potential risk and reward in the stock market. As is true of the fund selecting formulas, how we put our market timing model together is proprietary. But certainly anyone may use the CAPE ratio or the Q ratio or a moving average of some length. Put it all together, and come up with a strategy to get into and out of stocks.

Also, as we mentioned above with respect to fund selecting, we provide continuously updated market timing strategies in our newsletters and on our websites.

Again, I am not trying to be secretive, but I know that once something is recognized as providing superior returns, it tends to get arbitraged away. I don't want this to happen to us.

Conclusion

What should you do going forward? Find someone with at least a 15-year record of outperforming the market on a risk-adjusted basis.

Follow the advice.

Pass it on to your children.

From the 1700s through the present day, we have plowed through acres of the human experience. We have looked at human nature in action through secular bull and bear markets. We like to think we are in control of our emotions, but we really are not always rational animals. We live in greed and fear. So we have rejected the standard industry advice that says to buy and hold and don't compare funds and companies. Instead, we buy and sell and compare continuously. We view investing as a relay race wherein we try to invest with the leaders year after year. We believe the market has a thing called "value" and that we can measure it. This helps guide us in our decisions about when to invest and when to raise cash. It is acknowledgment that we have these all-too-human characteristics called "aging" and "circumstance." It does us no good for the brokers to have yachts while the investors go wanting and wondering what to do, while all the while still paying fees to their brokers.

I hope this book has loosened some rigid industry soil, provided some selecting and timing advice on what and when to plant such that the next hundred years go even better for all of us than the previous hundred. It's an old saying from much further back than a hundred years, nigh closer to 3,000 years,[5] but there really is nothing new under the sun. Most people still operate with fear and greed, but we now have some alternative tools by which to try to take advantage of this. If you agree, then this book will help as we accumulate, maintain, and pass on our wealth and knowledge to our children and as they do the same for theirs.

We hope to hear from you. If you would like further information about our selections and timing approaches, please send us an email at INFO@SelectionsAndTiming.com or INFO@401kSelections.com.

---

[5] The world's smartest man said, "There's nothing new under the sun." Solomon was in all his glory. Would he have jumped out of the plane with the hippie's backpack? No way to know.

APPENDIX A

Secular Stock Worksheet

We know that there are better times than others to invest in stocks and bonds, especially if your goal is to maximize returns and minimize risks. We also know that the efficient frontier is not static; it moves over time. In this appendix and the next, we want to provide you with some guidelines to consider when thinking about the question of where we are in the secular cycle. The answer you get will make a material difference in your wealth accumulation. Current answers are provided at our websites www.SelectionsAndTiming .com and www.401kSelections.com.

Technicals
- Rolling 5-, 10-, 15-, and 20-year returns
- Trend by moving averages

For example, Figure A.1 is a chart of the S&P 500 and its five-year rate of change (ROC) from January 1871 through January 2015.

As you can see, it does a fairly decent job of suggesting when we should start looking for the bear market to end. It is when the rate of change drops below −30%. This means that the S&P 500 is 30% below its price from five years before.

Fundamentals
- What is the CAPE ratio?
- What is the Q ratio?

FIGURE A.1 The Five-Year Rate of Change of the S&P 500, January 1871 Through January 2015

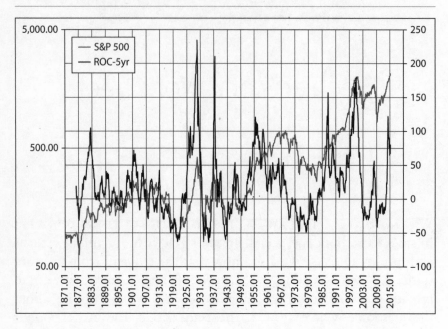

Source: Data for S&P 500 from Robert Shiller's website at http:// irrationalexuberance.com and data for ROC from the *No-Load Mutual Fund Selections & Timing Newsletter.*

◆ What is the forward P/E ratio?
◆ What is the trend of the leading economic indicators?

Social Climate
◆ Influential, well-known advisors saying to buy or sell stocks?
◆ War or peacetime (destruction or construction)?
◆ Status quo or game changer industry?

Sentiment (Contrary Indicator)
◆ Are the headlines consistently bearish or bullish?
◆ How does the market react?
◆ What are investors saying and doing?
◆ What are institutions doing?
◆ What is the NYSE margin debt?

These questions are meant to be a starting point, not an ending point. In other words, if the P/E ratio is in single digits and we are at peace, this should suggest something different to you than if the P/E ratio is above 30 and war has just broken out. If the five-year rate of change is +50% and the leading economic indicators are rolling into a downtrend, then this, too, should suggest something.

Having said all that, I would reiterate that because we do take a proactive rotational allocation approach to investing based on C, then all these things would be taken into account. If stock funds are not providing the return for the risk but bonds are, then C will reflect this. If stock funds are providing the most return for the risk taken, then that, too, will be reflected.

APPENDIX B

Secular Bond Worksheet

As with the stock market, we know that there are better times than others to invest in bonds. In this appendix and in Appendix A, we want to provide you with some worksheets to answer the question of where we are in the secular cycle. The answer you get will make a material difference in your wealth accumulation. Here are some questions to consider.

What is the secular bond trend?
   Rolling 5-, 10-, 15-, and 20-year returns
   Ratio of federal debt to GDP: Is it increasing or decreasing?

Social Climate
- Big names saying to buy or sell bonds?
- War or peacetime (destruction or construction)?

Are the domestic and world economies growing or shrinking?
   Are central banks reducing (loose money) or increasing (tight money) interest rates?
   The broad-based questions in Appendices A and B are for you to ponder and answer. But as I've been mentioning throughout this book, the C metric (risk-adjusted relative strength measure) takes these things and more into account through the monthly ranking process of the fund managers. The managers who are currently in tune with and invested according to the correct answers to these questions rise to the top in performance.

FIGURE B.1 Vanguard Total Bond Market Index Fund Investor Shares (VBMFX) Versus C-lect Bond for the Period from December 31, 2002, Through June 30, 2013

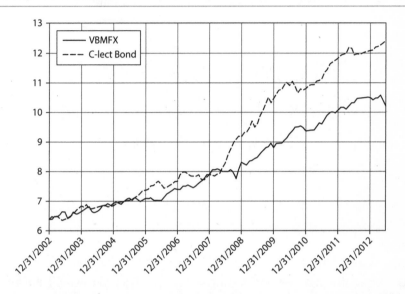

Source: Data for VBMFX from www.InvestorsFastTrack.com and data for C-lect Bond from the *No-Load Mutual Funds Selections & Timing Newsletter.*

As one might expect, the same proactive rotational allocation strategy based on C that is so useful for stock funds also works for the bond market. Figure B.1 shows VBMFX (Vanguard Total Bond Market Index Fund Investor Shares) and C-lect Bond for the period from December 31, 2002, through June 30, 2013. Like with stock funds, C-lect does not outperform each year, but has done so through the years. Past performance does not guarantee future performance.

This C-lect Bond program selects the top 6 of 35 bond funds as ranked by C, the risk-adjusted relative strength metric. The program forces at least a three-month holding period before possibly rotating from laggards to leaders. The 35 funds are made up of bond funds from different styles, such as high yield, international, Treasuries, corporates, and flexible funds.

As we saw in Chapters 2 and 3, bonds and stocks move in broad secular trends. The C metric is a way to tell us with whom to invest— the manager who is capturing the trends and valuations.

APPENDIX C

Mapping Your Personal Current Holdings to Where They Are Ranked

By now you know we rank mutual funds and ETFs by C, the risk-adjusted relative strength metric. We suggest using C to take a proactive rotational allocation approach that invests with the leaders and avoids the laggards.

The table that follows should help you with seeing where our strategy ranks your current holdings. Just go to our website at www.SelectionsAndTiming.com. Once you are a subscriber, you may enter your funds' ticker symbols. If we track each fund, you will see its rank. If we don't track it, just email the ticker symbol to us at info@selectionsandtiming.com. We may then begin to track that fund.

Once you know what each of your funds C rank is you may make a couple of decisions. Make lateral moves out of the laggards and into the leaders. A lateral move is simply maintaining roughly the same risk with the same amount invested but moving from a laggard fund into a leader fund. A laggard fund is one in which the returns are not justifying the risk taken. Continue to hold your top-rated funds as indicated by C. Just know that eventually those top leader funds will lag and will need to be replaced.

As the months, years, and decades go by, stay with the leaders and avoid the laggards.

Funds You Own	C Rank (see www.SelectionsAndTiming.com for roughly 800 mutual funds and ETFs)
1	
2	
3	
4	
5	
6	
7	
8	
9	
10	

APPENDIX D

Mapping Your 401(k) Choices

THERE ARE FOUR MAIN COMMENTS I'D LIKE TO MAKE FOR THOSE lucky enough to have a company-sponsored 401(k) retirement plan. (See www.401kSelections.com.) I'll then show an example of what it may mean to put C-lect to work for you in an actual 401(k).

1. **Meet the match.** Save at least as much as your employer matches. Otherwise, you are leaving free money on the table. Yes, there is a typical vesting period to actually own employer contributions, but the contributions you make are always yours.
2. **Ask for improvement.** Have your human resources department investigate plan alternatives. Ideally you want a 401(k) plan that provides four things:
   - ◆ Top funds in their respective investment styles
   - ◆ Wide diversification among fund styles
   - ◆ Low costs for funds and administration
   - ◆ Excellent informative education
3. **Think long term to retirement.** After all, having something is better than nothing. In other words, saving even a tiny amount like $10 a paycheck will be worth it. Of course, the more one saves the better, but the point is to save something. Put compounding to work for you by starting early.
4. **Avoid borrowing from your plan.** The argument for doing so is that you are paying yourself back with interest, but use this option only in dire emergencies.

For a free, no-obligation Special Report, please provide us with your company's name, a list of your 401(k) choices, and holding period restrictions your plan may have. We will provide a backtest to see whether a selecting process based on C will work for you too. If it does and if you decide it is worthwhile, we will work with you to bring the information into real time so that you may benefit from this going forward. Imagine your results when you meet the match and invest with the best funds over the years in your 401(k). Do this at www.401kSelections.com. We have backtested more than 20 as of this writing, and they all have benefited from the C-lecting strategy of proactively allocating your 401(k). Figure D.1 is one example showing the results over 22 years with a monthly contribution of $500.

Figure D.1 compares the S&P 500 (measured by SPY) and Vanguard Wellington Fund Investor Class (VWELX) with the proactive rotational allocation strategy based on C.

FIGURE D.1   A Comparison of a Buy-and-Hold Strategy in Either the SPY or VWELX with C-lecting the Top 2 Funds out of 27 Funds in an Actual 401(k), from January 1, 1993, Through December 31, 2014

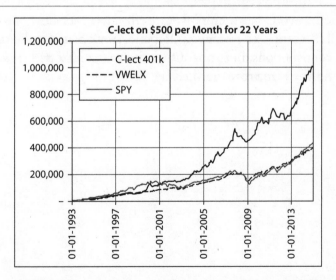

Source: Data for SPY and VWELX from www.InvestorsFastTrack.com and data for C-lect 401(k) from the *No-Load Mutual Funds Selection & Timing Newsletter* and www.401kSelections.com.

Each of the three choices started at $0.00. Into each position we made the same $500 per month contribution. For SPY and VWELX, we just bought and held. For C-lect, we rotated through the different funds based on C over the years from January 1, 1993, through December 31, 2014. Here are the final results.

C-lect grew to $1,003,000.
SPY grew to $428,000.
VWELX grew to $391,000.

I'm sure you agree that this is quite a difference for the same contribution. This just shows the principles found in this book at work as they were applied over the years to one well-known, actual 401(k) plan. Make your money work as hard for you as you do for it with C.

To be sure, there is no guarantee that future conditions will be similar to past conditions. We forced at least a two-month holding period on the C-lect rotation process. We bought and held two funds at any one time over the years. Past performance does not guarantee future performance.

Whether you are an employer or employee, see how your retirement plan compares at www.401kSelections.com. Make sure you have low costs and top funds. Over the years, stay with the leaders and avoid the laggards as ranked by C.

References

Bogle, John C. 1993. *Bogle on Mutual Funds* (McGraw-Hill).

Bogle, John C. 2012. *The Clash of the Cultures* (Wiley).

Bogle, John C., and David F. Swenson. 2009 (updated). *Common Sense on Mutual Funds* (Wiley).

Brown, Stephen J., William N. Goetzmann, and Alok Kumar. 1998. *The Dow Theory: William Peter Hamilton's Track Record Reconsidered* (Social Science Research Network: http://papers.ssrn.com/sol3/papers.cfm?abstract_id=58690).

Cottle, Sidney, Roger F. Murray, and Frank E. Block. 1988. *Graham & Dodd Security Analysis,* 5th ed. (McGraw-Hill).

Douglas, Mark. 1990. *The Disciplined Trader* (Simon & Schuster).

Easterling, Ed. 2005. *Unexpected Returns: Understanding Secular Stock Market Cycles* (Cypress House).

Ellis, Charles D. 1975. "The Loser's Game" (*Financial Analyst's Journal*, vol. 31, no. 4).

Ellis, Charles D. 1975. *Winning the Loser's Game* (McGraw-Hill).

Fink, Matthew P. 2011. *The Rise of Mutual Funds* (Oxford University Press).

Goodspeed, Bennett W. 1983. *The Tao Jones Averages: A Guide to Whole-Brained Investing* (Dutton Books).

Graham, Benjamin. 2006 (revised). *The Intelligent Investor* (Collins Business).

Greenblatt, Joel. 2010. *The Little Book That Still Beats the Market* (Wiley).

Hagstrom, Robert G. 1997. *The Warren Buffett Way* (Wiley).

Houtkin, Harvey I., and David Waldman. 1998. *Secrets of the SOES Bandit* (McGraw-Hill).

Hughes, John S., Jing Liu, and Mingshan Zhang. 2010. *Overconfidence, Under-Reaction, and Warren Buffett's Investments* (Social Science Research Network: http://papers.ssrn.com/sol3/papers.cfm?abstract_id=1635061).

Hulbert, Mark. Monthly newsletter, *Hulbert Financial Digest* (MarketWatch).

Keen, Sam. 1990. *To a Dancing God* (Harper Collins).

LeFevre, Edwin. 1980 (reprint). *Reminiscences of a Stock Operator* (Books of Wall Street, Vermont).

The Leuthold Group. *Stock Market Valuation: What Works and What Doesn't* (paper).

Lynch, Peter. 1993. *Beating the Street* (Simon & Schuster).

Maher, Matt, Harry White, Phil Fry, and Matt Wilkerson. 2013. "Asset Class Impacts on the 30-Year Efficient Frontier," *Journal of Accounting and Finance*, vol. 13, no. 2.

Malkiel, Burton G. 2007 (updated and revised). *A Random Walk Down Wall Street* (W. W. Norton).

Malkiel, Burton G., and Charles D. Ellis. 2009. *The Elements of Investing* (Wiley).

Mauboussin, Michael J. 2012. *The Success Equation: Untangling Skill and Luck in Business, Sports, and Investing* (Harvard Business Review Press).

Mauboussin, Michael J. 2012. *Think Twice* (Harvard Business Review Press).

Mauldin, John. 2004. *Bull's Eye Investing: Targeting Real Returns in a Smoke and Mirrors Market* (Wiley).

Napier, Russell. 2009. *Anatomy of the Bear: Lessons from Wall Street's Four Great Bottoms* (Harriman House).

O'glove, Thornton L. 1998. *Quality of Earnings* (Free Press).

O'Neil, William. 2009. *How to Make Money in Stocks,* 4th ed. (McGraw-Hill).

O'Shaughnessy, James P. 1997. *What Works on Wall Street* (McGraw-Hill).

Pring, Martin J. 1980. *Technical Analysis Explained* (McGraw-Hill).

Schwed, Jr., Fred. 1940, 2006 (reprint). *Where Are the Customers' Yachts?* (Wiley Investment Classics).

Shiller, Robert J. 2006. *Irrational Exuberance* (Crown Business).

Smith, Adam. 1976. *The Money Game* (Vintage).

Smithers, Andrew, and Stephen Wright. 2000. *Valuing Wall Street: Protecting Wealth in Turbulent Markets* (McGraw-Hill).

Stein, Ben, and Phil DeMuth. 2003. *Yes, You Can Time the Market* (Wiley).

Train, John. 1980. *The Money Masters* (Harper & Row).

Tyson, Eric. 2001. *Mutual Funds for Dummies* (Hungry Minds).

Weiss, Martin D. 2002. *The Ultimate Safe Money Guide: How Everyone 50 and Over Can Protect, Save, and Grow Their Money* (Wiley).

Websites with additional useful information, in alphabetic order:

AAII.com

crestmontresearch.com

ETrade.com

InvestorsFastTrack.com

FederalReserve.gov

Fidelity.com

hussmanfunds.com

ICI.org

Morningstar.com

PIMCO.com

Schwab.com

TRowePrice.com

Vanguard.com

Attributions

Among other permissions, the following attributions are noted.

For the S&P 500 Index:

> The S&P 500 Index is proprietary to and is calculated, distributed, and marketed by S&P Opco, LLC (a subsidiary of S&P Dow Jones Indices LLC), its affiliates, and/or its licensors and has been licensed for use. S&P® and S&P 500®, among other famous marks, are registered trademarks of Standard & Poor's Financial Services LLC, and Dow Jones® is a registered trademark of Dow Jones Trademark Holdings LLC. © 2013 S&P Dow Jones Indices LLC, its affiliates and/or its licensors. All rights reserved.

InvestorsIntelligence.com is a source for investor sentiment readings.

For Crestmont Research:

> The entire content of Crestmont's website, including but not limited to charts, graphs, analyses, etc., is subject to copyright with all rights reserved. All material available on this site may be used or referenced if the user references and acknowledges Crestmont Research and our website address (that is, "© 2014 www.CrestmontResearch.com" or "as presented by Crestmont Research www.CrestmontResearch.com").

For efficient frontier chart by decades showing that it shifts:

Source: Guggenheim Investments 2014 • guggenheiminvestments.com.

For the exchange-traded fund SPY usage:

Permission granted by State Street Global Markets LLC to use the ETF SPY fund documents, including the factsheet, prospectus, annual report, and historical distributions.

Index

Active funds, 114–126
Active management:
    C-lecting strategies as, 196
    and closet indexing, 108
    costs of, 130
    during market declines, 12
    necessity of, 5
    passive vs., 95, 157
Active management principles, 5–6
Advice, expert, 30n.4
Age:
    and buy-and-hold strategy, 114–115
    and C-lect strategies, 148–149, 185–186
    in diversification, 85–86, 111–113
    and investing, 176
    and moving averages, 163–164
    and risk reduction, 127
Age-based funds, 111, 190–191
Allocation(s):
    cash as, 56–57
    in diversification, 86–87
    as flexible vs. fixed, 47
    market timing vs., 158
    reasons for, 153–154
    risk management with, 175
    subdivisions in, 86–87, 133
    success of various strategies for, 56
"Asset Class Impacts on the 30-Year Efficient
    Frontier" (Maher, White, Fry, and
    Wilkerson), 85
Asset drift, 106–108
Assumptions (about markets), 3

Bacon, Sir Francis, 158n.3
Bear market(s):
    1900–1920, 39
    1929–1949, 40
    1968–1982, 41
    2000 and beyond, 42–44
    for bonds, 63–64
    characteristics of bull and, 37–44

    and C-lecting strategies, 183
    defined, 33
    losses during, 82–84
    "slope of hope" in, 30–31n.5
Beta (risk measurement), 135
Black Swans:
    and market timing, 155–156,
        172–173
    as risk, 131n.1
BlackRock, 125
Bogle, John C., 17n.7, 89n.2
Bond bear markets, 63–64
Bond bull markets, 63–64
Bond funds, 59, 61–62
Bond laddering, 62–63, 76
Bond market, 55–78
    bond basics, 57–60
    determining phase of, 76
    history of, 63–64
    investor sentiment in, 74–75
    myths about, 56–57
    one- to five-year cycles in, 72–73
    recommended strategy for,
        75–78
    strategy in, 60–63
    timing factors in, 64–72
Bond worksheet, 210–211
Bonds:
    basics of, 57–60
    cash vs., 99
    as hedge, 60
Borrowing, 55–56
Brokerage option, 7n.4
Buffett, Warren:
    annual letter to shareholders by, 90
    on market fluctuations, 92
    market inefficiencies used by, 125
    on preparing for Black Swans, 173
    skill vs. luck of, 91
    success of, 27–28n.2
    valuation indicator used by, 51

Bull market(s):
  1880–1900, 38–39
  1920–1929, 39–40
  1949–1968, 40–41
  1982–2000, 41
  2000 and beyond, 43
  for bonds, 63–64
  characteristics of bear and, 37–44
  and C-lecting strategies, 183
  defined, 33
  indicators of, 30–31n.5
  losses during, 83–84
Buy-and-hold strategy:
  and age factor, 114–115
  and C-lecting strategies, 182
  and diversification, 85–86
  limitations of, 22–25
  market timing vs., 158
  timing strategies vs., 160–161
  viability of, 14

C (Comets):
  defined, 7
  managing hybrid funds with, 141
  measurement of, 139–140
CalPERS (California Public Employees'
  Retirement System), 123
CAPE ratio (see Cyclically adjusted
  price-to-earnings ratio)
Capital fund distributions, 195
Cash:
  as asset, 56–57
  as asset class, 99–101
  as defensive measure, 128–129
  as diversification choice, 84
  in market timing, 157
  as riskless, 175
CDs, 56–57
China, 10–11
Circumstances (personal), 186–187
C-lect 2 Hybrid, 142–144, 198–199
C-lect 5 Fidelity, 198–199
C-lect 401(k), 216–217
C-lect Q1 401(k), 201–203
C-lect Q4 401(k), 201–203
C-lecting strategies, 127–152, 181–205
  and age, 185–186
  based on most return and least risk,
    135–140
  based on past performance, 132–135
  and buy-and-hold strategy, 182
  and circumstances, 186–187
  and compounding, 184–185
  and diversification, 127–128, 182
  and efficient frontier, 181–182
  for ETFs, 147–150
  fund selection with, 203–204
  and inflation, 187
  information for, 187–203

  for investing styles, 141–147
  for managers, 190
  managing the managers with, 191–192
  and market timing, 156, 204
  market valuation with, 192–195
  and math, 185
  for mutual funds, 140–141
  portfolio assembly with, 190–191
  for retirement plans, 200–203
  and rule of 72, 184
  traditional investing strategies vs., 128–132
  use of, 195–199
"Climbing the wall of worry," 30–31n.5
Closed funds, 108n.1
Closed-end funds, 29n.3
Closet indexing, 108–109
Comets [see C (Comets)]
Commissions, 120
Commodities business, 123
Competitive advantage, 122n.9
Compounding, 184–185
Congress, 118–119n.6
Congreve, William, 168n.5
Consumer price index (CPI), 66–67
Contrary indicators, 165
Control (with funds), 16–17
CPI (consumer price index), 66–67
Crestmont Research, 154
CS (relative performance comparison), 137–138
Cycles (in secular markets), 31–32
Cyclical markets:
  in bond markets, 72–73
  defined, 33
  and diversification, 82–84
  in secular markets, 34
Cyclically adjusted price-to-earnings (CAPE)
  ratio, 50–51, 169, 189

Day-trading, 89
Death cross (moving averages), 164
Debt instruments, 57
Divergences (indicators), 164–165
Diversification, 79–103
  allocation of funds in, 86–87
  and Black Swans, 172
  and C-lecting strategies, 127–128, 182
  and cyclical vs. secular markets, 82–84
  and fund selection, 88–95
  gains in fixed, 176
  limitations of, 80, 84–86
  losses in fixed, 174–175
  to manage risk, 127
  and manager selection, 101–102
  with style boxes, 109
  and timing, 95–101
  traditional view of, 79–82
Dividend yield, 52
Dogs of the Dow strategy, 159–160
Dow Jones, 14

Dow Theory (divergence), 165
Dutch East India Company, 13

Earnings yield, 52
EEM (iShares MSCI Emerging
    Markets ETF), 138
Eendragt Maakt Magt, 13n.6
EFA (iShares MSCI EAFE ETF), 138
Efficient frontier (EF):
    and C-lecting strategies, 181–182
    as flexible vs. static, 97–99
    historical use of, 45–47
    tracking changes in, 134
Efficient market hypothesis:
    and Dow Theory, 165
    as flexible, 80–81
Ellis, Charles D., 123
Emotions, 94–95
Employer matches, 214
Energy industry, 42–43
Exchange-traded funds (ETFs):
    average returns of, 130
    C-lecting strategies for, 147–150
    mutual funds vs., 1–2n.2, 9–10
    rise of, 125

Fed model, 52–53
Federal debt:
    and interest rates, 68–70
    as market indicator, 77
Fidelity, 106
Fidelity's Magellan Fund, 106
Fisher, Irving, 37n.9
Fixed income, 187
Fixed-income securities, 57
Fluctuations (*see* Market uncertainty)
Forecasting, 49–52
401(k) plans:
    brokerage option with, 7n.4
    C-lect strategy for, 148–150, 200–203
    employer matching in, 7n.3
    managing, with C, 7–9
    mapping of, 214–216
    (*See also* Retirement plans)
403(b) plans, 7–9
Fry, Phil, 85
Fund companies, 145–147
Fund performance:
    differences in, 2–5
    lagging, 117n.5
    of load vs. no-load funds, 18–19
    ranking, 116–117
    and size, 108
Fund selection:
    with C-lecting strategies, 203–204
    and diversification, 88–95
Fundamentals indicator (market timing),
    169–170
Funds of funds, 113–114

Gains:
    and average fund performance, 3–5
    calculating, 109–110
    in fixed diversification, 176
    improving, with market timing, 155
    tax considerations of, 150–151
GDP (gross domestic product):
    of China, 10–11
    and federal debt, 68–70
    as market indicator, 76–77
    as valuation indicator, 51
Global markets:
    correlation of, 95
    and world changes, 10–11
Gold (bubble in), 167, 168
Graham, Benjamin, 100
Great Depression:
    as bear market, 40
    disassociation from, 82
    effect of, on individual investors, 11
    unemployment during, 186–187
Greater fool strategy, 40n.13, 93
Greenspan, Alan, 42
Gross, Bill, 90, 91
Gross domestic product (*see* GDP)

Hedges, 60
Houtkin, Harry, 119–120
Humbling, of investors, 89–92
Hybrid funds:
    managed with C, 141
    performance comparisons for, 4
    as style box, 113

Index funds:
    costs of, 130
    hype of, 193–194
    as investment funds, 20–21
    limitations of, 25
    as passive management, 115–116
Indexes (divergences in), 164–165
Indicators (for market timing), 176–178
Inflation, 187
Information (for C-lecting strategies),
    187–203
Insider trading, 118, 118–119n.6
Interest rates:
    and bond prices, 60–61
    and consumer price index, 66–67
    and federal debt, 68–70
    and recessions, 64–66
    and stocks, as market indicator, 45
    and U.S. dollar, 67–68
Internal funds, of brokerage firms, 19
International markets, 110
Internet, 158–159
Inverse funds, 110–111
Inverted yield curve, 59–60
INVESCO PowerShares QQQ, 138

Investing styles:
  C-lecting strategies for, 141–147
  returns on various, 199–200
Investment funds, 1–26
  active, 114–126
  active management principles for, 5–6
  age-based, 111, 190–191
  bond, 59, 61–62
  choices in, 9–10
  closed, 108n.1
  closed-end, 29n.3
  fund of funds, 113–114
  historical fluctuations in, 10–12
  history of, 12–17
  internal, of brokerage firms, 19
  inverse, 110–111
  lifestyle, 111–113
  load, 18–19
  management of uncertainty with types of,
      110–114
  managing the managers for, 6–9
  marketing of, 94–95
  and money management, 17
  money market, 56–57
  no-load, 18–20
  no-transaction-fee, 9
  open-end, 29n.3
  passive, 114–126
  performance of, 2–5
  small-cap, 4
  target-date, 111
  traditional strategies for, 21–25
  transaction-fee, 9
  (See also specific fund and types of funds)
Investments:
  goal of, 131
  pooled, 13
Investor sentiment:
  in bond market, 74–75
  as market timing indicator, 165–167
  in secular markets, 37
  in stock worksheet, 208
Investors:
  effect of, on moving averages, 164
  following managers, 19–20
  humbling of, 89–92
Investors Intelligence, 166
Irrational Exuberance (Shiller), 189
iShares MSCI EAFE ETF (EFA), 138
iShares MSCI Emerging Markets ETF
      (EEM), 138
IWM (iShares Russell 2000 ETF), 138

Keynes, Lord John Maynard, 27n.1, 169, 181

Lateral trades, 151–152, 194
Legg Mason Value Fund, 48
Lifestyle funds, 111–113
Liquidity, 16–17

Load funds, 18–19
Losses:
  and average fund performance, 3–5
  in bull and bear markets, 82–84
  calculating, 109–110
  compounding results of, 154–155
  in fixed diversification, 174–175
  math to calculate recovery from, 185
  preventing, with market timing, 155–156
Luck, skill vs., 47–49, 84
Lynch, Peter, 91, 124

Maher, Matt, 85
Manager selection:
  as active process, 87
  and diversification, 101–102
Managers:
  approaches to market timing by, 156–158
  C-lecting strategies for, 190
  investors following, 19–20
  as temporary performance leaders, 101–102
  use of defensive tools by, 128–129
Managing the managers:
  with C-lecting strategies, 191–192
  for investment funds, 6–9
Market inefficiencies, 119–121
Market timing, 153–179
  alternative strategies for, 173–174
  and Black Swans, 172–173
  in bond market, 64–72
  in C-lect model, 143
  and C-lecting strategies, 204
  combinations of strategies for, 176–178
  divergences as indicators, 164–165
  and diversification, 95–101
  fundamentals of, 169–170
  investor sentiment as indicator, 165–167
  issues with, 159–160
  managers' approaches to, 156–158
  moving averages as indicators, 160–164
  myths about, 155–156
  news as indicator, 171–172
  overbought/oversold as indicators, 167–169
  popularity of, 48
  results of using, 174–176
  and stop losses, 176
Market uncertainty, 105–126
  active vs. passive funds to manage, 114–126
  and closet indexing, 108–109
  fund types to manage, 110–114
  and market valuation, 192–193
  and news, 171
  style boxes to manage, 109–110
  and style drift, 106–108
Market valuation, 192–195
Marketing, of funds, 94–95
Markets:
  reactions to, 155
  (See also specific types of markets)

Marshall Plan, 40
Math, 185
Measurability, 16–17
Mexican pesos, 109–110n.2
Modern Portfolio Theory (MPT), 45–47
Money management, 17
Money market funds, 56–57
Moving averages, 160–164
MPT (Modern Portfolio Theory), 45–47
Mutual funds:
    C-lecting strategies for, 140–141
    ETFs vs., 1–2n.2, 9–10

Net asset value (NAV), 62
New York Stock Exchange, 14
News:
    and investor sentiment, 166–167
    as market timing indicator, 171–172
No-load funds, 18–20
No-Load Mutual Fund Selections & Timing Newsletter, 4, 140
No-transaction-fee funds, 9

One- to five-year cycles, 72–73
Open-end funds, 29n.3
Overbought indicator, 167–169
Oversold indicator, 167–169

Par value, 59, 61–62
Passive funds, 114–126
Passive management, 95, 157
Past performance:
    C-lecting strategies based on, 132–135
    as selection standard, 88
P/E ratio (*see* Price-to-earnings ratio)
Pooled investments, 13
Portfolio assembly, 190–191
Portfolio map, 212–213
Positive yield curve, 59
Price, Michael, 125
Prices (and bond yields), 58–59
Price-to-earnings (P/E) ratio:
    cyclically adjusted, 50–51, 169, 189
    in Fed model, 52
    as fundamental, 169
    and market bubbles, 13–14
    Shiller, 50–51
Prince, Michael, 92

Q ratio, 51
QQQ (INVESCO PowerShares QQQ), 138

Railroads, 38–39
Rate of change (ROC), 44–45
Ratio:
    cyclically adjusted price-to-earnings,
        50–51, 169, 189
    of federal debt to GDP, 68–70
    Q, 51

Shiller P/E, 50–51
Tobin's Q, 51
(*See also* Price-to-earnings ratio)
Reactions (to market), 155
Real-time ratings, 136
Recessions, 64–66
Redemption fees, 21n.8
Relative performance comparison (CS),
    137–138
Retirement plans:
    CalPERS, 123
    C-lecting strategies for, 200–203
    403(b) plans, 7–9
    SPY vs., 216–217
    Vanguard Wellington vs., 216–217
Return(s):
    C-lecting strategies based on, 135–140
    measurements of, 137–140
    on SPY, 8, 198–199
    total, 109–110, 137
    on Vanguard Wellington, 8, 198–200
    on various investing styles, 199–200
    weighing with risk, 139–140
Reversion to the mean, 3, 151, 197
Risk:
    C-lecting strategies based on, 135–140
    inevitability of, 131n.1
    management of, with asset allocation, 175
    and market timing, 156
    measurements of, 135–136
    weighing with returns, 139–140
The Roaring Twenties, 39–40
ROC (rate of change), 44–45
Rotational allocation strategy, 47, 49, 141
Rule of 72, 184

Secular markets:
    cyclical markets in, 34
    defined, 24n.9, 33
    and diversification, 82–84
    strategies for, 45–47
Sentiment (*see* Investor sentiment)
Shakespeare, William, 55
Shiller, Robert, 32–33, 189
Shiller P/E ratio, 50–51
Short-term efficiency, 32–33
Short-term holding periods, 9–10, 21n.8, 145n.3
Short-term redemption fees, 145n.3
Sideways markets, 33
Skill, luck vs., 47–49, 84
"Slope of hope," 30–31n.5
Small Order Execution System (SOES), 120–122
Small-cap funds, 4
Social climate:
    in bond worksheet, 210
    in stock worksheet, 208
SOES (Small Order Execution System), 120–122
Solar energy, 173
S&P 500 Index, historical chart of, 36

SPY (SPDR ETF):
  C-lect 5 strategy vs., 147–148
  C-lect strategy vs., 149–150
  equity flows of, 15
  losses in, 143
  measuring volatility of, 136, 137
  retirement plans vs., 200–203, 216–217
  returns on, 8, 198–199
  in World Growth Index, 138
Standard deviation, 135
Standardization (of advantages), 85
STOCK Act, 118–119n.6
Stock market, 27–53
  after World War II, 71
  changes in, 118–119
  characteristics of bull and bear markets,
      37–44
  and the Fed model, 52–53
  forecasting in, 49–52
  historical data for, 35–36
  luck vs. skill in, 47–49
  recognition of phases of, 27–33
  terms used in, 33–35
  tools to analyze, 44–47
Stock worksheets, 207–209
Stocks:
  backtesting and buying, 148n.4
  cash vs., 99–101
  and interest rates, as market indicator, 45
Stop losses, 176
Style boxes, 109–110
Style drift, 106–108
Styles (investing) (see Investing styles)
Subdivisions (in allocations), 86–87, 133

T. Rowe Price, 125
Target-date funds, 111
Tax considerations, 150–151
Templeton, Sir John, 91–92, 124, 173
TIPS (Treasury Inflation-Protected Securities),
    74–75
Tobin's Q ratio, 51
Tools (for analysis), 44–47
Total returns, 109–110, 137
  (See also Return[s])
Traditional strategies (investing), 21–25

Transaction-fee funds, 9
Transparency, 16–17
Treasury Inflation-Protected Securities
    (TIPS), 74–75
Tulip mania, 13–14

Uncertainty (see Market uncertainty)
U.S. dollar, 67–68

V (volatility), 135–137
Value:
  of companies, 169–170
  of market, 192–195
  par, 59, 61–62
  of stock market, 126
Van Ketwich, Adriaan, 13n.6
Vanguard 500 Index Fund Investor Class
    (VFINX), 146
Vanguard Wellesley Fund, 106
Vanguard Wellington (VWELX):
  allocation of, 106
  C-lect 2 Hybrid vs., 144–145
  C-lect strategy vs., 149–150
  retirement plans vs., 200–203, 216–217
  returns on, 8, 198–200
VFINX (Vanguard 500 Index Fund Investor
    Class), 146
Vinik, Jeffrey, 106
Volatility (V), 135–137
VWELX (see Vanguard Wellington)

War, 38
War on Terror, 42, 72
WGI (World Growth Index), 138–139
Whipsaws, 161–163
White, Harry, 85
Wilkerson, Matt, 85
Winning the Loser's Game (Ellis), 123
World Growth Index (WGI), 138–139

Yield(s):
  and bond prices, 58–59
  dividend, 52
  earnings, 52
  inverted yield curve, 59–60
  positive yield curve, 59

About the Author

STEPHEN L. MCKEE IS MANAGING PARTNER OF WATERCOURSE WAY Holdings LLC, publisher of the top-rated *No-Load Mutual Fund Selections & Timing Newsletter*. He has been in the investment business for more than 30 years and has been mentioned in *Forbes, Wall Street Journal*, and other publications as a financial expert. He speaks at workshops across the country.

Steve's investment strategy is based on Modern Portfolio Theory and the efficient frontier concept. Recognizing that markets and managers change for better and worse, he developed the C rating metric, which is the risk-adjusted relative strength measure of mutual funds and ETFs. Stay with the leaders and avoid the laggards. He also applies this proactive rotational allocation strategy to well-known 401(k) plans.

Steve may be reached at 800-800-6563, SMcKee@ SelectionsAndTiming.com, or SMcKee@401kSelections.com.